ADULT READING SERIES

Challenger

Teacher's Manual

FOR BOOKS 1 – 4

REVISED EDITION

About the Author of the *Challenger* Series

Corea Murphy has worked in the field of education since the early 1960s. In addition to classroom and tutorial teaching, Ms. Murphy has developed language arts curriculum guides for public high schools, conducted curriculum and effectiveness workshops, and established an educational program for residents in a drug rehabilitation facility.

Ms. Murphy became interested in creating a reading series for older students when she began working with adults and adolescents in the early 1970s. The **Challenger Adult Reading Series** is the result of her work with these students.

In a very real sense, the students contributed greatly to the development of this reading series. Their enthusiasm for learning to read and their willingness to work hard provided inspiration, and their many helpful suggestions influenced the content of both the student books and the teacher's manuals.

It is to these students that the **Challenger Adult Reading Series** is dedicated with the hope that others who wish to become good readers will find this reading program both helpful and stimulating.

ISBN 0-88336-897-8

Copyright © 1986, 1991, 1994
New Readers Press
Publishing Division of Laubach Literacy
International
Box 131, Syracuse, New York 13210-0131

EACH ONE TEACH ONE

Printed in the United States of America

Manuscript editor: Mary Hutchison
Contributing writer: Carol Kidder
Design: Patricia Rapple
Cover design: Chris Steenwerth

9 8 7 6 5 4 3 2

Contents

6   **Introduction to the *Challenger* Series**

8   **Common Phonics Elements and Principles in English Words**

12   **Scope and Sequence Charts**

23   **1. Preparing to Teach**
Scheduling Considerations
The Lesson Components
Planning the Lessons
The Teacher-Student Relationship
Building a Good Working Relationship
Supplies
A Summary of Do's
Model Lesson Planning Worksheet

27   **2. Teaching the Lessons**
Sample Teaching Session Formats
Word Study
The Reading Selections
The Exercises
Some Final Thoughts
A Summary of Do's

36   **3. Writing**
Providing Opportunities for Writing
Understanding the Writing Process
Evaluating and Remediating Student Writing
Other Considerations
Correlated Writing Books
A Summary of Do's and Don'ts
Writing Revision Checklist
Editing Checklist
Teacher's Evaluation Guide

44   **4. Reinforcement Activities**
Word Index Activities
Reading and Writing Activities
Puzzles and Games
Student-requested Activities
A Summary of Do's

48   **5. Using the Lesson Notes**
Primary and Secondary Emphases
The Reading Selections
Developing Your Lesson Plan

Book 1

49   ***Challenger 1* Introduction**
Scheduling Considerations
Suggestions for Teaching the Lessons
Writing Activities
The Lesson Segments
Individual Lesson Notes

54   ***Challenger 1* Lesson Notes**
Lesson 1:   The Long and Short Vowels
Lesson 2:   More Work with Long and Short Vowels
Lesson 3:   More Work with Long and Short Vowels
Lesson 4:   Changing the First Consonant Sound
Lesson 5:   Changing the End Consonant Sound
Lesson 6:   Ending Consonant Blends
Lesson 7:   More Work with Ending Consonant Blends
Lesson 8:   Review of Vowels and Consonants
Lesson 9:   Vowel Sounds for *y*
Lesson 10:   Silent Letters
Lesson 11:   The *r*-Controlled Vowels
Lesson 12:   Vowel Combinations
Lesson 13:   The *r*-Controlled Vowel Combinations
Lesson 14:   Vowels Followed by the Letter *l*

Lesson 15:   Digraphs and Consonant Blends
Lesson 16:   Consonant Blends
Lesson 17:   More Consonant Blends
Lesson 18:   More Digraphs and Consonant Blends
Lesson 19:   Still More Consonant Blends
Lesson 20:   Sounds for *c* and *g*
First Review and Second Review

Book 2

75   *Challenger 2* Introduction
        Scheduling Considerations
        Suggestions for Teaching the Lessons
        Writing Activities
        The Lesson Segments
        Individual Lesson Notes
79   *Challenger 2* Lesson Notes
        Lesson 1:   Sneezing
        Lesson 2:   Cats
        Lesson 3:   The Number Seven
        Lesson 4:   A Few Facts about Beer
        Lesson 5:   Love Letters
        Review: Lessons 1–5
        Lesson 6:   Wigs
        Lesson 7:   Skunks
        Lesson 8:   Eggs
        Lesson 9:   Gold
        Lesson 10:   Mother Goose
        Review: Lessons 1–10
        Lesson 11:   Sleeping
        Lesson 12:   Honeybees
        Lesson 13:   Handwriting
        Lesson 14:   To Be a Slave
        Lesson 15:   A Very Strange Hobby
        Review: Lessons 1–15
        Lesson 16:   Whales
        Lesson 17:   Black Bart

Lesson 18:   One Idea about How the Earth Was Formed
Lesson 19:   Jails on the High Seas
Lesson 20:   The Father of Our Country
Review: Lessons 1–20

Book 3

99   *Challenger 3* Introduction
        Scheduling Considerations
        Suggestions for Teaching the Lessons
        Writing Activities
        The Lesson Segments
        Individual Lesson Notes
102   *Challenger 3* Lesson Notes
        Lesson 1:   Review of Long and Short Vowels
        Lesson 2:   Review of Consonant Blends and Digraphs: Part 1
        Lesson 3:   Review of Consonant Blends: Part 2
        Lesson 4:   Review of Consonant Blends: Part 3
        Lesson 5:   Review of Consonant Blends: Part 4
        Lesson 6:   Review of Consonant Blends and Digraphs: Part 5
        Lesson 7:   Review of Silent Letters
        Lesson 8:   Review of Vowel Combinations: Part 1
        Lesson 9:   Review of Vowel Combinations: Part 2
        Lesson 10:   The Sound for *au*
        Lesson 11:   Review of the *r*-Controlled Vowel
        Lesson 12:   Review of Vowels Followed by the Letter *l*
        Lesson 13:   Review of the Hard and Soft *c* and *g*
        Lesson 14:   The *gh* and *ght* Words

Lesson 15: Review of *r*-Controlled
            Vowel Combinations
Lesson 16: Common Word Beginnings:
            Part 1
Lesson 17: Common Word Beginnings:
            Part 2
Lesson 18: Common Word Beginnings:
            Part 3
Lesson 19: *Up-, Down-, Out-, Over-,*
            and *Under-*
Lesson 20: More Work with
            Compound Words
Review: Lessons 1–20

Book 4

123 *Challenger 4* Introduction
     Scheduling Considerations
     Suggestions for Teaching the Lessons
     Writing Activities
     The Lesson Segments
     Individual Lesson Notes

126 *Challenger 4* Lesson Notes
     Lesson 1:   The Heart
     Lesson 2:   Babe Ruth
     Lesson 3:   Time
     Lesson 4:   Insects
     Lesson 5:   The Brain Sees All
     Review: Lessons 1–5
     Lesson 6:   The Sun
     Lesson 7:   Thomas Edison
     Lesson 8:   Knives, Forks, and Spoons
     Lesson 9:   Manners
     Lesson 10: Flying Saucers
     Review: Lessons 1–10
     Lesson 11: Accepting Who You Are
     Lesson 12: Anne Frank: Part I
     Lesson 13: Anne Frank: Part II
     Lesson 14: The Ship of the Desert
     Lesson 15: Some Facts about
                 Southpaws
     Review: Lessons 1–15

Lesson 16: Some Thoughts about
            Dying
Lesson 17: The Number One Eater in
            America
Lesson 18: The Great Hunger
Lesson 19: Digestion
Lesson 20: Nail Soup
Review: Lessons 1–20

Answer Keys

146 Answer Key for Book 1

150 Answer Key for Book 2

159 Answer Key for Book 3

167 Answer Key for Book 4

Introduction to the *Challenger* Series

The *Challenger Adult Reading Series* is a program designed to develop reading, writing, and reasoning skills in adult and adolescent students. The first four books in the *Challenger* series emphasize *learning to read,* developing basic decoding, vocabulary, comprehension, and writing skills. Beginning with Book 5, the emphasis shifts to *reading to learn,* developing higher-level comprehension and reasoning skills while expanding the student's knowledge base.

Components of the Series

The *Challenger* series contains:
- 8 student books
- 5 teacher's manuals
- answer keys for Books 1–4 and 5–8
- the *Challenger Placement Tool*
- 8 puzzle books correlated to the student books
- 4 books of writing activities correlated to Books 1–4

The Student Books

Each book in this controlled vocabulary series contains 20 lessons, plus reviews. Each lesson includes:
- word study
- a reading selection
- a wide variety of exercises and activities

In Books 1, 3, 5, and 7, each lesson begins with a word chart that introduces new words according to specific phonics principles. In all books, new words that appear in the lesson are listed before each reading selection.

The reading selections in the odd-numbered books are mostly fiction. Books 1 and 3 contain original stories about a group of adults in a variety of situations. Most reading selections in Books 5 and 7 are minimally adapted well-known works of fiction. The even-numbered books contain engaging informational readings. The selections in Books 2 and 4 are on topics similar to those in magazines and encyclopedias. Most selections in Books 6 and 8 are adapted from highly respected works of nonfiction that enable students to broaden the scope of their knowledge.

The varied exercises and activities help students to develop their reading, writing, speaking, and listening skills and to increase their basic knowledge. Comprehension exercises based on the reading selections focus on the development of literal, inferential, and applied comprehension skills. In addition, comprehension exercises in Books 5 through 8 develop literary understanding, interpretation, and critical reading skills.

Other exercises are designed to increase vocabulary and develop reading and reasoning skills. They include vocabulary reviews; word associations; classifying, sequencing, and categorizing exercises; using context clues; forming analogies; using dictionaries and reference materials; and several types of puzzles.

There are reviews after every four or five lessons, except in Books 1 and 3. Each book has a final review. Also included in Books 1 through 5 are indexes of the words introduced so far in that book. The word indexes for Books 6 through 8 are included in the teacher's manuals. These word indexes can be used in developing reinforcement activities and vocabulary reviews.

The Teacher's Manuals

There is a single *Teacher's Manual for Books 1–4* and individual teacher's manuals for Books 5, 6, 7, and 8. These comprehensive manuals explain the concepts underlying the *Challenger* series and offer practical suggestions about procedures and techniques for working with students. Separate chapters deal with preparing to teach, teaching the lessons, writing, reinforcement activities, and using the lesson notes. These chapters should be read before you begin to use this program. Individual lesson notes containing suggestions for pre-reading, post-reading, and writing activities, and comments on specific exercises should be read before teaching the lessons. In the teacher's manuals, there are also introductions to each book, scope and sequence charts, and answer keys for each book. Finally, the *Teacher's Manual for Books 1–4* contains a chart of the common phonics principles and elements in English words.

Student Writing

Students are encouraged to write from the very first lesson. Early in the series, exercises focus on writing at the sentence level and are designed to simultaneously improve spelling, sentence structure, and students' skill in expressing themselves clearly. Most lessons in Books 5 through 8 have exercises that require students to write brief paragraphs. Suggestions for providing additional writing activities are given in the individual lesson notes.

Significant Educational Features

Flexibility and Adaptability

The *Challenger* series has been used successfully with students in many different types of instructional settings:
- adult volunteer literacy programs
- ABE, pre-GED, and GED programs
- secondary remedial reading programs
- secondary special education programs
- community college reading programs
- educational programs in correctional institutions
- workforce tutorial programs for employees

Challenger can be used in one-to-one tutoring situations, as well as in a variety of group settings. The lessons can be adapted to fit a variety of formats, allowing you to introduce additional activities and topics related to individual student interests and needs.

An Integrated Approach

Challenger integrates reading, writing, speaking, and listening skills. Reading comprehension is developed through oral discussion of inferential- and applied-level questions. These discussions help students to develop speaking and listening skills. Students build writing skills through follow-up writing activities. Critical thinking and reasoning skills are developed as students discuss the readings, the exercises, and their writing activities.

Sequenced Skill Building

Each lesson builds upon the skills developed and the content introduced in previous lessons. Students are continually challenged as the lessons increase in length and difficulty. As reading selections become longer, the content, vocabulary, and sentence structure become more sophisticated and demanding. The exercises and writing activities build on and expand students' knowledge and abilities. Students experience a sense of progress as they learn to apply their skills to new situations.

Highly Motivating Material

Students who have used the *Challenger* series have commented that this reading program has many characteristics that help to hold their interest and maintain their motivation. The characteristics they most frequently cite include:
- exceptionally motivating reading selections
- mature and diverse material
- information that increases background knowledge
- emphasis on using reasoning powers
- challenge of increasingly difficult materials
- feelings of success and confidence generated by the program

Placement

The *Challenger Placement Tool,* used in conjunction with information you have about a student's background knowledge, speaking and writing abilities, and motivation, can help you to decide where to place the student in the *Challenger* series. Scores on standardized reading inventories can also be used. For the first four books, scores in the following reading level ranges are appropriate:

Book 1: 2.0	**Book 3:** 3.0– 4.5
Book 2: 2.0–3.0	**Book 4:** 4.0–5.0

Keep in mind that numerical reading levels by themselves are not adequate descriptors of adult reading abilities. For students already using the series, scoring 85 per cent or better on the final review in each book indicates that the student is ready to go on to the next book.

> Although it is recognized that there are students of both sexes, for the sake of clarity and simplicity, we chose to use the pronouns *he, him,* and *his* throughout this book.

Common Phonics Elements and Principles in English Words

The English phonics system includes the sound-symbol relationships for the various vowels, consonants, consonant blends, and digraphs in English, plus the letter sequences and syllable patterns that indicate how words are most commonly pronounced. This chart lists single letters and common letter combinations together with key words that indicate how the letter or letters usually sound. When letters represent more than one sound, example words are given for each common sound. In addition, common short- and long-vowel syllable patterns are listed, along with basic spelling rules for adding endings to words.

Consonants

Consonant Letters That Represent One Sound

b	bed	**l**	lake	**t**	ten
d	dime	**m**	man	**v**	vase
f	feet	**n**	name	**w**	woman
h	hat	**p**	pen	**y**	you
j	job	**qu**	queen	**z**	zoo
k	kite	**r**	rope		

Consonant Letters with More Than One Sound

s	sun, rose	**Note:**	*s* can sound like /s/ or /z/.
x	six, example, xylophone		*x* can sound like /ks/, /gz/, or /z/.
c	can, cop, cup cent, city, icy	**Rule:**	*c* followed by *a, o,* or *u* sounds like /k/. *c* followed by *e, i,* or *y* sounds like /s/.
g	gas, got, gum ginger, germ, gym get, give, fogy		*g* followed by *a, o,* or *u* sounds like /g/. *g* followed by *e, i,* or *y* can sound like /j/. *g* followed by *e, i,* or *y* can also sound like /g/.
gu	guard, guess, guilt, guy		*gu* followed by a vowel sounds like /g/. The *u* is usually silent.

Consonant Blends

Consonant blends are two or three consonants (or a consonant and digraph) that commonly occur together. Each sound can be heard.

Initial Blends

bl	blue	**pl**	plate	**sp**	spoon
br	bride	**pr**	price	**spl**	split
chr	Christmas	**sc**	scar	**spr**	spring
cl	clock	**sch**	school	**squ**	square
cr	cry	**scr**	scream	**st**	step
dr	drop	**shr**	shrunk	**str**	street
fl	flame	**sk**	skate	**sw**	swim
fr	friend	**sl**	sleep	**thr**	throw
gl	glass	**sm**	smart	**tr**	track
gr	groom	**sn**	snow	**tw**	twin

Consonants
(continued)

Final Blends

ct	act	**nd**	hand	**rm**	farm
ft	left	**nge**	range	**rn**	corn
ld	gold	**nse**	sense	**rp**	burp
lf	self	**nt**	front	**rse**	course
lk	milk	**pt**	kept	**rt**	smart
lm	film	**rb**	curb	**sk**	ask
lp	help	**rce**	force	**sp**	clasp
lt	melt	**rd**	card	**st**	last
mp	lamp	**rf**	scarf	**xt**	next
nce	chance	**rk**	bark		
nch	lunch	**rl**	girl		

Consonant Digraphs

Consonant digraphs are two consonants that represent one sound.

ch	chair, machine, Christmas	**ph**	phone
ng	ring	**sh**	she
nk	bank	**th**	thing, the
		wh	whale, who

Silent Consonant Combinations

These are common consonant combinations that contain one or more silent letters. Hyphens indicate initial or final combinations.

-ck	clock	**-mb**	climb
gh	high, rough, ghost	**-mn**	autumn
-ght	sight, thought	**rh-**	rhyme
gn	sign, gnat	**sc-**	scent
kn-	know	**-tch**	catch
-lk	talk	**wr-**	wrong
-lm	calm		

Vowels

Vowel Letters and the Sounds They Represent

Each vowel letter represents several vowel sounds. The most common sounds are represented in the words listed below. All vowels can represent the *schwa* sound in unstressed syllables. The schwa is represented in many dictionaries by the symbol /ə/.

	Short Sound	Long Sound	Other Sounds	Schwa Sound
a	man	name	all, father, water	about
e	bed	me	cafe	open
i	six	time	ski	April
o	job	go	son, do, dog	second
u	but	rule, fuse	put	awful
y	gym	fly	any	

Vowels
(continued)

Vowel Combinations and the Sounds They Represent

Listed below are common vowel digraphs or vowel-consonant combinations. Many of these combinations produce long vowel sounds. If a combination represents more than one sound, a key word is given for each common sound.

Long Vowel Sounds

ai	rain
ay	day
ea	meat, great
ee	feet
ei	either, vein
eigh	eight
eu	feud
ew	blew, few
ey	key, they
ie	field, pie
igh	high
ind	find
oa	soap
oe	toe
oo	food
ue	due
ui	fruit

Other Vowel Sounds

ai	against
au	auto
aw	saw
augh	taught, laugh
ea	head
oi	boil
oy	boy
oo	book, blood
ou	you, country, out, soul, could
ough	though, thought, through, enough, bough, cough
ow	own, town
ui	build

r-Controlled and *l*-Controlled Vowels

When vowels are followed by *r* or *l*, the pronunciation of the vowel is usually affected.

air	fair	**err**	berry	**urr**	purr		
ar	car, dollar, warm	**ir**	girl	**al**	pal, bald		
arr	carry	**irr**	mirror	**all**	ball		
are	care	**oar**	roar	**ild**	mild		
ear	ear, earth, bear	**oor**	door	**ol**	old, roll, solve, doll		
eer	deer	**or**	horse, word, color				
er	very, her	**our**	hour, four, journal	**ull**	full, dull		
ere	here, were, there	**ur**	fur, fury				

Other Vowel-Consonant Combinations and the Sounds They Represent

-dge	badge	**-ci-**	magician, social	
-ed	hated, rubbed, fixed	**-si-**	session, television, Asian	
-gue	league	**-ti-**	caution, question, initial	
-que	antique	**su**	sugar, measure	
-stle	whistle	**-tu-**	picture	

Common Syllable Patterns in English

Some patterns of letters in syllables signal short vowel sounds. Others usually produce long vowel sounds. Recognizing the common short- and long-vowel syllable patterns can aid in decoding and spelling unknown words. It is usually the letter or letters that follow a vowel that determine pronunciation.

> **Key:** **V** = any vowel **C** = any consonant
> **(C)** = may or may not be a consonant

Syllables That Usually Produce Short Vowel Sounds

Closed syllables (syllables that end with one or more consonants)
VC: at, Ed, is, on, up
CVC: (also called 1-1-1 syllables) had, let, did, lot, but
CVCC: hand, less, with, lock, bump
            Exceptions: find, child, high, sign, old, poll, bolt, most

Syllables That Usually Produce Long Vowel Sounds

VCe: (silent *e* syllables) name, eve, time, hope, rule
VV(C): (double vowel syllables) paid, need, meat, die, boat, due, food
(C)V: (open syllables) ta/ble, fe/male, bi/cycle, go, o/pen
            Exceptions: Many unaccented open syllables: a/muse, to/day

A Syllable That Usually Produces the Schwa

Cle   (a consonant followed by *le*): table /tā bəl/, gentle /gĕn təl/

Rules for Adding Endings

The Doubling Rules

1. If a word has one syllable, one vowel, and one final consonant, double the final consonant before adding an ending that starts with a vowel. Do not double a final *w* or *x*. (This is also called the 1-1-1 Rule.)

> Examples: hop + ed = hopped *but* fix + ed = fixed
> run + ing = running   row + ing = rowing

2. If a word has more than one syllable, double the final consonant if the last syllable has one vowel, one final consonant, is accented, and the ending starts with a vowel.

> Examples: forgot + en = forgotten *but* offer + ing = offering
> begin + ing = beginning

The Silent *e* Rule

If a word ends in silent *e,* drop the final *e* before adding an ending that starts with a vowel.

> Example: joke + ing = joking
> secure + ity = security

The *y* to *i* Conversion

If a word ends in a consonant plus *y* (**C***y*), change the *y* to *i* before adding an ending, unless the ending starts with *i*. Note that this rule does not apply when a vowel precedes the *y*.

> Examples: lucky + er = luckier *but* cry + ing = crying
> happy + ness = happiness

SCOPE AND SEQUENCE: BOOK 1

Phonics	Lesson	1	2	3	4	5	6	7	8	9	10	11	12	13	14	15	16	17	18	19	20	R1	R2
1. Recognize long vowel sounds:	(CV and CVC¢)	★	★	★	★	★	☆	☆	★	☆	☆	☆	☆	☆	☆	☆	☆	☆	☆	☆	☆	☆	☆
	(CVVC)		☆				★	★	★	★	☆	☆	☆	☆	☆	☆	☆	☆		☆	☆	★	☆
2. Recognize short vowel sounds:	(VC and CVC)	★	★	★	★	★	☆	☆	★	☆	☆	☆	☆	☆	☆	☆	☆	☆	★	★	★	★	☆
	(CVCC)		☆				★	★	★	★	☆	☆	☆	☆	☆	☆	☆	☆	☆	☆	☆		
3. Recognize sounds for *y*		☆			★			☆		★					☆			☆		☆	★	★	☆
4. Recognize sounds for vowel groups:	*ee*	☆			★	★		☆	★		☆							☆	☆				☆
	ay, ey, oy, uy									★										☆	☆		
	ai, ie, oa, oi, ou, ue												★	☆				☆		☆			
	ea (as in *eat* and *head*)												☆	☆	☆			☆	☆	☆			
	oo (as in *food* and *foot*)											★	★					☆					
5. Recognize *r*-controlled vowel sounds:	*ar, are, or, er, eer, ir, ur*	☆						☆				★		☆				☆				☆	☆
	air, oar, oor													★									
	ear (as in *ear* and *bear*)													★									
	our (as in *sour* and *four*)													★									
6. Recognize vowel sounds followed by *l*: *al, el, ild, ol, ul, ull*															★								
7. Recognize sounds for single consonants		★	★	★	★	★	☆	☆	★	☆	☆	☆	☆	☆	☆	☆	☆	☆	☆	☆	☆	☆	☆
8. Recognize sounds for initial consonant blends:	*st, sk*															★							
	bl, cl, fl, gl, pl, sl																★	☆					
	br, cr, dr, fr, gr, pr, tr, str																	★					
	sm, sn, sp, sw, thr, tw																		★				
	chr, sc, scr, shr, spl, spr, squ																			★			
9. Recognize sounds for final consonant blends:	*nd, nt, ck, mp*						★	☆	☆		☆							☆					
	ng, nk							★															
	st, sk															★							
10. Recognize silent consonants: *kn, wr, mb, ght, tch*											★						★	☆					
11. Recognize sounds for digraphs:	*ch, sh*															★	☆	☆					
	th, wh																		★	☆			
12. Recognize sounds for *c* and *g*																					★	★	
13. Mark long and short vowel sounds				★					★					☆									

Word Analysis	Lesson	1	2	3	4	5	6	7	8	9	10	11	12	13	14	15	16	17	18	19	20	R1	R2
1. Recognize verb endings:	*-ed, -ing*	☆	☆	☆	☆	☆	☆	☆	☆	☆	☆	☆	☆	☆	☆	☆	☆	☆	☆	☆	☆	☆	☆
	-s																				☆		
2. Recognize noun endings:	*-s*	☆	☆	☆	☆	☆	☆	☆	☆	☆	☆	☆	☆	☆	☆	☆	☆	☆	☆	☆	☆	☆	☆
	-'s	☆	☆	☆	☆	☆	☆	☆	☆	☆	☆	☆	☆	☆	☆	☆	☆	☆	☆	☆	☆	☆	☆

KEY: ★ = Primary emphasis   ☆ = Secondary emphasis   ☆ = Integrated with other skills

Word Analysis, cont.

Lesson	1	2	3	4	5	6	7	8	9	10	11	12	13	14	15	16	17	18	19	20	R1	R2
3. Recognize contractions for:																						
not					☆	☆	☆	☆	☆	☆	☆	☆	☆	☆	☆	☆	☆	☆	☆	☆	☆	☆
is		☆					☆	☆			☆	☆	☆	☆	☆	☆	☆	☆	☆	☆		☆
am											☆	☆		☆			☆			☆		
will																				☆		
had												☆										
are																☆		☆	☆			☆
have																		☆				
would																				☆		
4. Recognize abbreviations:																						
Mr.	☆	☆		☆	☆		☆	☆	☆	☆	☆	☆	☆			☆	☆				☆	
Mrs., Ms.					☆		☆	☆	☆		☆	☆	☆		☆	☆		☆	☆			
Dr.																☆	☆					
5. Recognize other word endings:																						
-y, -ly									★													
-er													☆									
-ful, -less														★								
6. Recognize common word beginnings: un-, re-																			★			
7. Distinguish words that look similar/rhyme	★	★	★	★	★	★	★	★		★		★	★		★	★	★		★	★	★	☆
8. Form compound words																☆		☆				

Vocabulary

Lesson	1	2	3	4	5	6	7	8	9	10	11	12	13	14	15	16	17	18	19	20	R1	R2
1. Learn unfamiliar vocabulary	☆	☆	☆	★	★	★	★	★	★	★	★	★	★	★	★	★	★	★	★	★	☆	★
2. Identify synonyms								★	★					☆	★		☆			★	☆	★
3. Identify antonyms									★	★				★						★	★	★
4. Identify word associations										★			☆					☆	☆			
5. Learn/review common expressions														★								☆

Comprehension

Lesson	1	2	3	4	5	6	7	8	9	10	11	12	13	14	15	16	17	18	19	20	R1	R2
1. Decode words accurately when reading aloud	☆	★	★	★	★	★	★	★	★	★	★	★	★	★	★	★	★	★	★	★	★	★
2. Pronounce word endings when reading aloud	☆	☆	☆	☆	★	★	☆	☆	☆	★	☆	★	☆	☆	★	★	☆	☆	☆	☆	☆	★
3. Group words appropriately when reading aloud	☆	☆	☆	☆	☆	★	☆	☆	☆	☆	☆	☆	☆	★	☆	☆	☆	★	★	★	☆	★
4. Interpret punctuation correctly when reading aloud	☆	☆	☆	☆	☆	★	☆	☆	☆	☆	☆	★	★	★	★	★	★	★	★	☆	☆	★
5. Identify words using phonics and context clues	☆	☆	★	★	☆	★	★	☆	☆	☆	★	★	★	☆	★	★	★	★	★	★	☆	★
6. Read silently	★	★	☆	★	★	★	★	★	★	★	★	★	★	★	★	★	★	★	★	★	★	★
7. Follow oral directions	☆	☆	☆	☆	☆	☆	☆	☆	☆	☆	☆	☆	☆	☆	☆	☆	☆	☆	☆	☆	☆	☆
8. Improve listening comprehension	☆	☆	☆	☆	☆	☆	☆	☆	☆	☆	☆	☆	☆	☆	☆	☆	☆	☆	☆	☆	☆	☆
9. Discuss stories	★	★	★	★	★	★	★	★	★	★	★	★	★	★	★	★	★	★	★	★	★	★

KEY: ★ = Primary emphasis   ★ = Secondary emphasis   ☆ = Integrated with other skills

Comprehension, cont.

Lesson	1	2	3	4	5	6	7	8	9	10	11	12	13	14	15	16	17	18	19	20	R1	R2
10. Develop literal comprehension skills:																						
– Recall details	★	★	★	★	★	★	★	★	★	★	★	★	★	★	★	★	★	★	★	★		★
– Locate information in the story	★	★	★	★	★	★	★	★	★	★	★	★	★	★	★	★	★	★	★	★		★
11. Develop inferential comprehension skills:																						
– Infer word meanings from context clues	☆	☆	☆	☆	☆	☆	★	★	★	★	★	★	★	★	★	★	★	★	★	★	★	★
– Infer information from the story	☆	☆	☆	☆	☆	☆	☆	☆	☆	☆	☆	☆	☆	☆	☆	☆	☆	☆	☆	☆	☆	☆
– Use context clues to predict correct responses	☆	☆	★	★	☆	☆	☆	☆	☆	☆	☆	☆	★	☆	☆	☆	★	☆	★	★	★	☆
– Classify words under appropriate categories																	★					
12. Develop applied comprehension skills:																						
– Relate reading to personal experience	☆	☆	☆	☆	☆	☆	☆	☆	☆	☆	☆	☆	☆	☆	☆	☆	☆	☆	☆	☆		☆
– Draw conclusions	☆	☆	☆	☆	☆	☆	☆	☆	☆	☆	☆	☆	☆	☆	☆	☆	☆	☆	☆	☆		
13. Recognize number words	☆												☆				☆	★				☆
14. Learn/review basic factual information																		☆	☆	☆	☆	☆

Writing

Lesson	1	2	3	4	5	6	7	8	9	10	11	12	13	14	15	16	17	18	19	20	R1	R2
1. Write legibly	★	☆	☆	☆	☆	☆	☆	☆	☆	☆	☆	☆	☆	☆	☆	☆	☆	☆	☆	☆	☆	☆
2. Copy words accurately	★	★	★	★	★	★	★	★	★	★	★	★	★	★	★	★	★	★	★	★	★	★
3. Copy sentences accurately	★	★																				
4. Spell words with greater accuracy					★	★	★	★	★	★	★	★	★	★	★	★	★	★	★	★	★	★
5. Form new words by adding the endings:																						
-ed					☆	☆																
-ing							☆															
-y									★													
-er											★				★							
-est															★							
6. Change the y to i before adding:																						
-er											★				☆							
-est																		★			☆	★
7. Write number words								☆								☆				☆		
8. Use a and an appropriately					☆	☆	☆	☆														
9. Compose sentences												☆								☆	☆	☆

Note: Specific suggestions for additional writing assignments appear in the individual lesson notes for Book 1 and in Chapter 3 of this manual.

Study Skills

Lesson	1	2	3	4	5	6	7	8	9	10	11	12	13	14	15	16	17	18	19	20	R1	R2
1. Complete exercises:																						
fill-in-the-blank			☆	☆	☆	☆	☆	☆	☆	☆	☆	☆	☆	☆	☆	☆	☆	☆	☆	☆		☆
matching								☆	☆	☆	☆	☆	☆	☆	☆	☆	☆	☆	☆	☆	☆	☆
yes/no questions				☆																☆		
writing sentences								☆				☆				☆					☆	☆
true/false questions																					☆	☆
multiple choice questions																					☆	☆
analogies																						
2. Apply reasoning skills:																						
context clues	★	★	★	★	★	★	★	★	★	★	★	★	★	★	★	★	★	★	★	★	★	★
process of elimination						☆	☆	☆	☆	☆	☆	☆	☆	☆	☆	☆	☆	☆	☆	☆	★	☆
3. Use word indexes to check spelling					☆	☆	☆	☆	☆	☆	☆	☆	☆	☆	☆	☆	☆	☆	☆	☆		

KEY: ★ = Primary emphasis   ☆ = Secondary emphasis   ☆ = Integrated with other skills

SCOPE AND SEQUENCE: BOOK 2

Phonics	Lesson	1	2	3	4	5	R	6	7	8	9	10	R	11	12	13	14	15	R	16	17	18	19	20	R
1. Use phonic skills to decode unknown words		★	★	★	★	★	★	★	★	★	★	★	★	★	★	★	★	★	★	★	★	★	★	★	★
2. Recognize long and short vowel sounds		☆	☆	★	★	☆	★	☆	☆	☆	☆	★	☆	★	☆	☆	☆	☆	☆	☆	☆	☆	☆	★	☆
3. Identify long and short vowel sounds		★				★		☆	☆	☆	☆		☆	☆					☆						
4. Identify silent e		☆								☆															
5. Recognize/contrast r-controlled vowel sounds				☆	☆	☆		☆	☆	☆	★	☆	☆		☆	☆		☆	☆	☆	☆	☆	☆	☆	★
6. Recognize vowel sounds preceding l						☆		☆					☆					★	☆						
7. Contrast ow (as in cow and slow)				☆															☆						
8. Recognize aw words										☆				☆											
9. Contrast oo (as in food and foot)												★							☆						
10. Contrast other vowel sounds																						★			★
11. Recognize sounds for single consonants, consonant blends, and digraphs		★	★	★	★	★	★	★	★	★	★	★	★	★	★	★	★	★	★	★	★	★	★	★	★
12. Contrast sounds for single consonants, consonant blends, and digraphs		★	☆	☆	★	★	★	★	☆	☆	☆	☆	☆	☆	☆	☆	★	★	☆	☆	★			☆	
13. Recognize sounds for c and g		☆	☆	☆				☆	☆	☆	☆	☆	☆	☆		☆		☆	☆	☆				☆	
14. Recognize silent consonants and vowels		☆	☆	☆						☆	☆	☆	☆						☆						
15. Identify silent consonants and vowels												★	☆												

Word analysis	Lesson	1	2	3	4	5	R	6	7	8	9	10	R	11	12	13	14	15	R	16	17	18	19	20	R
1. Use syllabication to decode words		☆	☆	☆	☆	★	★	☆	★	★	★	★	★	★	★	★	★	★	☆	★	★	★	★	★	☆
2. Recognize abbreviations and contractions		☆	☆	☆	☆	★	★	☆	★	★	★	★	☆	☆	☆	☆	☆	☆	☆	☆	☆	☆	☆	☆	☆
3. Distinguish words that look similar/rhyme		★	★	★	☆	★	★	★	★	★	★	★	★	★	★	★				★	★	★		★	★
4. Recognize noun endings					★				★								★	★		★					
5. Recognize verb endings									★				☆					☆		☆		☆			
6. Recognize other word endings								☆		★		☆		☆			★	☆	☆	☆	☆	☆			★
7. Recognize common word beginnings																							☆		
8. Divide compound words								☆	☆										☆			☆			
9. Form compound words									☆	★															

Vocabulary	Lesson	1	2	3	4	5	R	6	7	8	9	10	R	11	12	13	14	15	R	16	17	18	19	20	R
1. Learn unfamiliar vocabulary		★	★	★	★	★	★	★	★	★	★	★	★	★	★	★	★	★	★	★	★	★	★	★	★
2. Infer word meanings from context clues		☆	★	★	★	★	★	★	★	★	★	★	★	★	★	★	★	★	★	★	★	★	★	★	★
3. Identify antonyms									★				☆		☆	☆						☆			☆
4. Identify synonyms									★	★		☆			☆						★	★			☆
5. Complete word associations								☆		★		☆		★						★				☆	
6. Complete analogies										★														★	
7. Learn/review idiomatic expressions/common sayings		☆	☆			☆					★			☆					☆					★	☆
8. Learn/review collective nouns																	☆								

KEY: ★ = Primary emphasis   ☆ = Integrated with other skills
★ = Secondary emphasis

Comprehension

Lesson	1	2	3	4	5	R	6	7	8	9	10	R	11	12	13	14	15	R	16	17	18	19	20	R
1. Follow oral and written directions	☆	☆	☆	☆	☆	☆	☆	☆	☆	☆	☆	☆	☆	☆	☆	☆	☆	☆	☆	☆	☆	☆	☆	☆
2. Group words appropriately when reading orally	☆	☆	☆	☆	☆	☆	☆	☆	☆	☆	☆		☆	☆	☆	☆	☆	☆	☆	☆	☆	☆	☆	☆
3. Interpret punctuation correctly when reading orally	☆	☆	☆	☆	☆	☆	☆	☆	☆	☆	☆		☆	☆	☆	☆	☆	☆	☆	☆	☆	☆	☆	☆
4. Identify words using context clues & phonics skills	☆	☆	☆	☆	☆	☆	☆	☆	☆	☆	☆	☆	☆	☆	☆	☆	☆	☆	☆	☆	☆	☆	☆	☆
5. Recognize title as topic of reading selection	★	☆	☆	☆	☆	☆	☆	☆	☆	☆	☆	☆	☆	☆	☆	☆	☆	☆	☆	☆	☆	☆	☆	☆
6. Improve listening comprehension	☆	☆	☆	☆	☆	☆	☆	☆	☆	☆	☆	☆	☆	☆	☆	☆	☆	☆	☆	☆	☆	☆	☆	☆
7. Discuss the reading passage	☆	☆	☆	☆	☆	☆	☆	☆	☆	☆	☆	☆	☆	☆	☆	☆	☆	☆	☆	☆	☆	☆	☆	★
8. Relate reading to illustrations				☆	☆		☆	☆			☆		☆											
9. Develop literal comprehension skills:																								
- Recall details	★	★	★	★	★	☆	★	★	★	★	★	☆	★	★	★	★	★	☆	★	★	★	★	★	★
- Locate information in the reading passage	★	★	★	★	★		★	★	★	★			★	★	★	★	★		★	★	★	★	★	
10. Develop inferential comprehension skills:																								
- Infer word meanings from context clues	☆	☆	☆	☆	★	☆	★	★	★	★	★		★	★	★	★	★		★	★	★		★	★
- Infer information from the selection		☆	☆	☆			☆	☆	☆				☆	☆	☆	☆			☆		☆			
- Draw conclusions based on selection	☆	☆	☆		☆	☆		☆	☆	☆		☆	☆	☆	☆		☆	☆	☆				☆	☆
- Use context clues to predict correct responses	☆	★	☆	☆			☆	☆	☆						☆									
- Classify words under topic headings			☆	☆			☆		☆						☆									
- Determine topic headings for words													☆	☆										
11. Develop applied comprehension skills:																								
- Relate reading to personal experience	☆	☆	☆	☆	☆		☆	☆	☆	☆	☆	☆	☆	☆	☆	☆	☆		☆	☆		☆		☆
- Draw conclusions based on personal experience	☆	☆	☆	☆	☆	☆	☆			☆		☆	☆							☆	☆		☆	
12. Learn/review basic factual information	☆	☆							☆				☆				☆	☆			☆			☆
13. Reorder words into meaningful sentences													☆			☆								
14. Sequence events accurately						☆																		

Writing

Lesson	1	2	3	4	5	R	6	7	8	9	10	R	11	12	13	14	15	R	16	17	18	19	20	R
1. Write legibly	☆	☆	☆	☆	☆	☆	☆	☆	☆	☆	☆	☆	☆	☆	☆	☆	☆	☆	☆	☆	☆	☆	☆	☆
2. Copy words accurately	☆	☆	☆	☆	☆	☆	☆	☆	☆	☆	☆	☆	☆	☆	☆	☆	☆	☆	☆	☆	☆	☆	☆	☆
3. Capitalize words appropriately	☆	☆	☆	☆	☆	☆	☆	☆	☆	☆	☆	☆	☆	☆	☆	☆	☆	☆	☆	☆	☆	☆	☆	☆
4. Spell words with greater accuracy	☆	☆	☆	☆	☆	☆	☆	☆	☆	☆	☆	☆	☆	☆	☆	☆	☆	☆	☆	☆	★	☆	☆	☆
5. Use homonyms correctly	☆	☆			☆						☆													
6. Spell number words accurately			☆			☆								☆		☆								
7. Form new words by adding the endings: −y													☆											
−er																			☆					
8. Change y to i before adding −er, −est, −ly															☆						☆			
9. Unscramble words/sentences			☆	☆	☆		☆	☆	☆	☆	☆	☆	☆	☆	☆	☆	☆		☆	☆	☆	☆	☆	☆
10. Write sentence answers to questions	☆	☆	☆	☆	☆	☆	☆	☆	☆	☆	☆		☆	☆	☆	☆	☆		☆	☆	☆	☆	☆	☆

Note: Specific suggestions for additional writing assignments appear in the individual lesson notes for Book 2 and in Chapter 3 of this manual.

KEY: ★ = Primary emphasis   ☆ = Secondary emphasis   ☆ = Integrated with other skills

Study Skills / Lesson	1	2	3	4	5	R	6	7	8	9	10	R	11	12	13	14	15	R	16	17	18	19	20	R
1. Increase concentration	★	★	★	★	★	★	★	★	★	★	★	★	★	★	★	★	★	★	★	★	★	★	★	★
2. Complete reading comprehension questions requiring: single words answers	☆	☆	☆	☆	☆	☆	☆	☆	☆	☆	☆	☆	☆	☆	☆	☆	☆	☆	☆	☆	☆	☆	☆	☆
phrases	☆	☆	☆	☆	☆			☆	☆	☆	☆	☆	☆	☆	☆	☆	☆	☆	☆	☆	☆	☆	☆	
complete sentences	☆	☆	☆	☆	☆	☆	☆	☆	☆	☆	☆	☆	☆	☆	☆	☆	☆	☆	☆	☆	☆	☆	☆	☆
3. Complete exercises: fill-in-the-blank	☆	☆	☆	☆	☆	☆	☆	☆	☆	☆	☆	☆	☆	☆	☆	☆	☆	☆	☆	☆	☆	☆	☆	☆
matching	☆	☆		☆	☆	☆	☆		☆			☆						☆			☆	☆		☆
multiple choice						☆		☆	☆			☆							☆		☆			☆
analogies									★			★							★		★			★
4. Apply reasoning skills to exercises: context clues	★	★	★	★	★	★	★		★	★	★	★	★	★	☆	☆	☆	☆	☆	☆	☆	☆	☆	☆
process of elimination	★	★	★	★	★	★		☆	★	☆	★	★	☆	☆	☆			☆	☆	☆	☆	☆		☆
5. Use a globe or atlas			☆	☆		☆	☆			☆	☆													
6. Use an encyclopedia				☆																			☆	
7. Use word indexes to look up correct spelling	☆	☆	☆	☆	☆	☆	☆	☆	☆	☆	☆	☆	☆	☆	☆	☆	☆	☆	☆	☆	☆	☆	☆	☆

KEY: ★ = Primary emphasis   ✭ = Secondary emphasis   ☆ = Integrated with other skills

SCOPE AND SEQUENCE: BOOK 3

Phonics

Lesson	1	2	3	4	5	6	7	8	9	10	11	12	13	14	15	16	17	18	19	20	R
1. Use phonics skills to decode unknown words	★	★	★	★	★	★	★	★	★	★	★	★	★	★	★	★	★	★	★	★	★
2. Recognize long and short vowel sounds	★	☆	☆	☆	☆	☆	☆	☆	☆	☆	☆	☆	☆	☆	☆	☆	☆	☆	☆	☆	☆
3. Recognize sounds for vowel combinations: *ai, ee, ēa, ĕa, ui*															★						
oa, ou, oi, oo									★		★										
au								★		★											
r-controlled vowel combinations																					
4. Recognize sounds for consonant blends: *st*		★																			
bl, br, cl, cr, fl, fr			★																		
gl, gr, pl, pr, sl, str				★																	
dr, tr, thr, sc, sk, sw					★																
sm, sn, sp, scr						★															
5. Recognize sounds for digraphs: *ch, sh*		★																			
th, wh						★ ☆															
6. Recognize sounds for *c* and *g*	☆												★								
7. Recognize vowel sounds preceding *l*												★									
8. Recognize silent consonants							★			☆				☆							
9. Recognize *r*-controlled vowel sounds											★				★						
10. Recognize *gh* and *ght* words							★							★							
11. Recognize *ow* sounds (as in *cow* and *slow*)																☆	☆				
12. Contrast vowel and consonant sounds																				★	★

Word Analysis

Lesson	1	2	3	4	5	6	7	8	9	10	11	12	13	14	15	16	17	18	19	20	R
1. Use syllabication to decode words	★	★	★	★	★	★	★	★	★	★	★	★	★	★	★	★	★	★	★	★	★
2. Recognize abbreviations and contractions	☆	☆	☆	☆	☆	☆	☆	☆	☆	☆	☆	☆	☆	☆	☆	☆	☆	☆	☆	☆	☆
3. Divide compound words	★	★	★	★	★	★	★														
4. Form compound words								★									★				
5. Divide words into syllables									★				★	★	★						
6. Combine syllables to form words										★						★					
7. Recognize common word endings: *-er*												★									
-est	☆	★																			
-y			★	★																	
-ly						★															
-ful and *-less*					★	★	☆	☆													
-en																					
8. Recognize common word beginnings: *re-*											★										
in-												★									
mis-													☆								
de-																					
ex-																					
com-, con-																★	★	★			
un-																★	★	★			
dis-, im-, in-																	★	★			
up-, down-, over-, under-																			★		

KEY: ★ = Primary emphasis   ★ = Secondary emphasis   ☆ = Integrated with other skills

Vocabulary

Vocabulary — Lesson	1	2	3	4	5	6	7	8	9	10	11	12	13	14	15	16	17	18	19	20	R
1. Learn unfamiliar vocabulary	★	★	★	★	★	★	★	★	★	★	★	★	★	★	★	★	★	★	★	★	★
2. Infer word meanings from context clues	★	★	★	★	★	★	★	★	★	★	★	★	★	★	★	★	★	★	★	★	★
3. Identify definitions/descriptions of terms	☆	☆	☆	☆			☆	☆		☆		☆	☆		☆	☆	☆	☆	☆	☆	☆
4. Identify synonyms					★						★									★	★
5. Identify antonyms						★						★								★	★
6. Distinguish between synonyms and antonyms							★	★					☆	★							
7. Complete analogies													☆								
8. Complete word associations									★	★							☆				

Comprehension

Comprehension — Lesson	1	2	3	4	5	6	7	8	9	10	11	12	13	14	15	16	17	18	19	20	R
1. Follow written directions	★	★	★	★	★	★	★	★	★	★	★	★	★	★	★	★	★	★	★	★	★
2. Identify words using context clues	★	★	★	★	★	★	★	★	★	★	★	★	★	★	★	★	★	★	★	★	★
3. Read stories independently	★	★	★	★	★	★	★	★	★	★	★	★	★	★	★	★	★	★	★	★	★
4. Complete exercises independently	★	★	★	★	☆	★	★	★	☆	★	★	★	★	★	★	★	★	★	★	★	★
5. Improve listening comprehension	☆	☆	☆	☆	☆	☆	☆	☆	☆	☆	☆	☆	☆	☆	☆	☆	☆	☆	☆	☆	☆
6. Group words appropriately when reading orally	☆	☆	☆	☆	☆	☆	☆	☆	☆	☆	☆	☆	☆	☆	☆	☆	☆	☆	☆	☆	☆
7. Interpret punctuation correctly when reading orally	☆	☆	☆	☆	☆	☆	☆	☆	☆	☆	☆	☆	☆	☆	☆	☆	☆	☆	☆	☆	☆
8. Develop literal comprehension skills:																					
– Recall details	★	★	★	★	★	★	★	★	★	★	★	★	★	★	★	★	★	★	★	★	★
– Locate specific information	★	★	★	★	★	★	★	★	★	★	★	★	★	★	★	★	★	★	★	★	★
9. Develop inferential comprehension skills:																					
– Infer word meanings from context clues	★	★	★	★	★	★	★	★	★	★	★	★	★	★	★	★	★	★	★	★	★
– Infer information from the story	★	★	★	★	★	★	★	★	★	★	★	★	★	★	★	★	★	★	★	★	★
– Use context clues to predict correct responses	★	★	★	★				★	★		☆							☆			
– Summarize the story																					
– Draw conclusions based on story				☆	☆				☆	☆		☆		☆				☆		☆	
– Predict outcomes				☆									☆	☆				☆			
– Classify words under topic headings											☆										
10. Develop applied comprehension skills:																					
– Relate reading to personal experience						☆			☆	☆				☆	☆	☆	☆				
– Draw conclusions based on personal experience					☆	☆			☆			☆			☆	☆					
11. Learn/review basic factual information																☆			☆		

Literary understanding

Literary understanding — Lesson	1	2	3	4	5	6	7	8	9	10	11	12	13	14	15	16	17	18	19	20	R
1. Distinguish between fiction and nonfiction	★	☆	☆	☆	☆	☆	☆	☆	☆	☆	☆	☆	☆	☆	☆	☆	☆	☆	☆	☆	☆
2. Identify/interpret characters' actions, motivations, and feelings	★	★	★	★	★	★	★	★	★	★	★	★	★	★	★	★	★	★	★	★	★
3. Identify/interpret plot	★	★	★	★	★	★	★	★	★	★	★	★	★	★	★	★	★	★	★	★	★
4. Relate title to content of story					★	★	★	★					★								
5. Identify/interpret setting (place)						★	★	★									☆		☆		☆	

KEY: ★ = Primary emphasis   ★ = Secondary emphasis   ☆ = Integrated with other skills

Writing	1	2	3	4	5	6	7	8	9	10	11	12	13	14	15	16	17	18	19	20	R
1. Write legibly	☆	☆	☆	☆	☆	☆	☆	☆	☆	☆	☆	☆	☆	☆	☆	☆	☆	☆	☆	☆	☆
2. Copy words accurately	★	★	★	★	★	★	★	★	★	★	★	★	★	★	★	★	★	★	★	★	★
3. Capitalize words appropriately	★	★	★	★	★	★	★	★	★	★	★	★	★	★	★	★	★	★	★	★	★
4. Spell words with greater accuracy	★	★	★	★	★	★	★	★	★	★	★	★	★	★	★	★	★	★	★	★	★
5. Form new words by adding the endings:																					
-ing	☆																				
-est		☆																			
-y			☆																		
-ly					☆	☆															
-ful, -less							☆	☆													
6. Change the y to i before adding -er, -est				☆						☆											
7. Unscramble words																		☆			
8. Write sentence answers to questions	★								★	★	★	★	★	★	★	★	★	★	★	★	★

Note: Specific suggestions for additional writing assignments appear in the individual lesson notes for Book 3 and in Chapter 3 of this manual.

Study Skills	1	2	3	4	5	6	7	8	9	10	11	12	13	14	15	16	17	18	19	20	R
1. Increase concentration	★	★	★	★	★	★	★	★	★	★	★	★	★	★	★	★	★	★	★	★	★
2. Skim story to locate information	★	★	★	★	★	★	★	★	★	★	★	★	★	★	★	★	★	★	★	★	★
3. Complete exercises:																					
- Reading comprehension questions	☆	☆	☆	☆	☆	☆	☆	☆	☆	☆	☆	☆	☆	☆	☆	☆	☆	☆	☆	☆	★
- Fill-in-the-blank	☆	☆	☆	☆	☆	☆	☆	☆	☆	☆	☆	☆	☆	☆	☆	☆	☆	☆	☆	☆	★
- Matching	☆	☆	☆	☆	☆	☆	☆	☆	☆	☆	☆	☆	☆	☆	☆	☆	☆	☆	☆	☆	☆
- Multiple choice	☆	☆	☆	☆	☆	☆	☆	☆	☆	☆	☆	☆	★	☆	☆	☆	☆	☆	☆	☆	★
4. Apply reasoning skills to exercises:																					
context clues	★	★	★	★	★	★	★	★	★	★	★	★	★	★	★	★	★	★	★	★	★
process of elimination	★	★	★	★	★	★	★	★	★	★	★	★	★	★	★	★	★	★	★	★	★

KEY: ★ = Primary emphasis   ★ = Secondary emphasis   ☆ = Integrated with other skills

SCOPE AND SEQUENCE: BOOK 4

Phonics / Lesson	1	2	3	4	5	R	6	7	8	9	10	R	11	12	13	14	15	R	16	17	18	19	20	R
1. Use phonic skills to decode unknown words	★	★	★	★	★	★	★	★	★	★	★	★	★	★	★	★	★	★	★	★	★	★	★	★
2. Identify long and short vowel sounds	☆	☆	★	☆												☆								☆
3. Recognize sound for -le		★							☆				☆							☆				
4. Identify silent letters													☆											
5. Distinguish sounds for g									☆					☆										

Word Analysis / Lesson	1	2	3	4	5	R	6	7	8	9	10	R	11	12	13	14	15	R	16	17	18	19	20	R
1. Use syllabication to decode words	★	★	★	★	★	★	★	★	★	★	★	★	★	★	★	★	★	★	★	★	★	★	★	★
2. Divide words into syllables	☆	☆	☆	☆	☆			☆				☆				☆				☆			☆	
3. Combine syllables to form words	★			☆							☆		☆											
4. Recognize common word endings: -er	★	★																						
-y			☆			☆																		
-ing				☆																				
-est, -ness, -ship, -ment													☆							☆				
-ful																			☆					
-less																								
5. Recognize common word beginnings								☆											☆					
6. Form compound words														☆		★								
7. Recognize singular and plural forms									★	☆							☆							

Vocabulary / Lesson	1	2	3	4	5	R	6	7	8	9	10	R	11	12	13	14	15	R	16	17	18	19	20	R
1. Learn unfamiliar vocabulary	★	★	★	★	★	★	★	★	★	★	★	★	★	★	★	★	★	★	★	★	★	★	★	★
2. Infer word meanings from context clues	★	★	★	★	★	★	★	★	★	★	★	★	★	★	★	★	★	★	★	★	★	★	★	★
3. Identify definitions/descriptions of terms	★			★	★	★	★	☆					☆					★				★		★
4. Produce definitions/descriptions of terms	★																★		☆	★		★		
5. Learn/review idiomatic expressions/common sayings																								
6. Identify synonyms		★			★	★						★		★										
7. Identify antonyms		★			★	★						★		★										
8. Distinguish between synonyms and antonyms																								
9. Complete word associations		★								★	★										★		★	
10. Complete analogies				★				★									★		☆					
11. Complete double crostic											☆		☆											
12. Learn/review multiple meanings and pronunciations										☆														
13. Learn/review abbreviations															☆			☆					☆	

Comprehension / Lesson	1	2	3	4	5	R	6	7	8	9	10	R	11	12	13	14	15	R	16	17	18	19	20	R
1. Identify words using context clues	★	★	★	★	★	★	★	★	★	★	★	★	★	★	★	★	★	★	★	★	★	★	★	★
2. Read selections independently	★	★	★	★	★	★	★	★	★	★	★	★	★	★	★	★	★	★	★	★	★	★	★	★
3. Complete exercises independently	★	★	★	★	★	★	★	★	★	★	★	★	★	★	★	★	★	★	★	★	★	★	★	★
4. Improve listening comprehension	☆	☆	☆	☆	☆	☆	☆	☆	☆	☆	☆	☆	☆	☆	☆	☆	☆	☆	☆	☆	☆	☆	☆	☆
5. Group words appropriately when reading orally	☆	☆	☆	☆	☆	☆	☆	☆	☆	☆	☆	☆	☆	☆	☆	☆	☆	☆	☆	☆	☆	☆	☆	☆
6. Interpret punctuation correctly when reading orally	☆	☆	☆	☆	☆	☆	☆	☆	☆	☆	☆	☆	☆	☆	☆	☆	☆	☆	☆	☆	☆	☆	☆	☆

KEY: ★ = Primary emphasis   ★ = Secondary emphasis   ☆ = Integrated with other skills

Comprehension, cont.

Lesson	1	2	3	4	5	R	6	7	8	9	10	R	11	12	13	14	15	R	16	17	18	19	20	R
7. Develop literal comprehension skills:																								
– Recall details	★	★	★	★	★	★	★	★	★	★	★	★	★	★	★	★	★	★	★	★	★	★	★	★
– Locate specific information	★	★	★	★	★	★	★	★	★	★	★	★	★	★	★	★	★	★	★	★	★	★	★	★
– Sequence events				★															★					
8. Develop inferential comprehension skills:																								
– Infer word meanings from context clues	★		★	★	★	★	★	★	★	★	★	★	★	★	★	★	★	★	★	★	★	★	★	★
– Infer information from the reading	★	★	★	★	★	★		★	★	★	★	★	★	★	★	★	★	★	★	★	★	★	★	★
– Draw conclusions based on reading	★			★																	★	★	★	★
– Use context clues to predict correct responses			★		★		★	★			★	★	★					★	★	★	★	★	★	★
– Determine topic headings for words					★																			
– Classify words under topic headings							★				★			★								★		
– Determine cause and effect relationships																								
9. Develop applied comprehension skills:																								
– Draw conclusions based on personal experience	★				★				★	★	★			★						★				
– Relate reading to personal experience			★		★				★	★			★		★	★				★			★	
– Sequence events					★				★	★														
10. Learn/review basic factual information	★	★	★	★	★	★	★	★	☆	☆	★	★	☆	☆	★			★	☆			☆		★
11. Locate/infer information from a menu																							★	

Writing

Lesson	1	2	3	4	5	R	6	7	8	9	10	R	11	12	13	14	15	R	16	17	18	19	20	R
1. Write legibly	☆	☆	☆	☆	☆	☆	☆	★	★	☆	☆	☆	☆	☆	☆	☆	☆	☆	☆	☆	★	☆	★	☆
2. Copy words accurately	★	★	★	★	★	★	★	★	★	★	★	★	★	★	★	★	★	★	★	★	★	★	★	★
3. Capitalize words appropriately	★	★	★	★	★	★	★	★	★	★	★	★	★	★	★	★	★	★	★	★	★	★	★	★
4. Spell words with greater accuracy	★	☆	★	★	★	★	★	★	★	★	★	★	★	★	★	★	★	★	★	★	★	★	★	★
5. Form new words by adding the endings:	★																							
-er		★	☆	☆																				
-y			☆	☆																				
-ing							☆																	
6. Change f to v to form plurals										☆														
7. Change the y to i before adding:									☆				☆							☆				
-er, -est, -ness																★			☆					
-ly																								
8. Unscramble words																							★	
9. Write sentence or paragraph answers to questions	★	★	★	★	★	★	★	★	★	★	★	★	★	★	★	★		★		★				★

Note: Specific suggestions for additional writing assignments appear in the individual lesson notes for Book 4 and in Chapter 3 of this manual.

Study Skills

Lesson	1	2	3	4	5	R	6	7	8	9	10	R	11	12	13	14	15	R	16	17	18	19	20	R
1. Increase concentration	☆	☆	☆	★	★	★	☆	★	★	☆	☆	★	★	★	★	★	★	★	★	★	★	★	★	★
2. Skim passage to locate information	★	★	★	☆	★	★	☆	★	★	☆	★	☆	★	★	★	★	★	★	★	★	★	★	★	★
3. Apply reasoning skills to exercises: context clues	★	★	★	★	★	★	★	★	★	★	★	★	★	★	★	★	★	★	★	★	★	★	★	★
process of elimination	★	★		★	★	★	☆	★	★	★	★	★	★					★	★	★	★	★	★	★
"intelligent guessing"	★																							
4. Use a dictionary to look up word meanings		☆		☆			☆			☆	☆	☆	☆	☆	☆	☆	☆	☆	☆	☆	★	☆	☆	☆
5. Use an atlas or globe															☆									

KEY: ★ = Primary emphasis   ★ = Secondary emphasis   ☆ = Integrated with other skills

Chapter 1

Preparing to Teach

These suggestions are offered to help you prepare to teach using this program. We hope that you will find these suggestions helpful. Some of them may need to be modified to fit your particular situation.

Scheduling Considerations

Most beginning readers progress best when you meet with them for one hour five times a week at a regularly scheduled time. A schedule in which learners meet only two or three times a week or at different times each week can work, but often progress is slower than for learners who work with a teacher at the same time each day.

In volunteer programs, meeting daily is often impossible. In this setting, try to schedule at least two sessions a week. If only one session a week is possible, encourage learners to set aside some time each day to read. Emphasize that daily practice will be essential for progress in developing reading skills.

The Lesson Components

Each lesson in *Challenger* has three basic components: word study, a reading selection, and skill-building exercises.

1. **Word Study.** In Books 1 and 3, word study includes a chart with words that contain specific phonetic elements, plus words for study—words being used in the lesson for the first time in the series. Lessons in Books 2 and 4 do not have word charts, but they do have words for study.

2. **The Reading Selection.** Books 1 and 3 contain pieces of short fiction. Books 2 and 4 have nonfiction informational reading selections.

3. **The Exercises.** Each lesson has several exercises designed to develop decoding, vocabulary, comprehension, and reasoning skills. The first exercise in Books 2–4 is a comprehension exercise based on the reading selection. Suggested questions that can be used in oral discussion to assess comprehension are included in the lesson notes for Book 1.

Because *Challenger* is a very flexible program, there are several ways to handle the lesson material when working with your students. With students beginning in Book 1, you may cover one lesson in each session. Or you may briefly review the preceding lesson, then spend the bulk of the session on the new lesson. Particularly with students working in Books 2–4, you may spend part of the session on material addressing student-specific goals or needs. Another option is to spend the first part of the session discussing the reading selection and exercises done for homework, and the second part of the session introducing the reading selection and previewing the exercises for the next lesson.

It will take a few sessions to determine the pace and procedures that work best for your students. Keep in mind, however, that following a consistent procedure helps learners because they tend to work much better when they have a sense of routine.

Planning the Lessons

It is important to prepare thoroughly to teach each lesson. The following steps should help you prepare for teaching a lesson.

1. Read the lesson notes found in this manual for suggestions to help you teach a particular lesson. Go over the answers in the Answer Key.

Planning the Lessons (continued)

Decide what you want to emphasize (your objectives), list activities, and prepare any materials you will need.

2. Plan pre-reading activities to introduce the reading selection. Try to anticipate questions students may have about the exercises.

3. Decide what you want to emphasize (reading comprehension, spelling rules, etc.) and plan how you will do it.

4. Look over any notes you made after the preceding class to see if there is anything that students need to review.

5. Plan a writing activity based on suggestions in Chapter 3 of this manual or in the lesson notes.

6. Decide upon any reinforcement activities you may want to use and complete any preparation needed. (Suggestions for reinforcement activities are given in Chapter 4.)

7. After the session, make notes about approaches and strategies that worked well and areas that need reinforcement for individual learners and for the group as a whole.

On page 26, there is a Model Lesson Planning Worksheet that you may want to use.

Try to allow a few minutes before students arrive to prepare yourself mentally and emotionally for the session. As the teacher, your main function is to serve as a bridge between the student and the lesson material. How well the session goes is often determined by how relaxed and focused you are on the work.

The Teacher-Student Relationship

Establishing a good teacher-student relationship is absolutely essential for students' progress. Mature students rely heavily on teachers' support and encouragement to bolster their self-confidence and reinforce their motivation, particularly in periods of extreme frustration.

Completing the lessons takes a lot of work. Encourage students to view their time with you and their homework assignments as daily workouts or practice sessions. Sports and music, which require daily practice, are helpful analogies. No matter how much progress is being made, most learners experience a sense of frustration at one time or another. Your encouragement will help them to get through those periods when they feel like giving up.

Above all, these lessons should be seen as opportunities for learners to move smoothly toward their reading goals. They do not have to demonstrate mastery of the material in one lesson in order to go on to the next lesson. Mastery comes with consistent practice. It is crucial for you to think in terms of improvement rather than mastery and to regard mistakes as natural and helpful. Some learners will be very sensitive to mistakes in their work. They will need continual reinforcement of the concept that we all learn from our mistakes.

Finally, remember that reading comprehension depends to a large extent on the background information a student has. As you come to know your students better, you can identify gaps in background knowledge that you can help to fill through reinforcement activities, discussion, and pleasure reading or other supplemental reading. Plan the sessions with the students' personal goals and needs in mind.

Building a Good Working Relationship

- Avoid treating learners with either condescension or pity. Remember that adult learners have a wealth of experience to draw upon.

- Greet students pleasantly and spend a few minutes talking before you begin the session. You might discuss what has happened in your students' lives or in your life, what they have read that they found

Building a Good Working Relationship
(continued)

particularly interesting, or how their homework went. Then use a phrase such as "Shall we get started?" to indicate that it is time to begin the session.

- In a tutorial or small-group situation, work from the learner's book rather than your own. This practice conveys a "we're in this together" spirit.
- Use positive reinforcement during the sessions. Remind learners of the progress they are making. When they are particularly discouraged, do this in a concrete way by showing them how many pages they have completed or how their writing has improved.

Supplies

General Supplies

- An alphabet chart with upper-case and lower-case letters is helpful for beginning readers and writers.
- Have a dictionary available and, if possible, a set of encyclopedias. These valuable resources provide additional information and sometimes pictures about many of the words, people, events, and other things mentioned in *Challenger*.
- A globe or an atlas will enable learners to find the geographical location of places mentioned in the lessons.

Be prepared to teach students how to use these resources. Encourage them to do research as often as their interest, abilities, and time permit.

Teacher Supplies
You will need:

- your copies of the *Challenger* student book and Teacher's Manual
- your lesson plan
- blank paper for making notes during the session
- a pen or pencil for making marginal notes and marking corrections in the students' books. (Avoid red ink as it is frequently associated with bad memories of school.) Colored highlighters are also helpful for marking troublesome words.

Student Supplies
For each class, students need:

for writing

- their *Challenger* book
- a pen or pencil
- their writing notebook. We recommend using a loose-leaf binder with wide-lined paper for writing assignments and reinforcement activities.

yes

A Summary of Do's

✓

- Do schedule as many sessions each week as possible.
- Do develop a consistent lesson format.
- Do take time to decide the pace that works best for your learners.
- Do prepare for each class.
- Do take a few moments to relax before each class.
- Do develop a good working relationship with your students because it is essential to their reading progress.
- Do make sure that the environment in which you teach is as conducive to good learning as possible.

Model Lesson Planning Worksheet

	Activities	Notes
1. Homework Review		
A. The Reading Selection Objectives:		
B. Post-reading Activities Objectives:		
C. Review of Exercises and New Words Objectives:		
2. Writing Activity Objectives:		
3. Reinforcement Activity Objectives:		
4. Homework Preview		
A. Word Study Objectives:		
B. Pre-reading Activities Objectives:		
C. Previewing the Exercises Objectives:		

Chapter 2

Teaching the Lessons

*How you teach the lessons in **Challenger** will depend on a number of issues. Whether you are tutoring a single student or working with a small group, what book your students are working in, the number of times you meet with them each week, and various other concerns will have to be taken into consideration.*

Sample Teaching Session Formats

Because of its flexibility, *Challenger* lends itself to a variety of teaching session possibilities. The following sample format outlines a procedure that can be used with a small group of students who all are working on the same lesson in *Challenger 2– 4.*

The Current Lesson

1. **Homework Review.** For most lessons, read aloud some or all of the reading selection assigned for homework. Go over the Exercise 1 comprehension questions and discuss the reading selection. Suggestions for discussion are given in the individual lesson notes. Go over the other exercises, paying particular attention to any new material introduced in the lesson.
2. **Summarizing.** Have students summarize what they learned from the lesson.
3. **Writing Activity.** Suggestions for writing activities are given in Chapter 3 of this manual and in the individual lesson notes.
4. **Reinforcement Activity.** If time permits, give students additional practice in an area of difficulty.

The New Lesson

1. **Word Study.** Introduce or review the phonics principles and have students read words from the word chart (for Book 3).
2. **The Reading Selection.** Have students read the Words for Study. Introduce the reading in the new lesson using one or more pre-reading activities. Assign the reading of the selection for homework, or read the selection orally and assign a second reading of the selection for homework.
3. **Preview Homework Exercises.** Preview the exercises in the new lesson with students to be sure they understand how to do them. Teach any new principles or rules pertaining to the exercises. Suggest topics for a writing activity.

Whenever possible, try to reserve the last segment of each session for pleasure reading. In the beginning, you may read a story, poem, or article of interest to your students. As students' confidence increases, you might take turns reading "just for fun" material. Select material that deals with students' hobbies, work, or specific goals. For instance, if a student has mentioned wanting to read to his children, bring in age-level appropriate stories and help the student practice reading them. If a student loves to cook, help him to read recipes from a cookbook.

Do not expect to know in the beginning how much time to allot for each segment of the lesson. All students are different, and understanding how to pace the lessons takes time. By observing students' responses and rates of accuracy and improvement, you will become able to predict how much time a given segment of the lesson should take.

Particularly for students working in Book 1, it may be preferable to spend two class sessions on one lesson. That way, the first session begins with the word study, followed by pre-reading activities. Next you and your student read the story orally and discuss it. The exercises can then be previewed for homework or the student can complete them during the session. In the next class session, you can go over the exercises, have the student summarize what was learned in the lesson, and do writing and reinforcement activities.

Specific suggestions for teaching students working in Book 1 are included in the Introduction to Book 1, which begins on page 49.

Below are suggestions for teaching the main components of each lesson in *Challenger*. These components include word study, the reading selection, and the exercises. Dealing with writing assignments and suggestions for reinforcement activities are discussed in Chapters 3 and 4.

Word Study

The *Challenger* series places significant emphasis on word recognition skills, since a major obstacle to reading improvement is a poor sight vocabulary. New words are introduced in the odd-numbered books through the word charts, and in all books in the Words for Study section preceding each reading selection.

The Word Charts

In Books 1 and 3, word charts appear at the beginning of each lesson. The words in the chart illustrate particular phonics principles being introduced or reviewed in the lesson. Many of the chart words are also used in the story and the exercises.

The phonics approach to decoding used throughout *Challenger* is based on learning to recognize the following:

- the basic sound-letter relationships
- common letter combinations regularly found in English words
- common syllable patterns that indicate how words are pronounced

The chart on pages 8–11 lists the main sound-symbol relationships, plus letter combinations and syllable patterns that influence decoding.

The phonics approach provides an organizing principle for introducing new words in this controlled-vocabulary series. By learning some basic phonics principles, students develop the necessary tools for sounding out new words, reviewing forgotten words, and handling increasingly difficult material. Since the phonics method is based on a problem-solving approach to decoding, the tendency to blurt out the first word that comes to mind gives way to a more reasoned discovery of how to decode words.

The following procedure is suggested for working with the word charts.

1. Students say the guide sound for the first group of words.
2. Students sound out the words containing the guide sound. Use your judgment in deciding how many words students should read. They don't have to read all the words in any given chart. They can sound out the remaining words as they encounter them in the readings or the exercises.
3. When students have completed the chart, do a brief review of the words they have read. You can point to words at random and have students read them. Or you may say a word and have students locate it.
4. You may want students to practice writing some of the chart words. Writing selected words reinforces both the letter patterns and word recognition.

Word Study
(continued)

Particularly for word charts that focus on vowel sounds, we recommend that you have students begin with the vowel sound when sounding out words. Starting with the vowel sound helps students to develop the problem-solving approach. Many beginning readers identify the initial sound in the word and then guess the rest. Often it is a wrong guess. By emphasizing the vowel sound, adding the ending sounds, and then working on the initial sounds, students decode with much greater accuracy. The following example is based on Lesson 2 of Book 1.

1. Students say the guide sound for the first row in the chart, /ā/.
2. They cover up the *d, t,* and *e* of the word *date* and say the vowel sound, /ā/.
3. They uncover the letters to the right of the vowel, *te,* and say the vowel sound plus the consonant, /āt/.
4. Then students uncover the *d* and say /dāt/.
5. If necessary, review the function of the silent *e*.

Beginning students sometimes have difficulty putting the sounds together. Assist them by modeling the pronunciation of the words and having students repeat them.

Some students can sight-read many of the chart words in the early lessons of Books 1 and 3. These students may resist learning the phonics approach. Assure them that they will not have to sound out words they can sight-read, but that this method will give them a way to attack new words. Use the following steps when working on word charts with students who have a basic sight vocabulary.

1. Have students read the words in the order in which they appear. Point out the letter and syllable patterns of the words they already know how to decode.
2. When students miss a word, teach the guide sound and have them sound out the word, beginning with the vowel sound when the chart focuses on vowel sounds.
3. During the random review, have students review all the sounds whether or not they had difficulty with them.
4. Provide reinforcement activities that focus on the sounds and words that gave students difficulty.

When working on the word charts, concentrate on developing word attack skills. Since students probably know the meanings of most of the chart words, avoid spending a lot of time on definitions. There are opportunities for developing vocabulary skills in context later in the lessons. If students ask for the definition of a chart word, state the meaning and use the word in a sentence.

The Words for Study

The Words for Study section contains words that appear in the story and exercises for the first time in this controlled-vocabulary series. They are listed in the order and form in which they appear in the lesson.

Students may be able to sight-read some of these words. As students progress, they may be able to sound out the unfamiliar words that adhere to phonics principles they have studied. If students cannot sight-read or sound out a word, say the word and have students repeat it a few times. Either state the meaning, or ask students to try to figure out the meaning as the word is used in context in the lesson.

Since Words for Study are listed in the form in which they appear in the lesson, some of them have endings such as *-s, -ed,* or *-ing.* Make sure students notice and read the endings on words that have them.

Word Study
(continued)

Sometimes a student's pronunciation of a word will differ from yours. Offer the standard pronunciation only if the student asks for it. Mispronunciation becomes important if it interferes with a student's reading comprehension or spelling. In these instances, encourage students to use the standard pronunciation.

Using Key Words

Students can use words they already know as key words to help them sound out and remember new words. A key word is a familiar word that helps students remember a specific sound/symbol relationship. Key words should be short, common words the student can read easily. Students should usually select the key words themselves.

Key words are especially helpful for the following phonics elements: *r*-controlled vowels, *l*-controlled vowels, silent letter combinations, and vowel combinations, particularly combinations that spell more than one sound. For instance, in Lesson 12 of Book 1, the vowel combination *ea* is shown with two lists of words. You might suggest that students select one word from each list, such as *eat* and *head,* to use as key words. When students encounter the words *deal* and *least* in Lesson 14, they can write their key word *eat* in the margin to remind them that those words have the long *e* sound.

The Reading Selections

The stories in Book 1 are designed to be read aloud in class and then discussed orally. Specific instructions for handling the readings in Book 1 can be found in the Introduction to Book 1, beginning on page 49.

The readings in Books 2–4 may be handled in a number of ways, depending on your students' needs and the amount of time you have with them. It is a good idea to provide for two readings of each selection, one to develop fluency and one for comprehension. The readings can be both oral and silent, with one done in class and the other for homework. Tell students that even experienced readers often have to read things more than once, particularly when reading instructions, textbooks, forms, and so forth.

Each reading selection should be introduced with appropriate pre-reading activities and followed with post-reading activities.

Pre-reading Activities

It is important to introduce each reading selection using one or more pre-reading activities. The type of pre-reading activities you select will depend upon whether students are reading the fiction in Books 1 and 3 or the informational readings in Books 2 and 4. Pre-reading activities for individual lessons are suggested in the lesson notes.

Pre-reading activities should accomplish one or more of the following objectives:
- to stimulate students' interest by drawing on their prior experience or understanding of the subject
- to give students a purpose for reading
- to provide essential background information

The first pre-reading activities usually will be to have students read the Words for Study and the selection's title and then predict what the reading will be about or tell what they think the title means.

You can link the subject of the reading to students' personal experiences by asking "Have you ever done/been/thought/felt . . .?" questions. You can give students a purpose for reading by setting a task for them as they read. For instance, in Lesson 5 of Book 3 you might say, "As you read, think about what kind of person Ginger is." For Lesson 9 of Book 4 you could say, "Try to remember times when you have seen children eating in these ways."

Students will better understand some of the readings in Books 2 and 4 if pertinent historical or geographical background is provided. For example, a discussion of Hitler's attempt to destroy Europe's Jewish population during World War II should precede the reading of the excerpts from Anne Frank's diary in Lessons 12 and 13 of Book 4.

Reading the Selection

There are a variety of ways to handle the reading selections, and the procedure used should vary from lesson to lesson, particularly for students working in Books 1 and 2. The following methods have proved effective with beginning readers.

- Read to the students. By reading aloud while students follow along in the text, you model good oral reading and facilitate comprehension.
- Read one sentence aloud while your student follows along. Then have your student read the sentence aloud. This method is sometimes called "echo reading."
- You and your student read the selection aloud together ("duet reading").
- A group of students reads a selection aloud together.
- Alternate reading aloud sentences or short paragraphs with a student.

When the first reading is done as homework, you may want to introduce some of the selections by reading aloud the first paragraph or two. Tell the students that you will read only the beginning of the story while they follow along in the book. Then ask one or two questions to make sure students have understood what you read. By reading aloud, you can create interest in the reading at the same time you are modeling good reading.

Post-reading Activities

1. **Oral Reading.** Have students in Books 1 and 2 read the selection aloud before starting to discuss it. This gives you an opportunity to note their strengths and weaknesses and also to help them develop good oral reading habits. Students in Books 3 and 4 should also read at least part of the selection aloud for most lessons. How often you do this and how much of the selection is read aloud depends upon time and the needs of your students.

2. **Summarize.** Have students summarize the reading by identifying and stating the main points. Discuss any predictions they made about the reading based on the Words for Study and the title.

3. **Exercise 1.** For students working in Books 2–4, go over their responses to the reading comprehension questions in Exercise 1.

4. **Discuss the Reading.** Have a general discussion of the reading to make sure students have understood what they have read and to give them practice in developing listening and speaking skills. Ask literal-, inferential-, and applied-level questions to assess students' comprehension. Suggested questions are given in the lesson notes for each lesson.

   Literal-level Questions. These questions deal with the most basic kind of comprehension, that is, remembering what the author said. In answering literal questions, students do not need to infer information or apply what they have read to prior knowledge. Answers to literal questions can be found in the reading selection, and you should encourage students to look back at the reading for the answers.

Start with a general question such as "What does this sentence tell you?" or "What happened in this paragraph?" Then move on to questions about specific details. Literal questions about the stories in Books 1 and 3 can deal with characters, events, settings, or other details. Examples of detail-specific questions are: "Where does this story take place?" "What are the characters' names?" "What did Kate do with the cake?"

Literal questions about the readings in Books 2 and 4 also can deal with specific details. You might ask, "Why do skunks spray their liquid?" "How did Black Bart get started holding up stagecoaches?" "What do some people think flying saucers might be?"

Inferential-level Questions. These questions require students to use information in the reading to draw conclusions that are not actually stated. Examples of inferential questions pertaining to the story in Lesson 9 of Book 1 are: "Why didn't Eddie want Kate to bake the cake for the party?" "Do you think Bob will think it's funny that they bought him toys for his birthday?"

Inferential questions for the informational reading in Lesson 9 of Book 2 are: "Why didn't John Sutter want people to know gold had been found on his land?" "Explain what 'made a strike' means in this story."

Applied-level Questions. These questions help students relate what they have read to their own experiences. Examples of applied questions are: "Do you know people like the characters in this story? Describe them." "Tell about a similar experience you have had." "What would you do if you were in this situation?"

Applied questions for the informational readings might be: "How would your life be different if Edison hadn't invented the light bulb?" "Describe an ad that made you want to buy or do something."

Literal-, inferential-, and applied-level questions help students respond to the reading selections and develop critical reading skills. With practice, students learn to use information from their reading to support their own thoughts. They also begin to see connections between the situations in the readings and their own life experiences. When they make such connections, reading becomes an enjoyable activity that helps them to think more clearly and that motivates them to learn more.

Facilitating Group Discussion

To create an atmosphere in which the reading selections and students' reactions to them can be discussed freely and openly, consider these suggestions.

- Plan questions to get the discussion started, but be flexible in order to take advantage of students' interests and curiosity.
- Make sure students understand two basic ground rules: that one person speaks at a time and that they treat each other's opinions with respect.
- Encourage participation, but don't force it.
- Keep the discussion focused.
- Avoid asking questions that can be answered with yes and no.
- Allow students to react to each other's opinions and comments. Avoid dominating the discussion yourself.

View discussions as you view the students' other work—in terms of improvement, or growth, instead of mastery. It takes time to develop a good discussion group in which participants really listen to each other and gain the necessary confidence to express themselves genuinely. It also takes time for students to learn the kinds of questions to ask and the types of information to contribute. You can help them by modeling appropriate questions and responses during the early sessions, then making fewer and fewer contributions as students become more skillful.

When tutoring an individual student, discussion of the reading is just as essential. It is important for the learner to develop speaking and listening skills and to be able to express his thoughts about and reactions to what he has read. It may be harder to get an individual student to participate at first, but as you learn more about his interests and abilities, you can prompt the discussion with these in mind.

The Exercises

In addition to reading comprehension exercises, there are other exercises in the lessons that build decoding, vocabulary, and comprehension skills. Many of these other exercises help learners to develop their reasoning abilities by requiring them to think and infer, to use context clues, to practice the process of elimination, and to apply what they already know to new situations.

Previewing the Exercises

Generally, the exercises are assigned as homework. Allow enough time at the end of the session to preview the exercises so that students understand how to do them. Since exercise formats are repeated frequently, you should only have to explain the directions for any given format the first few times it occurs. When introducing a new exercise format, you may want students to complete the first one or two items to be sure they understand what to do.

When an exercise is based on phonics principles or spelling rules, an example may be given. When previewing this type of exercise, ask questions about the example to make sure students understand the process being illustrated.

For example, in Lesson 5 of Book 1, Exercise 1 deals with adding *-ed* to words. When previewing this exercise, have students look at the examples and ask: "Were any letters dropped or added to the root word when *-ed* was added?" When they have studied the examples and answered the question, tell them, "When adding *-ed* to words that end in silent *e,* drop the silent *e* before adding *-ed*. If a word has one syllable, one vowel, and one final consonant, double the final consonant before adding *-ed*."

Students may want to write these spelling rules in their writing notebooks.

Doing the Homework

Homework is the learners' responsibility. They must understand and accept the concept that regular practice outside of class time is essential for them to improve their reading skills. You may want to review the importance of practice by comparing homework with practicing a sport or musical instrument.

Adult learners often profit by doing their homework with someone else who is working in the same book. They can help each other sort out any difficulties that may arise. Discussing problems and giving explanations reinforce understanding and recall of the material for both learners.

Sometimes adult learners try to do their homework right after a full day of work, while trying to make dinner, or just before going to bed.

Encourage them to schedule a definite study time in quiet surroundings when they will not be exhausted or distracted by other activities or responsibilities.

If once in a while a student doesn't complete the homework exercises, don't be concerned. If a student generally neglects the homework, however, you can suggest alternative plans for getting it done and help the student find a workable study time and place. Occasionally, an adult learner simply can't do any work outside the class session. If this is the case, both you and the student must recognize and accept the fact that progress will be slow.

The following reminders may be helpful from time to time.

- Students should complete all homework items to the best of their ability. Leaving an item blank is not nearly so helpful as guessing wrong and correcting an answer in class.
- Items in a given exercise do not always have to be done in order. Teach students how to use the process of elimination. For appropriate exercises, tell students to do the items they are sure of first, checking off answers as they use them. Then, for questions they are unsure of, they can select the most logical answers from the choices that are left.
- Students should check over their homework after finishing all the exercises to be sure they haven't skipped any answers.

Going Over the Homework

It is important to go over all work that students do. They need feedback in order to correct mistakes and to build good reading and writing habits. They also need to know that their efforts are important enough for you to spend time on.

Going over the homework provides the opportunity to review and reinforce concepts introduced and practiced in the exercises. When a student misses several items in an exercise, it is a signal that additional reinforcement is necessary.

If you are tutoring an individual student, have him read his answers aloud. If you work with a group, the whole group can go over most of the exercises together. Have students take turns reading their answers aloud. They should read whole sentences in exercises that have them. Tell students to correct their own work.

When going over students' work, be careful not to concentrate on their mistakes to the extent that you overlook their overall progress. Positive reinforcement is particularly important during this time.

Take your time and enjoy this part of the lesson. Take advantage of any opportunities that arise to link items in the exercises to students' own experiences or to previous discussions. It is always helpful for students to see the relationship between their reading and their lives beyond the classroom.

The Lesson Summary

Have students summarize the lesson. This helps to facilitate learning and remembering. Ask them to say what the lesson was about in their own words. Then ask, "What did you learn from this lesson? What was hard for you?" Review any important concepts that they left out.

Some Final Thoughts

Giving Explanations

It is important to respond as promptly and clearly as possible to questions that students raise in class. When questions arise, give explanations that are brief and to the point. Don't be afraid to say, "I don't know, but I'll find out" when you don't have the answer to a specific question. For instance, if a student asks why some words have a silent *gh,* you can respond, "I don't know, but I think it has to do with their origins. If you're interested, we can check that in the dictionary later."

The Need for Positive Reinforcement

It is important to remember the value of positive reinforcement in all work that students do. Develop the habit of saying "good" or "right" after each correct response. Even if students make an error, there is usually something positive you can say. For example, you can say, "You've almost got it, but let's read the second sentence again."

Stress the notion of progress, since students are progressing as they complete each lesson. From time to time, you may want to suggest that they look back to the work they did in earlier lessons in the book or compare the writing they are doing now with what they did earlier in their writing notebooks.

The Importance of Observation

It is important to pay close attention to how well students are progressing through the lessons in order to provide reinforcement activities when necessary and to adapt procedures as students become ready for greater challenges. Keep the following questions in mind to help you assess students' progress.

• Can students sound out or sight-read more words with less help?
• Are students correcting more of their own mistakes?
• Are students more adept at discussing the readings?
• Do students answer more questions correctly?
• Are students' writing skills gradually improving?

As you become attuned to students' progress, it will become easier to predict the areas that will need special reinforcement as well as those that students will probably grasp easily. You will thus be able to adapt the pace and procedures of the lessons to students' developing skills.

• Do have a general discussion of the reading to assess students' comprehension, and ask literal-, inferential-, and applied-level questions.
• Do make sure students understand how phonics helps them to improve their word-attack skills.
• Do make sure students know why they need to do homework.
• Do make sure students know exactly how to do the homework exercises.
• Do help students to develop good study habits.
• Do maximize learning by having students correct their own work.
• Do take time to review homework without rushing.
• Do give explanations when students request them.
• Do provide positive reinforcement regularly and naturally.
• Do consciously monitor students' progress.

Chapter 3 Writing

*The **Challenger** series emphasizes helping students to develop their reading skills. Opportunities for sustained writing in the student books are necessarily limited. This chapter gives suggestions for integrating more writing practice into the lessons on a regular basis.*

Providing Opportunities for Writing

Generally, basic reading students progress more rapidly if they have a writing activity as part of each lesson. There are several purposes for including writing practice.

- Writing is part of literacy. Writing reinforces and enhances reading skills.
- Writing helps students to formulate and express their thoughts more precisely. It also helps to develop reasoning skills as students learn to monitor whether or not their writing makes sense.
- The writing that students do in their lessons can help them with other writing, such as for letters, reports, job applications, and résumés.
- Through sustained writing, students can develop and polish their writing skills.

Even students with severely limited writing skills can begin to write from their very first lesson. Provide opportunities for free writing that doesn't have to be polished. Encourage students to get used to expressing their thoughts in writing. Students who write on a regular basis will come to understand that the purpose of both reading and writing is to communicate ideas.

Students working in Book 1 can keep dialogue journals and dictate language experience stories. Dialogue journals act as written conversations between you and the student. Since the journals are kept confidential, students can write anything they want to. Because you do not correct or change anything they write, they are freed from the fear of making mistakes. In your responses to students' journal entries, you can model correct written English while showing an interest in what students are telling you. Students gradually come to see writing as a means of communicating their ideas rather than as a chore.

Language experience activities, based on topics the students are interested in, use material and vocabulary familiar to the students. In a language experience activity, beginning students name a topic and dictate a story. You write down the story, and they can later read it. Somewhat more advanced students can dictate several words or phrases related to a topic, and you can create a word map for the topic from the dictated words. The students can write stories based on the word maps. Then the students can read the stories they have written.

In addition to the above activities, students with limited writing skills can write brief notes, grocery lists, reminders for appointments, instructions to family members, and so forth. The individual lesson notes include suggestions for writing activities to supplement the lessons. Other topics of interest to the students, such as personal letters or current events, are also appropriate writing activities. As students progress through the *Challenger* books, writing activities can be increasingly longer, more polished, and more complex.

Students should keep their writing assignments in a writing notebook. A loose-leaf binder with wide-lined notebook paper works well. They should keep all drafts of a given activity in their notebooks. Have them date their work so that they can see how their writing improves over time.

Understanding the Writing Process

As students become more confident about putting their thoughts and ideas in writing, they can focus on such issues as organization and development of their material and the technical aspects of writing.

In order for students to become more competent writers, you will need to help them understand the writing process. Inexperienced writers often fail to understand that a lot of planning and revision goes into producing a polished piece of writing. They want their first draft to be perfect and concentrate so heavily on not making mistakes that they cannot express their ideas freely. You will need to help them understand that the writing process has several stages, starting with doing pre-writing activities, then writing a first draft, revising, editing, and doing a final version. When students are ready and when there is an appropriate activity, guide them through some or all of the steps below.

Pre-writing Activities

Selecting a Topic. Choosing a topic depends upon the type and purpose of the activity. The topic may be linked directly to the current lesson, but it doesn't have to be. In any case, the topic should be something the writer is interested in and knows something about.

Defining the Purpose and Audience. It is extremely important, particularly for inexperienced writers, to have a clear understanding of the purpose of the writing activity and the audience for whom it is intended. Understanding the purpose of the writing helps the writer to generate ideas and clarify the topic. Keeping the audience in mind helps to avoid one of the most common mistakes inexperienced writers make: leaving out important information that the reader needs to know.

Generating and Organizing Ideas. Brainstorming and idea mapping are useful techniques for generating and organizing ideas relating to the topic. Working in pairs or small groups, students can discuss the topic, jotting down ideas as they are mentioned. They can map their ideas by circling the main ideas and clustering around them the details that support those ideas. Then they can plan the order in which they want to present the main ideas. It often helps new writers to do this by developing a brief outline from the idea map.

Clarifying the Topic. The writer needs to clarify the topic by writing a complete sentence that expresses the main theme or concept that he wants to communicate. This can be done either before or after the brainstorming and idea-mapping steps. If it is done before, the writer should reread the statement after the idea-mapping process and, if necessary, revise it to include any new ideas that arose.

Writing and Revising

First drafts of any writing activity that will be revised and edited should be double-spaced to allow ample room for editing. In a tutoring situation, you will want to read and react to the first draft so that you can guide the student in the revision process. If you have a group of students, they can share their work with each other. Working in pairs or small groups, writers can read their drafts aloud to one another and react to each other's writing on the basis of content and organization. The Writing Revision Checklist on page 41 can serve as a guide for this process. You can adapt the checklist to the needs and abilities of your students and to the requirements of specific writing assignments.

When writers have revised their first drafts, they can then exchange papers and act as editors, checking for mechanical problems such as missing words, spelling, capitalization, and punctuation. The Editing Checklist on page 42 can be used as a guide or adapted to your students' abilities. Give writers the opportunity to make changes before collecting the edited version.

Evaluating and Remediating Student Writing

When responding to student writing, be sure to make positive comments before noting areas for improvement. Your reactions should be based more on the content, style, and organization of the writing than on the mechanical aspects. You can use the Teacher's Evaluation Guide on page 43 or adapt it to suit your needs.

Have a short conference with each student individually to discuss written assignments. Begin by stressing the good points, giving positive feedback and reinforcement. Select one weakness for the writer to work on in the next writing activity. The most helpful areas will be those that will significantly improve the student's writing when mastered.

Deal with each student's mechanical problems as they occur in the student's writing. Provide additional practice for the student that addresses a specific problem. If most of your students have a particular mechanical problem, you can teach a mini-lesson about it.

The following are a few general suggestions for helping students with mechanical problems.

Spelling Difficulties

When students misspell words they have studied in *Challenger,* have them look up the correct spelling in the Word Index. If students misspell a word they haven't studied, point out any parts of the word that are correctly spelled and praise the logic of any phonetically reasonable misspellings.

For instance, if a student spells *friend* as *frend,* point out that the spelling represents the way the word sounds, but that there is a silent letter in *friend.* Help the student to find the correct spelling in the Word Index or the dictionary and have him practice writing it correctly a few times. Suggest that students keep a list of words that they find hard to spell in a special section of their writing notebooks or on index cards. Help students learn how to use a dictionary when they are ready. This is an important skill for them to have.

Students who misspell a great many words will probably need remedial spelling help in addition to their work in *Challenger.* One approach is to ask an adult learner which words he most wants to learn to spell. These will usually be high utility words for that learner. Learning to spell these often-used words will improve the learner's spelling rapidly.

Students who can spell very few words correctly should still be given regular and varied opportunities to write. Accept their level of competence, which may include many invented spellings, and do not make them correct every misspelled word. Instead, look for general patterns of misspellings and try to correct those one at a time. Tackling a general problem helps students to spell correctly all the words that fall into that category, rather than learning to spell one word at a time. *Patterns in Spelling,* a program published by New Readers Press, may be very helpful for these students.

Grammatical Errors

Grammatical errors occur because of the way the student has learned the language. For instance, students who say "he don't" or "they was" will also write that way. Bad grammatical habits take a lot of oral and written practice to replace. You can provide additional practice for these students, as well as modeling correct grammar in the classroom.

Short Sentences

Students who write short, choppy sentences may need help in thinking of more information to add in order to make their writing more interesting. When working in pairs, one student can ask questions of the other about the information contained in a first draft. By discussing the topic, the student can come up with additional details or descriptive information to add to the next draft.

Run-on Sentences and Fragments

Run-on sentences usually sound all right to the students who have written them, so you will need to help them see that, by using commas and periods where necessary, readers can follow the thoughts more easily. To illustrate how punctuation helps the reader, have the student read the sentences aloud, pausing only at commas and taking a breath only at a period. If you prefer, you can demonstrate by reading aloud the same way. When students understand the function of punctuation marks, have them revise the run-on sentences as necessary.

Have students read sentence fragments aloud also, and then ask, "Is that a complete thought?" Help them to fill in the missing information orally and then rewrite the fragment as a complete sentence.

Omitted Words

All writers omit words occasionally because the mind thinks faster than the hand can write. Often, students notice a missing word when reading their writing aloud. Sometimes, however, a student will read a word that's not there without realizing that it is missing. In this case, you can point to each word in the sentence as the student reads it. Encourage students to reread their writing after they have written a draft. Students who often omit words should point to each word as they reread what they have written.

Confusing Sentences

When a student writes a confusing sentence, say, "I don't know what this means. Can you explain it to me?" Once you understand the intent, start a more coherent version of the sentence and have the student finish it and read the revision. Ask if it now says what the student intended to say. If not, work on the sentence until the revision accurately expresses the student's original idea.

Other Considerations

Writing, like reading, should be evaluated in terms of improvement rather than mastery. Most students read far better than they write. Allow them to develop from their own starting points, making them aware of their strengths as well as patiently helping them to work on their weaknesses.

Here are a few other suggestions to consider in helping students with their writing.

• As often as possible, have writers read their writing aloud. Students usually enjoy doing this, and it gives them a chance to hear whether

Other Considerations (continued)

or not their writing makes sense. Insist on honest but courteous reactions from the other students.

- With the writers' permission, use writing from previous or present students as models to demonstrate a specific writing activity. Seeing the work of their peers helps students understand how the activity is to be done.
- Compile worksheets of sentences or paragraphs that illustrate common problems. For extra practice, students can work together to correct the errors and better understand how to avoid common writing problems.
- Provide the opportunity for students to publicly display or occasionally publish their final drafts.

Correlated Writing Books

Writing workbooks containing skill-building activities correlated to *Challenger 1–4* are available from New Readers Press. Each of the four writing books contains two pages of exercises for each lesson in the corresponding *Challenger* book. Writing skills are developed sequentially throughout the four books.

A Summary of Do's and Don'ts

- Do provide regular opportunities for writing activities appropriate for students' levels of ability.
- Do have students keep writing notebooks for all their writing assignments.
- Do allow students to get used to expressing themselves in writing through free-writing activities that don't have to be polished.
- Do have students occasionally revise and edit their writing.
- Do be sure students understand the purpose of the writing activity and keep the audience in mind as they write.
- Do have students work together in pairs or small groups to generate ideas and to react to each other's writing.
- Do find something to praise in each piece of writing.
- Do base your responses primarily on content, style, and organization.
- Don't overemphasize mechanical errors.
- Do select a specific area for each student to work on to improve writing skills.
- Do provide opportunities periodically for students to display or publish their writing assignments.

Writing Revision Checklist
(to be used to react to early drafts)

	Author		Reader	
	Yes	Needs Work	Yes	Needs Work
Is the topic clearly stated?				
Does each paragraph have a sentence that tells clearly what the paragraph is about?				
Are there enough supporting details, examples, or reasons?				
Are all ideas related to the topic?				
Have all the important questions that readers might ask been answered?				
Is there a beginning, a middle, and an end?				
Are all ideas arranged in a logical order?				
Does the writing seem complete?				
Are there connecting words to help readers relate the ideas to each other?				
Are there some long, medium, and short sentences?				
Are there different kinds of sentences (for instance, questions or commands)?				
Have interesting, colorful, and appropriate words been chosen?				
Rather than some words being used again and again, have different words been used to express the same idea?				

Editing Checklist
(to be used to guide the final draft)

	Author		Reader	
	Yes	Needs Work	Yes	Needs Work
Is the topic clearly stated?				
Do all the ideas relate to the topic?				
Do added ideas make the author's meaning clearer?				
Does any new order of sentences or paragraphs improve the writing?				
Is the revised draft easier to understand?				
Is the revised draft more convincing?				
Are all words spelled correctly?				
Are all sentences punctuated correctly?				
Are capital letters used whenever necessary?				
Is each sentence a complete thought?				
Have all run-on sentences been fixed?				
Do pronouns refer clearly to someone or something?				
Are all action words used correctly?				

Teacher's Evaluation Guide

1. Purpose
- Is the main theme of the composition clearly stated?
- Does the writing reflect a clear sense of the intended audience?

2. Content/Ideas
- Are there clearly stated main ideas supporting the main theme?
- Are main ideas supported by reasons, examples, and other details?
- Are main ideas and supporting material related to the main theme?
- Is content appropriate to the theme and the audience?

3. Organization and Development
- Does each paragraph have a single main idea plus supporting material?
- Are main ideas and supporting material in a logical order?
- Are transitions used when appropriate?
- Is there an introduction and a conclusion, if appropriate?

4. Sentence Structure
- Are all sentences complete thoughts?
- Is there a variety of sentence structures?

5. Language
- Are the words accurate and appropriate to the theme and audience?
- Is the language clear, concrete, and concise?

6. Check Mechanical Problems

___ Spelling	___ Sentence fragments
___ Punctuation	___ Run-on sentences
___ Capitalization	___ Verb tense usage
___ Subject-verb agreement	___ Pronoun usage

7. Positive Reinforcement
- What are the best things about this composition?

8. For Next Time
- What one thing should the writer concentrate on improving in the next writing activity?

Chapter 4 — Reinforcement Activities

These activities reinforce students' understanding and retention of the lesson material and give further practice in areas of weakness. When planning reinforcement activities, keep in mind that they should be fun. Select activities that students can enjoy, and avoid those that might cause frustration. Be sure to keep a record of activities you develop that work well.

Word Index Activities

After every four or five lessons in each book, there are word indexes of all the words introduced up to that point. Activities based on these word lists can reinforce word recognition skills and review meanings. Some activities based on the word indexes require little or no preparation. Others require some preparation on your part, but students appreciate your taking time to design activities specifically for them.

Word Review

Have a student pick any column in the word index that directly precedes the current lesson and read all the words. Students should mark words they can't sight-read or sound out with relative ease. After they have read the entire column, review the troublesome words. A note of caution: Students with certain learning disabilities have great trouble reading words in isolation and may need to review words in context.

Guess the Word

Have a student pick a column of words. Then select a word from that column and give a clue for the word. Have the student find the word in the column and read it. Try to give clues that relate to the student's environment or experience, since this association makes retention easier. A variation on this is for you to pick a column of words, then have the student select individual words and give clues.

Spelling Bees

Oral spelling bees can be particularly helpful when a specific pattern or principle is emphasized. For instance, all the words might contain the same consonant blend or have doubled consonants before an ending. Spelling bees should be spontaneous, brief—10 words is usually sufficient—and informally presented. They should not resemble quizzes.

Flash Card Activities

Flash cards can be made by neatly printing words on 3 x 5 index cards. The following are examples of activities to do with flash cards.

Beat the Clock. Having a student read a series of related words on flash cards is a good way to reinforce specific phonics skills and to develop sight vocabulary. Students often enjoy flash card activities using a timer. They like to see how many correct answers they can produce before the time runs out.

Phonics Review. If a student has trouble mastering a particular sound-symbol relationship or phonics principle that has been introduced and studied, this activity can be very helpful. Select 15 or 20 words that demonstrate a phonics principle, such as *r*-controlled vowels, the silent *e*, or vowel pairs. You can use the word charts in Books 1 and 3 as a source for words, as well as the word indexes. Continue to use the phonics flash cards until the student can sight-read the words automatically.

Categories. You will need 15 flash cards for this activity. Refer to the appropriate word index to make sure you use words the student has studied. Think of three categories, and then select five words the student can associate with each category. For instance, the three categories might be people, parts of the body, and things to eat.

To begin, lay out the 15 cards in three columns of five cards each. Have the student read the words on all the cards first. Then name the first category. You might say, "I want you to put all the words that pertain to people in the first column." When this has been done correctly, name the second category. After this category has been completed, have the student try to figure out the category for the remaining words.

Concentration. This game provides word recognition reinforcement for students who have trouble differentiating between similar words. It is based on the card game of the same name and can be played by two to four people. You will need duplicate sets of flash cards to give you two cards for each word being reviewed. The cards should be laid out facedown. Players take turns turning up two cards at a time. If the cards match, the player removes the pair from the playing area. If the cards do not match, they are turned facedown again. When all the cards have been matched, the player with the most pairs wins. The level of difficulty can be increased by using pairs of similar words such as *dairy* and *diary*.

Make a Sentence. In this activity, each flash card contains a single word. All the words together are used to form a sentence. Be sure to include words the student finds troublesome. Include capitalization and punctuation signals on the flash cards so the student can use these clues to figure out the correct arrangement. As the student's skills improve, increase the complexity of the sentences.

Reading and Writing Activities

The following activities can help to build reading, comprehension, and writing skills. These skills include sequencing, recognizing cause and effect, summarizing, sentence combining and expanding, and comparing and contrasting ideas.

What's the Order?

For this sequencing activity, entire sentences are printed on index cards. The sentences need to be carefully worded so that they will make sense when placed in an appropriate order. Lay out the cards in random order and have students read each sentence. Then they should put the sentences in an order that makes sense. Have them read all the sentences aloud in the order they have selected. Below is a set of sentences that illustrate sequencing in chronological order.

I rode a bus to the park. (4)

I had so much fun that I got home very late. (5)

I phoned a friend to see if he wanted to go. (2)

My friend refused to go. (3)

I wanted to go to the park. (1)

Occasionally, there may be more than one way the sentences can be arranged to make sense. Any sequence that a student can justify should be considered acceptable.

Matching

This activity can help develop awareness of cause-and-effect relationships. It requires five sentences and 10 index cards. Write the sentence beginnings on five cards and the sentence endings on the remaining cards. After students have arranged the cards to form five complete sentences, they should read them aloud. Below is a set of sentence beginnings and endings to illustrate this activity.

1. Andy wanted to celebrate because (C)
2. Jack always put on a hat when he went out because (A)
3. Mack really needed to take time and relax more because (D)
4. Joan wasn't asked to go to the party because (E)
5. Linda wanted to take a course at the high school because (B)

A. he was starting to lose his hair.
B. she wanted to learn more about reading.
C. he had just won a new television set.
D. he was always losing his temper.
E. her friends knew she was out of town.

When preparing your own sentences, be sure there is only one sensible ending for each sentence beginning. Each example above starts with an effect. This activity can also be done by starting the sentences with causes and having students match the effects. Below is an example.

1. Andy had just won a new television set, so
A. he wanted to celebrate.

Key Words

This activity can help students to write summary statements of the main ideas in paragraphs or reading selections. Select four or five key words in the reading, and write them on an index card or the chalkboard. Ask students to write a sentence about the reading, using all the key words. The following example is based on Lesson 15 of Book 2.

Key words: hobby   barbed wire   people   collect
An appropriate response would be: "Some people collect different kinds of barbed wire as a hobby."

Sentence Combining

Making one sentence out of several short sentences is good practice for students who tend to write short, choppy sentences. Prepare a set of short sentences, each containing one idea. Have students combine them into a single, longer sentence. Compare results, keeping in mind that there are usually several different acceptable responses. The following example is based on Lesson 2 of Book 3.

Jerome walked into the room.
Jerome saw Steven.
Steven had his shirt on.
Steven had his shorts on.
He was standing on his head.

Appropriate responses would be: "Steven, who had his shirt and shorts on, was standing on his head when Jerome walked into the room." Or: "When Jerome walked into the room, he saw Steven, wearing his shirt and shorts, standing on his head."

This activity can be done orally or by students writing their responses and then reading them aloud.

Sentence Expanding

This is another activity to help students write longer, more complex sentences. Write a kernel sentence on the chalkboard and have students add descriptive words and phrases to expand the basic idea. The kernel sentence can be related to the reading selection in the current lesson, such

Reading and Writing Activities (continued)

as "People have hobbies." Or it can be something learners can relate to easily, such as "The car was damaged." Suggest that students add details that answer such questions as how, why, which ones, when, and so forth.

Compare and Contrast

Some reading selections lend themselves to comparison and contrast activities. Students might list the differences between mammals and fish after reading the selection on whales in Lesson 16 of Book 2. Or they might list similarities and differences between two characters in the stories in Books 1 and 3.

Puzzles and Games

Puzzles

Word puzzles are an excellent way to reinforce both meaning and spelling. *Puzzles for Challenger 1–8,* eight books of puzzles correlated to each lesson in the *Challenger* series, are available from New Readers Press. Also, puzzles and other activities can be found in magazines sold in drugstores and supermarkets. You can create similar puzzles with vocabulary from past and current word indexes.

Word and Information Games

Students often enjoy games modeled after television shows such as "Jeopardy" and "Wheel of Fortune." These games take some time to prepare but are a great way to reinforce vocabulary and information.

Students can create their own "Jeopardy" games by preparing sets of questions and answers based on the reading selections. They can also create categories of vocabulary words. For example, all the answers in a category might begin with the letters *st.* Other categories might include people's names, things to eat, places to visit, and compound words.

A game based on "Wheel of Fortune" can be played using words and phrases from the lessons. On a piece of paper, draw boxes representing each letter in a phrase. In place of spinning a wheel, "contestants" draw from a stack of cards on which dollar values are written. Be sure to include some "lose a turn" and "extra turn" cards, as well as a "bankrupt" card. As students guess letters correctly, write the letters in the boxes. This type of activity is an excellent way for students to become more aware of letter patterns in English words.

Student-requested Activities

From time to time, students may need help with specific personal needs, such as filling out application forms or reading a letter or brochure. These are excellent reinforcement activities because they help students to apply the skills they are building and they remind students of the relevance of reading and writing to their daily lives.

Encourage students to let you know in advance, whenever possible, if they plan to bring in this type of material. In that way, you can plan the lesson to allow time for helping the student complete the task. Sometimes the activity will be something, such as filling out a form, that all of the students in the group can benefit from. Often, however, you will need to plan time to meet with the individual student who needs the help.

A Summary of Do's

- Do plan reinforcement activities to build comprehension skills and to give extra practice in areas of weakness.
- Do keep a record of activities that work well.
- Do encourage students to develop some of the activities.
- Do encourage students to bring in material they need your help with and to let you know in advance that they will do so.

Chapter 5 Using the Lesson Notes

The sections that follow contain individual notes for each lesson. These notes give suggestions for teaching the material in the lesson. Keep in mind that the lesson notes are only suggestions. If you try one of the ideas a few times and find it doesn't work with your students, disregard it.

Primary and Secondary Emphases

In most cases, the items listed under the "Primary emphasis" heading receive the greatest emphasis in the lesson and require the most teaching. Except for the early lessons in Book 1, reading comprehension and vocabulary development receive primary emphasis in most lessons. The first time a particular principle, task, or skill is introduced, it is also listed under "Primary emphasis." Items listed under "Secondary emphasis" often are skills that have been introduced previously and are now being reinforced.

The Reading Selections

The lesson notes contain suggestions for pre-reading and post-reading activities. It is a good idea to vary the methods used for presenting the reading selections and assessing comprehension. Carefully monitoring your students' progress will help you to develop sound procedures for improving reading and comprehension skills.

Developing Your Lesson Plan

As you prepare for a teaching session, refer to the notes for the lesson or lessons you will be working on and decide which suggestions you want to incorporate into your lesson plan. It is a good idea to write down the specific ideas and suggestions you plan to use. The Model Lesson Planning Worksheet on page 26 may be helpful. List the objectives you hope to achieve for your students and decide on how to handle each segment of the lesson. Plan the activities you will use to reach the objectives, and gather any materials you may need. Note particularly how you plan to teach any new concepts presented in the lesson. Also make note of any suggestions that might be helpful to the students when they are doing their homework.

Under the heading "Notes," jot down any remarks or reminders about particular difficulties students may have had with the lesson. Also note specific words or skills for which you may want to develop reinforcement activities. Be sure to keep notes of any procedures and techniques that seem to work well so that you can use them again.

Challenger 1 — Introduction and Lesson Notes

Challenger 1 is designed for adult and adolescent students reading at or above a 2.0 reading level as determined by standardized reading inventories. Students beginning in this book should know how to blend sounds together to form words, have a basic understanding of sound-symbol relationships, and be able to discriminate between short and long vowel sounds. They should also be able to read some words by sight. Book 1 is appropriate for students who test at level 1 or 2 on the *Challenger Placement Tool*.

Book 1 emphasizes learning to recognize phonics elements and principles, developing phonetic decoding and reading comprehension skills, and building vocabulary. Book 1 lessons include the following significant features.

- New vocabulary is introduced in each lesson by means of word charts organized on the basis of phonics principles. The phonics principles provide students with an important tool for decoding words, enabling them to progress more rapidly than a random introduction of unrelated words would allow.
- Words are reviewed throughout the lessons so students learn to sight-read them or sound them out with minimal difficulty.
- Oral reading of stories helps to establish accurate, fluent reading.
- Stories gradually increase in length and complexity.
- Oral discussion of stories is used to aid and assess comprehension.
- Exercises give students practice in skills such as adding endings, distinguishing between similar words, and identifying synonyms and antonyms.

Scheduling Considerations

At least for the early lessons, Book 1 works best in a tutorial setting. This allows you to give your undivided attention to the student and pace the work according to the student's needs.

Students working in Book 1 usually need 1½ hours of time to complete each lesson. If your sessions are an hour long, you can plan two sessions per lesson, allowing time for writing activities, such as dialogue journal writing and language experience activities, as well as reinforcement activities that provide extra practice to develop skills.

As students progress beyond the mid-point of Book 1, a group setting with three to five students may work well if such a setting is possible. This way, students receive support and stimulation from one another, making learning a more enjoyable activity.

Suggestions for Teaching the Lessons

Each of the 20 lessons in Book 1 includes a word chart, a story, and reading and writing exercises. Many of the chart words are reviewed in the story and exercises in a lesson. The stories, which describe happenings in the lives of a group of friends, give students experience with reading lighthearted fiction. Most adults are familiar with the story form and should be able to relate to many of the incidents they read about.

The Word Charts

Each lesson begins with a word chart containing new words that illustrate specific phonics principles. For each lesson, you should explain the phonics principles being introduced or reviewed in the chart. Pages

8–11, Common Phonics Elements and Principles in English Words, may be a helpful reference for you. Have students sound out the words following the procedures recommended in Chapter 2 of this manual. Then do a random review of the words before proceeding to the story segment of the lesson.

The Words for Study

Point out that the Words for Study are new words that appear in the story or in the exercises that follow. Have students sight read as many of these words as possible. If a student can't sound out or sight-read one of the words listed, simply say it and have the student repeat it a few times while looking at the word. Most students should be able to sound out the majority of phonetically regular words by the middle of the book.

Reading the Story

Pre-reading suggestions are given in the lesson notes for Book 1. As part of the pre-reading activities, have students predict what the story will be about based on the Words for Study and the title. Students can also make predictions about what other vocabulary words they might expect to find in the story. You may also give a brief introduction to the story or ask a question that provides the student with a purpose for reading.

Oral reading is stressed in Book 1 in order to develop good reading patterns. Second readings of the stories should be assigned for homework. The following are some suggestions for handling the oral readings and discussions of the stories. It's a good idea to vary your procedure from lesson to lesson to avoid boredom or frustration. It may take a while to find the procedures with which your student feels comfortable.

- Read aloud the first paragraph of the story. Ask a question or two to determine if the student has understood what you read. Have the student read the next sentence aloud. Continue taking turns reading sentences until the end of the story. Help the student to sound out words or use context clues when necessary. Discuss what is happening at good breaking points in the story. At the end, briefly summarize the story with the student and then discuss it. Questions for discussion are suggested in the individual lesson notes.

- As your student becomes more proficient, you can alternate reading whole paragraphs. Again, discuss what is happening at good breaking points in the story.

- If your student has a great deal of trouble reading aloud, you might try echo reading. In this procedure, you read aloud one sentence while the student follows along in the book. The student then reads aloud the same sentence. Continue in this manner until the story is finished, stopping to discuss what is happening at appropriate points in the story.

- You can also help your student build fluency and confidence by reading aloud together. With this method, be sure to note words the student has trouble with, so you can reinforce recognition of them after you have read and discussed the story together.

- Have students with weak decoding skills read a paragraph twice, once for accurate decoding, and once for meaning. Discuss content only after the second reading. After discussing the whole story, ask the student to reread one or two sentences that were troublesome.

As students become better at decoding and hear you model good oral reading, their fluency improves. Then they can read more of the story themselves. For students whose comprehension skills need to be developed, continue to ask questions at good breaking points in the stories.

Assessing Comprehension

Comprehension is assessed through oral discussion in Book 1. Brief, informal discussions about the stories are far less threatening than having to give written answers to comprehension questions. Lead the discussion by asking literal-, inferential-, and applied-level questions as described in Chapter 2. Suggestions for all three types of questions are given in the individual lesson notes.

Encourage students to give precise answers and to see relationships that are developed across sentence or paragraph boundaries. The following dialogue, based on Lesson 1, illustrates how you can do this.

Teacher: What happened in the first paragraph?
Student: Some guy overslept.
Teacher: Good. What's his name?
Student: Bob.
Teacher: So what happened to Bob because he overslept?
Student: He was late for work.
Teacher: Right. Bob was late for work because he overslept.

In this dialogue, the teacher models a precise answer for the student and draws attention to the cause and effect relationship in the content of the story. Through dialogues such as this, you can assess comprehension, help students develop precision in their answers, and build awareness that the purpose of reading is to obtain meaning.

Dealing with Oral Reading Difficulties

It is important that students develop good reading habits from the beginning. The most important habit for them to develop is that of monitoring their reading for meaning. While they read, they should continually ask themselves if what they have read makes sense. Since fluency is also very important, avoid interrupting students' reading unnecessarily. Whenever possible, allow students to read through a whole passage, and then have them reread certain sentences in which they misread words. The following are some suggestions for dealing with typical oral reading problems that beginning readers have.

Decoding Problems. There are two common types of decoding problems: incorrect decoding and not recognizing a word. When an incorrectly decoded word interferes with meaning, ask, "Does that make sense?" If students substitute a word with a similar meaning, such as reading "riding the bus" for "taking the bus," simply ignore the substitution. If students don't recognize a word from a word chart, help them to sound it out using the word chart procedure. If they don't recognize a word listed under Words for Study, simply pronounce it for them. Make a note of words or sounds that give students frequent trouble and emphasize these words in reinforcement activities.

Skipping Words. When students occasionally skip words, make a mental note of it. When they finish the first reading, have them reread a sentence or two to see if they read the skipped words the second time through. If they do not, point out the skipped words and have them read the sentence again. Check to be sure they understand the passage.

Misreading Little Words. Short words often give the most trouble. Students need to learn that comprehension is affected when they misread words such as *in* for *on* and *form* for *from*. Again, you can have students reread a sentence when they finish the story to see if they read the words correctly. If a student consistently makes many errors of this type, particularly errors involving letter reversals, it may signal a learning disability. In that case, the student should be tested for that possibility.

Ignoring Punctuation Marks. In oral reading, the most important punctuation marks are the comma, the period, and the question mark. If students ignore these marks, explain how they function and model how the voice responds to these marks.

Ignoring Word Endings. Note any endings, such as *-ed* or *-ing,* that students fail to read in the story and have them reread words with those endings after they have finished the story. Students who drop endings in their everyday speech may need extra practice and reinforcement to overcome this problem.

The Exercises

Generally, the exercises should be previewed during the class session and completed for homework. Book 1 students are not responsible for reading the directions that precede each exercise. The directions are for your benefit. Students who are capable of reading the directions, however, should do so during the homework preview.

Explain in your own words how to do each exercise. If there is a column of answer words, have students read the words. When an item has been done as an example, have the students read it. Explain, or have the student explain, how it was done. In the early lessons, have students complete one item in each exercise to be sure they know how to do it. When all of the exercises have been previewed, have students explain briefly what they are supposed to do in each one.

Remind students that they are to answer all questions. If students have a tendency to skip items they don't know, explain that they should make "intelligent guesses." Show them how the use of context clues and the process of elimination are strategies for selecting correct answers.

Go over all the homework exercises during the next class session. Have students correct all wrong answers. For the first 10 lessons, 70 per cent accuracy is acceptable. Eighty per cent accuracy is a reasonable expectation for the last 10 lessons. If students score below these levels more often than not, divide each lesson over more class sessions and increase the number of reinforcement activities.

Writing Activities

Providing writing opportunities on a regular basis is important for beginning readers. Dialogue journals and language experience stories are appropriate writing activities for students in Book 1. Both types of activities are discussed in Chapter 3 of this manual. In addition, the lesson notes suggest topics related to the lesson material that students might write about.

The Lesson Segments

The procedure for each session should be as consistent as possible. Most sessions will have the following segments. You may want to vary the order to suit your particular situation.

1. **Homework Review.** Go over the exercises in the previous lesson that were done as homework.
2. **Word Study.** Introduce the new lesson and explain the phonics principles presented in the word chart. Have the student read some or all of the chart words and then the Words for Study.
3. **Reading the Story.** Do one or more pre-reading activities to introduce the story in the new lesson. Have the student read the story aloud and then discuss it.
4. **Writing Activity.** Have the student do some free writing, or work with the student on a pre-writing activity such as idea mapping or dictating a language experience story.

The Lesson Segments
(continued)

5. **Reinforcement Activity.** When time permits, focus on an area of difficulty in a way that is fun for the student. See Chapter 4 for suggestions.

6. **Homework Preview.** Go over the exercises to be done for homework to be sure the student knows how to do them.

Individual Lesson Notes

The individual lesson notes, which begin on page 54, contain suggestions and procedures for teaching the lessons in Book 1.

Lesson 1: The Long and Short Vowels

Primary emphasis
- Long and short vowel patterns
- Single consonant sounds
- Oral and silent reading comprehension
- The silent *e* rule

Secondary emphasis
- Accurate, legible writing
- Context clues
- Distinguishing between similar words
- Writing and study skills

Word Chart

Note: **V** = any vowel, **C** = any consonant

1. Long vowel patterns introduced:
   - The silent *e* (**VCe**): *name, time, woke, rule*
   - Open syllables (**CV** and **V**): *be, I, go*
   - Double vowel (**VV**): *see, need*

2. Short vowel pattern introduced:
   - Closed syllables (**VC, CVC**): *at, yes, is, Bob, but*

3. Special notes:
   - The word *a* is usually pronounced /ə/.
   - There are two pronunciations of long *u:* /oo/ and /yoo/.
   - Help students sound out *Eddie*, since *ie* hasn't been introduced yet.

Words for Study

1. Most of the words here are not phonetically regular. Pronounce those that students don't recognize and have them repeat each word several times while looking at it.
2. Point out the apostrophe in *o'clock* and the abbreviation *Mr.*

Pre-reading Activities

Ask or say to students:

1. Have you ever been late because you overslept? What happened?
2. Read this story to find out why Bob is late for work and what happens to him.

Post-reading Activities

Ask or say:

1. Tell what happened to Bob after he overslept.
2. How did Bob get to work?
3. Why did Bob stay in a job he hated?
4. About what age do you think Bob and Eddie are? Why do you think so?
5. What do you think Bob will do now? Why?
6. Do you know anyone who has recently lost a job? What did that person do?
7. Do you think someone should be fired for being late to work?

Language Experience or Writing Activity

Complete one of these sentences.

I agree that Bob should be fired because . . .

I disagree that Bob should be fired because . . .

Additional Activities

1. Read to your students for pleasure at the end of each lesson, beginning with this lesson. Suggested material: short stories, articles of interest to students, poems, news stories, etc.
2. Make folders for storing language experience stories and students' writings.

Exercises

1 Read and Write

Students should copy the sentences accurately, paying special attention to capitalization and punctuation.

2 Read and Write

- Have students read the words on the left. Some are words students haven't studied yet. Review the long vowel silent *e* rule.
- Suggest that students read each sentence, saying "blank" for each line. Read the first sentence: "Blank did not have blank to go to the park." Then have students read the sentence with *Tim* and *time* filled in and write the words on the correct lines. Assign the rest of the exercise for homework, or have the students finish it with your help.

Summarizing the Lesson

Help students to reflect on what they have learned. Ask, "What were the most important things you learned in the lesson?"

Lesson 2: More Work with Long and Short Vowels

Primary emphasis
- Long and short vowel patterns
- Single consonant sounds
- Oral and silent reading comprehension
- The silent *e* rule

Secondary emphasis
- Legible, accurate copying
- Distinguishing between similar words
- Context clues
- Writing and study skills

Word Chart

1. Long vowel patterns reviewed: the silent *e* (**VCe**), double vowel (**CVVC**)

2. Short vowel patterns reviewed: closed syllables (**VC** and **CVC**)

3. Short vowel pattern introduced: one vowel, two consonants (**CVCC**): *which*

4. Special notes:
   - Long *u* is pronounced /oo/ and /yoo/.
   - Help students sound out *when* and *which,* since the digraphs *wh* and *ch* are new.

Words for Study

1. Pronounce the words that students don't recognize and can't sound out. Have them repeat each word several times.

2. Point out the *-ed* ending on *relaxed* and the apostrophe in *let's.* Ask if students know what two words make up *let's.* If they don't, tell them *let's* is another way to say *let us.* Have them write *let us* and compare with *let's* to find the difference. Explain that the apostrophe stands for the missing *u* in *let's.*

Pre-reading Activities

Ask or say:

1. What do you remember about Bob and Eddie from Lesson 1?

2. In this story, Bob has a job interview. Have you ever had a job interview? How did you feel before the interview? Read this story to find out how Bob feels before his interview.

Post-reading Activities

Ask or say:

1. Tell what happened in this story.
2. Where did Dan Rose live?
3. What did Bob tell his dad he would do if Mr. Rose offered him the job?
4. Do you think Bob and Eddie have been friends for a long time? Why or why not?

5. What did Eddie do to help Bob relax before the job interview? Did it help?

6. Who do you think arranged the appointment between Bob and Dan Rose?

7. Do you think Bob should take a job he does not know how to do? How might he learn how to do it?

8. What are some of the questions Dan Rose might ask when interviewing Bob for a job to fix bikes?

Language Experience or Writing Activities

1. Dictate a language experience story about finding a job.

2. Tell about a job you like or do not like.

Additional Activities

1. Obtain job application forms for students to practice filling out. Help students to prepare the form and suggest that they keep it for future reference.

2. Discuss what to expect at a typical job interview. Help students prepare answers for the types of questions usually asked at job interviews.

Exercises

2 **Read and Write** (word sounds)

During your preview of this exercise, have students read all the words in the column on the left. Some are new words. Review the long vowel silent *e* rule. Remind students to read the first sentence as, "Mom needed a *blank* box for the roses."

Summarizing the Lesson

Discuss with students what they learned from the lesson. Do a random review of chart words and the Words for Study.

Lesson 3: More Work with Long and Short Vowels

Primary emphasis
- Long and short vowel patterns
- Single consonant sounds
- Oral and silent reading comprehension
- The silent *e* rule

Secondary emphasis
- Distinguishing among similar words
- Context clues
- Writing and study skills

Word Chart

1. Long vowel patterns reviewed: **VCe**, **CVVC**
2. Short vowel pattern reviewed: **CVC**

Pre-reading Activities

Ask or say:

1. What do you remember about Eddie from the stories in Lessons 1 and 2? Allow students to reread the sections of those stories that mention Eddie. Help students scan the stories to find Eddie's name.
2. As you read, decide if you think Bob spends a lot of time with Kate.

Post-reading Activities

Ask or say:

1. Tell how Kate and Eddie met.
2. Where did Kate work?
3. How often does Eddie see Kate?
4. Was Eddie driving the jeep when he saw Kate at the lake? How do you know?
5. Who are the most important characters in this story?
6. What are some things you learned about Eddie, Kate, and Dave?
7. Do you think it was wise for Kate to ride off with Eddie when she had just met him? Why or why not?

Language Experience or Writing Activities

1. Tell about what you like to do with your friends.
2. Tell about a special day you remember.

Additional Activities

1. Ask students to describe how they imagine the location of this story. Ask, "What time of year do you think it was? What kind of weather? What were people wearing?"

2. Introduce the use of dialogue journals. See Chapter 3 for details.

Exercises

1 Read and Write

Each of these sentences has three blanks. The words to be filled in are similar and could easily be confused. During the homework preview, have students read the words in each group to be sure they can distinguish among them. Then have students complete the first two sentences to be sure they understand what to do.

2 Read and Write (marking vowels)

During the homework preview, explain the long, short, and silent vowel marks. Tell students to read each word and listen for the vowel sounds before marking them.

Summarizing the Lesson

Discuss with students the most important things they learned from this lesson. Review difficult words or concepts.

Lesson 4: Changing the First Consonant Sound

Primary emphasis
- Long and short vowel patterns
- Single consonant sounds
- Oral and silent reading comprehension
- The silent *e* rule

Secondary emphasis
- Distinguishing among similar words
- Context clues
- Writing and study skills

BOOK 1

Word Chart

1. Have students read down each column of three rhyming words, so they will recognize the similarities in sound and spelling and begin to develop an awareness of word patterns.

2. Long vowel patterns reviewed: **VCe, CVVC, CV**

3. Short vowel patterns reviewed: **CVC, CVCC**

4. Make sure students know that *qu* is pronounced /kw/ in *quite* and *quit* and that *ph* is pronounced /f/ in *phone*.

Words for Study

1. The name *Louise* is difficult for many students. Have them repeat it several times while looking at it.

2. *didn't:* Review the word *apostrophe* and ask if students know what two words make up *didn't*. If they don't, tell them that *didn't* is another way of saying *did not*. Have them write *did not*. Compare *didn't* with *did not* to find the difference. Explain that the apostrophe stands for the missing *o* in *didn't*.

Pre-reading Activity

Ask or say:

Do you remember making something that turned out so bad that you were embarrassed someone would see it? In this story, Kate tries to bake a cake for the first time. Read to find out what happens to Kate's cake.

Post-reading Activities

Ask or say:

1. Tell what happened in this story.

2. Why do you think Kate refused Aunt Louise's help in baking the cake?

3. Compare how Kate felt about accepting help at the beginning of the story with how she felt at the end.

4. Do you think Kate will try to bake another cake soon? Why or why not?

5. The next time Kate decides to bake a cake, what do you think she will do differently?

6. Do you think Kate will laugh about this someday?

7. Can you remember a time when you refused help because you wanted to do something yourself? How did it turn out?

Language Experience or Writing Activities

1. Tell about an experience similar to Kate's. Think about the first time you cooked, sewed, painted, or repaired something.

2. Do you have any funny stories about cooking? What did you do with the food that was made?

Additional Activity

Read the last sentence in the first paragraph of the story. What does the exclamation mark tell you? How should this sentence be read aloud?

Exercises

1 **Read and Write** (word sounds)

Some words in the left column are new. Have students read all the words during the homework preview.

2 **Yes or No**

These lighthearted questions are for reading practice. There are no "correct" answers.

Summarizing the Lesson

Discuss with students the most important things they learned in this lesson. Ask students to summarize what they have learned so far about words with long and short vowels. Review the word-pattern concept.

Lesson 5: Changing the End Consonant Sound

Primary emphasis
- Long and short vowel patterns
- Single consonant sounds
- Oral and silent reading comprehension
- Distinguishing among similar words

Secondary emphasis
- The ending -ed
- Context clues
- Writing and study skills

Word Chart

1. Have students read down each long vowel column to get a sense of the changes in the final consonant sounds. Then do the same for the short vowel columns.

2. Long vowel patterns reviewed: **VCe, CVVC**

3. Short vowel patterns reviewed: **CVC, CVCC**

Words for Study

1. *it's* and *don't*: Use the procedure outlined in Lessons 2 and 4 to teach these contractions. Stress that *it's* is the contraction for *it is,* not the possessive form for *it (its).*

2. *Mrs.* and *Ms.*: Be sure students know these abbreviations. Review *Mr.* from Lesson 1.

Pre-reading Activity

Ask or say:

To whom do you go for help and advice? In this story, Bob asks Aunt Louise about a small problem. As you read the story, think about what kind of person Aunt Louise is.

Post-reading Activities

Ask or say:

1. What are two things the story mentions about Aunt Louise?

2. What was Aunt Louise doing when Bob arrived?

3. Where was Bob just before he visited Aunt Louise?

4. What time of day did Bob visit Aunt Louise? How do you know?

5. Bob said he had a problem at work and needed help. What did Aunt Louise think the problem was?

6. What are some things you learned about Aunt Louise in the story?

7. Do you think Aunt Louise is a good listener? Why or why not?

8. Does the story tell us what advice Aunt Louise gives Bob? If the story continued, what advice would you expect her to give him? What advice would you give him?

Language Experience or Writing Activity

Can you think of someone in your life like Aunt Louise? Write or tell about why you like this person or about an incident when this person listened to you and gave you advice. Did you follow the advice? What happened?

Exercises

1 Read and Write (add -ed)

During the homework preview, tell students that they are going to practice adding -ed to words they have studied. Go over the examples, helping students to discover the spelling patterns. For each example ask, "Were any letters added, dropped, or changed when -ed was added?" When students have discovered the pattern for each column, state the patterns as follows:

- For column 1 words, simply add -ed to the base word.
- For column 2 words, drop the silent e before adding -ed.
- For column 3 words, double the final consonant before adding -ed.

Have students do item 2 in each column. Then have students read the remaining words in each column with the -ed added, to be sure they understand how to do the exercise.

Summarizing the Lesson

Discuss what students learned from the lesson. Review the patterns for adding -ed that were introduced.

Lesson 6: Ending Consonant Blends

Primary emphasis
- Ending consonant blends *nd, nt, ck, mp*
- Short and long vowel patterns
- Oral and silent reading comprehension

Secondary emphasis
- The ending *-ed*
- Distinguishing among similar words
- Context clues
- Writing and study skills

Word Chart

1. Explain that each consonant can be heard in a consonant blend. Have students read down the columns of rhyming words, concentrating on the sounds of the blends.
2. The **CVCC** words in this chart all have short vowel sounds except the *ind* words, which have a long vowel sound. Be sure to point this out to students.
3. Ask students what missing letters the apostrophes stand for in *can't, don't,* and *won't.*

Pre-reading Activities

1. Review what students learned about Eddie in Lessons 1–3.
2. Ask: Have you ever played bingo or the lottery? Have you ever been to a racetrack? In this story, Eddie has good luck at the track. Read to find out if he stops betting before his luck changes.

Post-reading Activities

Ask or say:

1. Tell what happened in this story.
2. Before Eddie hopped on a bus for the track, he tried to get money for the roses another way. What was it?
3. Find a sentence in the story that shows Eddie didn't know much about betting on horses.
4. At the beginning of the story, what did Eddie plan to do with the money he won?
5. What did Eddie plan to do with his money after he won the second time?
6. If Eddie had won a third time, what do you think would have happened next?
7. Why do you think Eddie kept playing until he lost?
8. Do you think Eddie made good decisions? Would you have done anything differently?

Language Experience or Writing Activities

1. Does Eddie believe in luck? Do you believe in luck? Write or tell about a time you felt lucky.
2. Discuss and list gifts people give that are not purchased at a store (suggestions: time, help, support, friendship, volunteer work, blood). Complete one of the following sentences.

   I want to give the gift of . . .

   I give the gift of . . .
3. How do you feel about gambling?

Additional Activities

1. Read an excerpt from a story or article about horse racing with or to your students.
2. Ask: Do you believe in lending money to friends? What problems can result?

Exercises

1 **Read and Write** (add *-ed*)

Review the three patterns for adding *-ed* introduced in Lesson 5.

Summarizing the Lesson

After discussing what students learned from the lesson, review the ending consonant blends and the patterns for adding *-ed.*

Lesson 7: More Work with Ending Consonant Blends

Primary emphasis
- Ending blends *ng* and *nk*
- Oral and silent reading comprehension
- Short vowel patterns (**CVCC**)

Secondary emphasis
- The ending *-ing*
- Distinguishing among similar words
- Context clues
- Writing and study skills

Word Chart

1. The *ng* and *nk* endings may be difficult for students to pronounce.
2. Students may need help sounding out the *th* in *thing, thank,* and *think,* since this unvoiced *th* has not been introduced yet.
3. Point out that the *w* in *wrong* is silent.

Pre-reading Activities

Ask or say:

1. Do you know what "getting up on the wrong side of the bed" means? How do you feel when you get up on the wrong side of the bed?
2. As you read this story, look for things that happen to Dave that make him decide he has gotten up on the wrong side of the bed.

Post-reading Activities

Ask or say:

1. In your own words, retell the story starting with the ringing alarm clock.
2. What do you think *funk* means in this sentence: "The clock rang, and Dave woke up in a funk"?
3. How did Dave get to work after he junked his jeep? What does "junked his jeep" mean?
4. List the things that made Dave decide he had gotten up on the wrong side of the bed.
5. In what room did the cat cause the trouble? Was Dave in that room when the cat broke the jam pot? How do you know?
6. Do you think Dave lives alone with his cat? Why or why not?
7. Is Dave a neat person? What information from the story did you use in deciding your answer?
8. Do you think Dave made the right decision? What would you do in the same situation?

Language Experience or Writing Activities

1. What kinds of things make you angry in the morning?
2. Write or tell about a time when you got up on the wrong side of the bed.
3. Write or tell about how you like to spend your days off.

Additional Activity

Ask: What if Dave had gotten up on the right side of the bed? Have students retell the story from this point of view.

Exercises

1 **Read and Write** (add *-ing*)

Review the rules for adding the *-ed* ending and tell students that they apply to adding *-ing* as well. Point out *fix* in the first column. Tell students that although it looks like the words in column 3 (**CVC** words), *x* is not doubled before adding the ending.

Summarizing the Lesson

Discuss with students the most important things they learned in the lesson. Review rules for adding endings that begin with a vowel.

Lesson 8: Review of Vowels and Consonants

Primary emphasis
- Long and short vowel patterns
- Single consonant sounds
- Oral and silent reading comprehension

Secondary emphasis
- Distinguishing among similar words
- Context clues
- Synonyms
- Writing and study skills

Word Chart
1. Have students read down the columns of rhyming words.
2. Long vowel patterns reviewed: **VCe**, **VVC**
3. Short vowel patterns reviewed: **CVC**, **CVCC**

Words for Study
Have students tell the differences in spelling and pronunciation between *were* and *where*. Point out that *here* represents a third pronunciation of *-ere*. Provide practice in sentences if students confuse these words.

Pre-reading Activities
Ask or say:
1. Have you been to an amusement park? What was it like?
2. In this story, Aunt Louise and Jack go to an amusement park. As you read, decide if you think Jack and Aunt Louise have known each other for a long time.

Post-reading Activities
Ask or say:
1. Find a place in the story that suggests Jack and Aunt Louise are old friends.
2. Was Aunt Louise sensitive about her age? How do you know?
3. When Jack noticed that Aunt Louise was getting mad, what did he do?
4. What are some of the things Jack and Aunt Louise did at the amusement park?
5. Why did Jack say it was time to go home?
6. Aunt Louise said, "It seems as if we just got here!" When people say this, what does it usually mean?

Language Experience or Writing Activities
1. Complete the following sentence. Something I have always wanted to do is . . .
2. When does time seem to go by very slowly for you? Very fast? Write about an experience you remember.

Exercises
2 **Read and Write** (use *a* and *an*)

Teach when to use *a* and when to use *an* during the homework preview by giving examples such as "Eddie ate *an* apple, but Bob ate *a* banana."

3 **Read and Write** (mark vowels)

Review the long, short, and silent vowel marks.

4 **Read and Write** (synonyms)

During the homework preview, introduce this matching exercise by going over the example. Point out the check mark before *huge*. Then have students do item 2. Make sure they understand that they are to match words having the same meaning. Remind them to check off each word they use.

Explain the process of elimination. Tell students they don't have to do the items in order. They can do the ones they know first, skipping those they are not sure of. Then they can go back and do the skipped ones when fewer choices remain.

5 **Read and Write** (write sentences)

Although students will be composing complete sentences, most of the words they will need to use are in the questions to be answered. Teach or review the use of initial capital letters and end punctuation for sentences.

Summarizing the Lesson
Discuss with students what they learned from the lesson. Review the uses of *a* and *an* and the concept of forming words by changing the initial consonants.

Lesson 9: Vowel Sounds for y

Primary emphasis
- Vowel sounds for *y: y, ay, ey, oy, uy*
- *-y* as a suffix
- Words that end in *-ly*
- Oral and silent reading comprehension

Secondary emphasis
- Context clues
- Synonyms
- Writing and study skills

Word Chart

1. The letter *y* as /ī/ and the vowel combinations *ay, ey, oy,* and *uy* are introduced.
2. Explain that days of the week are capitalized.
3. Point out that *y* is considered a consonant at the beginning of such words as *yesterday*.

Words for Study

Tell students that *what's* is the contraction for both *what is* and *what has*.

Pre-reading Activities

Ask or say:

1. Do you remember the story in Lesson 4 about Kate's attempt to bake a cake? Find a reference to that episode in this story.
2. In this story, read to find out how Bob's friends plan to celebrate his birthday.

Post-reading Activities

Ask or say:

1. Retell this story in your own words.
2. Two people offer to bake a cake for the party. Who are they?
3. Why do you think Eddie wanted Aunt Louise to bake the cake instead of Kate?
4. Is knowing how to bake a cake important to Kate? Why do you think so?
5. Did everyone agree on how to spend the six dollars? Who did not agree? Why?
6. Find the place in the story that suggests that everyone went along on the shopping trip.
7. How do you think Bob will feel when he opens his gifts?

Language Experience or Writing Activities

1. What is the strangest birthday gift you ever received?
2. Write about a birthday you remember.

3. Complete the following sentence. If I could spend my birthday doing anything I wanted, I would . . .

Additional Activities

1. Introduce abbreviations for the days of the week.
2. Bring a calendar to class. Help students figure out which day of the week their birthdays fall on and write sentences using this information.
3. List ideas for celebrating birthdays that don't cost much money.

Exercises

1 Read and Write (add *-y* to words)

Point out that the *y* in these words sounds like long *e*. Have students explain what to do when adding *-y* to the words in each column. If necessary, review what they learned about adding *-ed* and *-ing* in earlier lessons.

2 Read and Write (words that end in *-ly*)

During the homework preview, have students read the words that end in *-ly* in the left column.

3 Read and Write (words that end in *-y*)

During the homework preview, introduce the rule for changing *y* to *i* before adding any ending unless the ending starts with *i*.

4 Read and Write (synonyms)

Review the process of elimination during the homework preview. Have students complete any two items to make sure they remember how to do this type of exercise.

Summarizing the Lesson

Have students reflect on what they learned in the lesson. Ask them to state the spelling rules about adding endings that start with a vowel and about changing *y* to *i* before adding an ending.

Lesson 10: Silent Letters

Primary emphasis
- Silent letters *kn, wr, mb, ight, tch*
- Oral and silent reading comprehension

Secondary emphasis
- Distinguishing among similar words
- Context clues
- Antonyms
- Word associations
- Writing and study skills

Word Chart

1. Have students identify the silent letters in each cluster. They may want to draw a line through each silent letter.

2. Point out that *ight* spells /īt/ in many common words.

3. Tell students that *tch* is a common spelling for /ch/ at the end of a syllable with a short vowel.

Pre-reading Activities

Ask or say:

1. In this story, Eddie thinks clearly and reacts fast in a dangerous situation. Read to find out what happens to Eddie just when he thinks his troubles are over.

2. As you read, find a place in the story where time seems to move very slowly for Eddie.

Post-reading Activities

Ask or say:

1. Tell the story beginning with when Eddie stops at the red light.

2. Why didn't Eddie drive away when the man waved a knife?

3. Find the place in the story where time seems to move very slowly for Eddie.

4. Where did Eddie's car end up? What kind of shape was it in after the accident?

5. Compare the night out Eddie had planned with what really happened.

6. Eddie stays calm for a while. At what point in the story do you think this changes?

7. If you were in Eddie's situation, what would you have done?

8. If the story continued, what do you think would happen next?

9. What do you think Kate might have done when Eddie didn't show up?

Language Experience or Writing Activities

1. Write or tell about a time when things did not turn out as you expected.

2. Continue the story. What are some things to do after a car accident? What did Eddie do about contacting Kate? What happened to the man with the knife?

Additional Activities

1. Discuss cause and effect. Then read the sixth paragraph in the story to find a cause and an effect.

2. If passing the driver's license test is a goal of any of your students, begin to use a driver's manual in your lessons. Start with the pages on traffic signs. (*Studying for a Driver's License,* a book available from New Readers Press, is designed to help low-level readers pass the oral or written driver's test.)

Exercises

2 Opposites

This matching exercise should be done like the synonym matching exercises in Lessons 8 and 9. Be sure students understand they are to match *opposites* this time. If necessary, review the process of elimination during the preview.

3 Word Study (words that don't fit)

During the homework preview, explain that in each row of words, there is one word that does not fit with the rest. Have students read the example and explain why *yesterday* is the right answer. Have them do the second item and, if necessary, the third item.

Summarizing the Lesson

Discuss with students what they learned from the lesson. Do a random review of words that contain silent letters.

Lesson 11: The *r*-Controlled Vowels

Primary emphasis
- The *r*-controlled vowels in *ar, are, or, er, eer, ir, ur*
- The endings *-er* and *-ier*
- Oral and silent reading comprehension
- Spelling (changing *y* to *i*)

Secondary emphasis
- Context clues
- Writing and study skills

Word Chart

Explain that when the letter *r* follows a vowel, the sound of the vowel is somewhat affected. Also point out that *er, ir,* and *ur* are pronounced the same way.

Words for Study

Teach the contractions *I'm* and *there's* using the same procedure as in earlier lessons.

Pre-reading Activities

Ask or say:

1. Do you know how to play cards? This is a story about a card game.
2. As you read this story, think about how each of the three adults behaves toward Mary.
3. As you read, decide if you think Aunt Louise is a good neighbor.

Post-reading Activities

Ask or say:

1. Why did Mary ask to stay at Aunt Louise's house?
2. When she knocked on Aunt Louise's door, Mary was dirty. How did she get dirty?
3. Compare how the three adults behaved toward Mary.
4. Do you agree with how Aunt Louise handled Mary's request for beer? How would you handle such a request?
5. Do you consider Aunt Louise a good neighbor? Explain.

Language Experience or Writing Activities

1. Does anyone in your neighborhood remind you of Aunt Louise? Write or tell about why this person reminds you of her.
2. Does Mary remind you of a child in your life? Write or tell about why this person reminds you of Mary.

3. Complete the following sentence. A game I like to play is . . .

Additional Activity

Some communities have programs for children whose parents work early or late. Does your community have such a program? What are other ways concerned parents deal with child care? List advantages and disadvantages of each.

Exercises

1 Read and Write (add *-er* to words)

Review the silent *e* and doubling rules used when adding endings. Point out *few* and *box* in the first column. Explain that *w* and *x* are not doubled.

3 Read and Write (change *y* to *i* and add *-er*)

During the homework preview, go over both parts of this exercise thoroughly. Have students read the example in the first part and tell what is different about the spelling of *handier*. If necessary, review the *y* to *i* conversion introduced in Lesson 9. Then have students write *happier*.

Next, explain that when students have written all the *-ier* words, they should fill in the blank in each sentence below with the *-ier* word that fits best. Have them read sentence 6. Then, have them find the sentence in which *happier* fits best. They should write *happier* in the blank in sentence 2.

Summarizing the Lesson

Discuss with students the most important things they learned from this lesson. Ask them to explain the procedures for adding endings that start with a vowel and for adding endings to words that end in a consonant plus *y*.

Lesson 12: Vowel Combinations

Primary emphasis
- Vowel combinations *ai, ea, ie, oa, ue, oi, oo, ou*
- Context clues
- Oral and silent reading comprehension

Secondary emphasis
- Distinguishing between similar words
- Writing sentences
- Writing and study skills

Word Chart

1. The upper section contains long vowel combinations except for the second column of *ea* words. Point out that the first vowel is long in the long vowel pairs and the second vowel is silent. Encourage students to select key words such as *eat* and *head* for both *ea* sounds.

2. The lower section contains some of the more troublesome vowel combinations. Encourage students to pick key words for both *oo* sounds and for this pronunciation of *ou*.

Words for Study

Point out that *all right* is two words. Teach the four contractions following the usual procedure.

Pre-reading Activities

Ask or say:

1. Have you ever picked a fight with someone just because you were in a bad mood?

2. In this story, Kate is in a bad mood. Read to find out how Eddie changed her mood.

Post-reading Activities

Ask or say:

1. Tell the story in your own words.

2. Find the paragraph that mentions three reasons why Kate was in a bad mood. What are the three reasons?

3. What did Kate do before she shouted? Why? Did it help?

4. What is Eddie's good news?

5. How did Eddie change Kate's mood?

6. Was Kate excited about Eddie's new job? How do you know?

7. If Kate had been in a better mood, what do you think she would have done differently?

8. What could Kate have said or done to prevent the fight? What could Eddie have said or done to prevent the fight?

Language Experience or Writing Activities

1. What are some things that put you in a bad mood?

2. Write or tell about a time when you heard some good news that cheered you up.

3. List and discuss Kate's problems in terms of problems she can solve and problems beyond her control.

Exercises

1 **Read and Write** (context clues)

During the homework preview, have students read the words at the left. Tell them to use these words to complete this little story. Have them complete the first sentence, checking off the words at the left as they use them. Note that in the third paragraph it doesn't matter whether they write *soap* and *water* or *water* and *soap*.

3 **Read and Write** (write sentences)

This exercise is like Exercise 5 of Lesson 8. Appropriate answers can be "I like it better when the sun is out" or "I like it better when the moon is out." Also appropriate would be "I never go to the movies; I rent tapes instead." Accept all reasonable responses.

Summarizing the Lesson

Discuss with students what they learned from the lesson. Do a random review of words from the chart. Make note of vowel combinations that give students trouble, and plan reinforcement activities for extra practice.

Lesson 13: The r-Controlled Vowel Combinations

Primary emphasis
- The r-controlled vowel combinations *air, ear, oar, oor, our*
- Oral and silent reading comprehension
- Context clues

Secondary emphasis
- Distinguishing among similar words
- Word associations
- The -er ending
- Reviewing factual information
- Writing and study skills

Word Chart

1. There are two pronunciations for both *ear* and *our*. Encourage students to choose and learn a key word for each sound.

2. In "A Review of Sounds," keep in mind that even though the sounds are being reviewed, many of these words are new. Vowels followed by the letter *w* have not been formally studied. However, the student has studied *saw* and *now*, so the words listed under these key words should cause no difficulty.

3. The consonant blends *sm* and *sch* haven't been studied yet. If necessary, help students to sound out *smart* and *school*.

Pre-reading Activities

Ask or say:

1. In this story, Dave is tired of the routine in his life. Do you ever get tired of the routine in your life?

2. As you read this story, notice how Dave's opinion of his artwork changes.

3. Read this story to find out why Dave thinks night school is going to be a lot of fun.

Post-reading Activities

Ask or say:

1. Before he began night school, how did Dave spend his evenings?

2. What are some reasons Dave decided to go to night school?

3. What did Dave think his picture looked like? What did he think Joan's picture looked like?

4. What did Dave lie about? Why do you think he lied?

5. Compare how Dave feels about his social life at the beginning of the story with how you think he feels about it at the end.

6. Dave is tired of watching TV. Do you watch TV? Do you get tired of it also? What are some things you like to do instead?

7. Did Dave's opinion of his painting change after talking to Joan? Do you think people form opinions about themselves as well as their work from what other people say?

Language Experience or Writing Activities

1. In this story we learned the reasons Dave went back to night school. There are many reasons people go back to school. Tell about why you or someone you know decided to go back to school.

2. Dave's picture of a pear did not look good to him at first. He wanted to tear it up and quit. Have you had similar feelings when you attempted something new? Did you quit or stay with it? Did your feelings about what you were doing change?

Exercises

1 **Read and Write** (word sounds)

Explain that the words in the boxes are to be used for the sentences directly to the right. Have students do the first set during the preview.

2 **Read and Write** (words that end in -er)

Have students read the words at the left. Explain that one of the meanings of the ending -er is "a person who does something." This exercise illustrates that meaning.

3 **Word Study** (words that don't fit)

Remind students to pick out the word that doesn't fit with the other words.

Summarizing the Lesson

Discuss with students what they learned from the lesson. Encourage students to include in their summaries bits of information they might have learned from the sentences in Exercise 1 or the questions in Exercise 2.

Lesson 14: Vowels Followed by the Letter *l*

Primary emphasis
- Vowels followed by *l: al, el, il, ild, ol, ul, ull*
- Context clues
- Oral and silent reading comprehension

Secondary emphasis
- The endings *-ful* and *-less*
- Synonyms and antonyms
- Common expressions
- Writing and study skills

Word Chart

1. When the letter *l* follows a vowel, the sound of the vowel often is affected. Have students choose and learn key words for any of these combinations that cause difficulty.

2. Students can remember the sounds for *ild* and *ol* better if they mark the vowels long.

Pre-reading Activities

Ask or say:

1. How do you feel about paying bills? In this story, we learn that paying bills is a job Jack hates. Do you hate to pay bills? Why or why not?

2. As you read, compare how Jack and Eddie feel about paying bills.

Post-reading Activities

Ask or say:

1. Where does this story take place?

2. How did Eddie feel toward Jack? What information from the story did you use to decide?

3. Why did Eddie think Jack was laughing? Was he right?

4. Why did Jack laugh while paying his bills?

5. Compare Jack's and Eddie's attitudes toward paying bills.

6. Why do you think Jack and Eddie thought a 10 cent phone bill was funny?

7. Do you think Jack expects to hear from the phone company about the mistake in the bill? Why or why not?

8. If you were in the same situation as Jack, would you do the same thing? Why?

9. What if the telephone company had overcharged Jack instead of undercharging him? How do you think Jack's reaction would have been different?

Language Experience or Writing Activities

1. Complete the following sentence. My attitude toward paying bills is . . .

2. Bring to class a few sample bills. Discuss important things to remember when paying bills such as the due date, keeping records, and the interest on the balance. Then discuss terms such as *balance, charges, finance, remit, interest rate,* and *grace period.*

Exercises

1 Read and Write (the ending *-ful*)

Point to *-ful* in the directions, and have students read it. Then have them read the words at the left with the ending *-ful* added. Explain that when they have written all the words with *-ful* added, they should use those words in the sentences. Have them read the example sentence. If they are confused, have them complete an item on their own.

2 Read and Write (the ending *-less*)

Preview this exercise in the same way as Exercise 1. During the homework review, ask students to explain the difference between *harmful* and *harmless.* Then ask them the difference between *careful* and *careless* and between *helpful* and *helpless.* Point out that endings often change the meanings of words.

5 Sayings

Tell students that the words at the left are used in common expressions. Have them read the example and complete the next item. Remind them to use the process of elimination as they do the exercise. Discuss any of the sayings that are unfamiliar during the homework review.

Summarizing the Lesson

Discuss what students learned from the lesson. Do a random review of the chart words.

Lesson 15: Digraphs and Consonant Blends

Primary emphasis
- Digraphs and consonant blends *ch, sh, st, sk*
- The endings *-est* and *-iest*
- Oral and silent reading comprehension
- Context clues

Secondary emphasis
- Distinguishing among similar words
- Synonyms
- Writing and study skills

Word Chart

1. Have students pronounce the digraphs and consonant blends before they sound out the words.
2. Note that these digraphs and blends are found at both the beginning and end of words.

Words for Study

Teach *couldn't* and *I'll* as you have other contractions.

Pre-reading Activities

Ask or say:

1. What does it mean to "save the day"? Can you think of a time when you or someone you know "saved the day"?
2. While reading the story, decide if you think Kate was foolish or brave.

Post-reading Activities

Ask or say:

1. Retell the story in your own words.
2. How did Kate save the day?
3. What is the first clue in the story that something is wrong at the store?
4. What did the store manager offer Kate as a reward?
5. Do you think Kate considered herself to be in danger when she shouted at the robbers?
6. At what point in the story do you think Kate first realized that she had been in danger?
7. Did the store manager and the other customers seem to think Kate had acted bravely? Did Eddie think Kate had acted bravely? Compare and discuss why everyone in the store except Eddie was happy after the robbers left.
8. Kate had a wish about buying a chair. What was her wish? At the end of the story, did Kate's wish come true?
9. Do you think Kate was foolish, brave, or both? Explain your answer.

Language Experience or Writing Activities

1. Ask if any students have witnessed a crime. Ask how that experience affected their understanding of the story. Students can write about their experience.
2. Ask students to think about shopping and then complete one of the following sentences.

   I like to shop for . . .

   I do not like to shop for . . .
3. Do you believe there should be stricter laws controlling guns? Explain your opinion.

Exercises

1 **Read and Write** (the ending *-est*)

Review the *-er* ending introduced in Lesson 11. Point out the relationship between *-er* meaning *more* and *-est* meaning *most*. If necessary, review the rules for adding endings that start with a vowel.

2 **Read and Write** (change *y* to *i* and add *-est*)

Review the *y* to *i* conversion if necessary.

Summarizing the Lesson

Discuss what students learned from the lesson. Review the digraphs and consonant blends introduced in the word chart.

Lesson 16: Consonant Blends

Primary emphasis
- Consonant blends *bl, cl, fl, gl, pl, sl*
- Oral and silent reading comprehension
- Compound words
- Context clues

Secondary emphasis
- Distinguishing among similar words
- Writing sentences
- Writing and study skills

Word Chart

Have students pronounce the consonant blends before they sound out the words. Point out that these blends are at the beginning of words.

Words for Study

1. Be sure students know that the abbreviation *Dr.* stands for *doctor* and that the first letter should be capitalized.
2. Teach the contraction *haven't* following the usual procedure.

Pre-reading Activities

Ask or say:

1. Have you ever been hurt because you were rushing? In this story, Bob is rushing to work and slams his hand in the car door.
2. As you read this story, look for two reasons Bob felt as if he were going to faint.

Post-reading Activities

Ask or say:

1. Explain how Bob's accident happened.
2. In what two places does this story take place?
3. Did Bob see the doctor?
4. The story mentions two reasons why Bob felt like fainting. What are the two reasons?
5. Do you think June does a good job of nursing Bob's hand in this story? Explain.
6. Do you agree with Aunt Louise's saying "Bad times can turn into good times a lot more often than people think"? What was the bad time for Bob? What was the good time?
7. Do you think Bob did the right thing after his accident? What would you do differently?

Language Experience or Writing Activities

1. Has rushing ever caused you trouble? Explain.
2. Tell about a time when you met an old friend after many years.

Additional Activities

1. Aunt Louise's friends are always quoting her. Read some sayings or proverbs in class. Discuss the meaning of each.
2. Ask if students ever had to deal with a first-aid emergency. Discuss first aid for bleeding and other emergencies. You might want to get a first-aid manual or brochures from the American Red Cross. The American Red Cross can also provide other information about first aid.

Exercises

1 Read and Write (word sounds)

Remind students that they did a similar exercise in Lesson 13.

2 Read and Write (compound words)

During the preview, teach the concept of compound words. Explain that a compound word is made up of two smaller words. List several compound words that students have encountered such as *girlfriend, birthday, herself, payday,* and *something.*

Explain that students will choose words from list A and add words from list B to them to form compound words. Then they will use the compound words to fill in the blanks in the sentences.

Have students read the example sentence and note that *down* and *town* are joined to form the compound word. Have them complete items 2 and 3 to make sure they understand how to do this exercise. Tell students to check off words as they use them and to use the process of elimination.

Summarizing the Lesson

Discuss what students learned from the lesson. Point out that when compound words are formed, the spelling of the words does not change as sometimes happens when adding endings.

Lesson 17: More Consonant Blends

Primary emphasis
- Consonant blends *br, cr, dr, fr, gr, pr, tr, str*
- Classifying words
- Oral and silent reading comprehension
- Context clues

Secondary emphasis
- Distinguishing among similar words
- Reviewing factual information
- Writing and study skills

Word Chart

Have students pronounce these initial consonant blends before sounding out the words.

Words for Study

1. Review compound words by having students identify the two words in *upset* and *anywhere*.

2. Teach the contraction *hadn't* following the usual procedure.

Pre-reading Activities

Ask or say:

1. Review the stories in Lessons 1 and 2. In this story, we learn how Bob has been doing in his new job.

2. In this story, Bob carefully plans his date with June. Read to find out what Bob forgot to plan.

3. What does it mean to "freeze in your tracks"? Read this story to find out what caused Bob to freeze in his tracks.

Post-reading Activities

Ask or say:

1. Tell what happened in the story.

2. It was Saturday morning, and Bob thought the night would never come. Does he want the night to come? What does this sentence tell you about how Bob is feeling?

3. Dan Rose yelled at Bob for five minutes. Was Bob worried about losing his job? Explain your answer.

4. Find a sentence that shows that Bob is doing well in his job repairing bikes.

5. What were some of the decisions Bob had to make as he prepared for his date?

6. Find a place in the story that shows Bob is a considerate person.

7. What caused Bob to freeze in his tracks?

8. At the end of the story, Bob has an important date with June and no money. What do you think he will do next?

Language Experience or Writing Activities

1. List some ideas for solving Bob's problem.

2. Do you remember a day when time seemed to pass quickly or slowly? Describe it.

3. Even when he was at work, Bob took pride in how he looked. Do you think how a person dresses for a job matters? Think of some jobs where it does matter and some jobs where it does not matter.

Exercises

2 **Read and Write** (classify words)

Have students read the headings for the three categories and the words in the column on the left. Explain that they should decide under which heading each word in the column fits best. Have them explain why *barn* is listed under "Farm." Then have them read *bus stops* and note that it could go under either "Town" or "School." Suggest that they should therefore skip it for now and go on to the next item. Students should have no difficulty seeing that *churches* should be listed under "Town."

3 **Read and Write** (best and least)

Explain that this exercise calls for students' own opinions. Tell them to write what they like best on the lines at the left of each group. Then they should write what they like least on the lines at the right. There are no right or wrong answers.

Summarizing the Lesson

Discuss with students the variety of things they learned from this lesson.

Lesson 18: More Digraphs and Consonant Blends

Primary emphasis
- Digraphs and consonant blends *wh, th, thr, tw, sm, sn, sp, sw*
- The words for numbers 1 through 20
- Oral and silent reading comprehension
- Context clues

Secondary emphasis
- Distinguishing among similar words
- Compound words
- Reviewing factual information
- Writing and study skills

Word Chart

1. Some people pronounce the *wh* digraph as /w/; others pronounce it as /hw/. Either way is acceptable.
2. Note that the words in the first *th* row have the voiced *th* sound. Words in the other two rows have the soft, or unvoiced, *th* sound.

Words for Study

Review compound words by having students identify the two words in *afternoon, everybody,* and *nothing*.

Pre-reading Activities

Ask or say:

1. The title of this story is "A Way with Kids." What does it mean to have a way with kids? Do you think you have a way with kids? Why or why not?
2. As you read this story, think about how Jack solves his problem with Billy. Think about what you would say or do if you were in Jack's place.

Post-reading Activities

Ask or say:

1. Summarize the story in your own words.
2. Why was Jack taking care of Billy?
3. What two things did Billy do to Jack as soon as the family left?
4. Where does this story take place? How do you know?
5. Do you think Mary's mother had trouble with Billy? Why or why not?
6. What advice did Mary's mother give Jack before she left? In your opinion, was this useful advice?
7. Have you ever been in a situation similar to Jack's? What did you learn about children from your experience?

8. Do you think Jack will be asked to watch Billy again? Do you think he would accept? Why or why not?

Language Experience or Writing Activity

Jack needed to make a decision when things got difficult. He chose to use self-control and not lose his temper. Write or tell about a time when you used self-control or when you should have used self-control but didn't.

Additional Activity

Have the class discuss the subject of children's behavior problems. List what works and what doesn't work.

Exercises

2 Numbers

Have students read the words for the numbers 1 through 20. Then do a random review by writing several of the words for them to read without the figures. Make sure students write the word rather than the figure when they do the exercise.

3 Read and Write (compound words)

Remind students to add words from list B to the words in list A to form compound words and then use the compound words to fill in the blanks in the sentences.

Summarizing the Lesson

After discussing what students learned from the lesson, do a random review of the chart words and of the words for 1 through 20.

Lesson 19: Still More Consonant Blends

Primary emphasis
- Consonant blends *sc, scr, shr, spl, spr, squ, str, chr*
- The prefixes *un-* and *re-*
- Oral and silent reading comprehension
- Context clues

Secondary emphasis
- Distinguishing among similar words
- Word associations
- Reviewing factual information
- Writing and study skills

Word Chart

These consonant blends can be troublesome. Spend as much time as necessary for students to feel confident in recognizing and pronouncing them.

Words for Study

Teach the contraction *we're* following the usual procedure.

Pre-reading Activities

Ask or say:

1. Have you ever had to deal with an emergency? Share what you learned from the experience.
2. As you read this story, think about what Kate did that showed good sense in an emergency.

Post-reading Activities

Ask or say:

1. Tell what happened in the story.
2. Did Kate witness the accident?
3. What was the first thing Kate did after the accident? What did she do next?
4. Kate called the police. Did they ever arrive? Explain why the police probably did not come.
5. If this had been a real accident, what did Kate do that would have been helpful? What did Kate do that would have caused trouble?
6. Kate wished Aunt Louise were home because she would know what to do. What does this tell you about the relationship between Kate and Aunt Louise?
7. Describe the scene of the accident. Think about what Kate overlooked. If a movie crew was filming, what else would be there?
8. If you were in Kate's place, what would you have done differently?

Language Experience or Writing Activities

1. Kate wished Aunt Louise were there because she would know what to do. Think about a person you depend on and write about that person.
2. Write a list of important things to try to remember when dealing with an emergency.
3. Do you think "How Kate Got to Be a Movie Star" is a good title for this story? Did the title interest you in reading the story? Is this really a story about how Kate got to be a movie star? What is it about? Write another title for this story.
4. Did you ever witness an accident? How was your reaction the same or different from Kate's in this story?

Exercises

3 **Read and Write** (words that don't fit)

Remind students to choose the word that doesn't fit with the rest of the words in each row.

4 and **5** **Read and Write**

Students should write words on all the lines at the left before using them in the sentences. Point out that there are no spelling changes when *un-* and *re-* are added to the beginnings of words. Discuss how adding *un-* and *re-* changed the meanings of words during the homework review.

Summarizing the Lesson

After students summarize what they learned in the lesson, do a random review of the words with consonant blends. Make note of any blends that students have difficulty producing and develop reinforcement activities for extra practice.

Lesson 20: Sounds for *c* and *g*

Primary emphasis
- The sounds for hard and soft *c* and *g*
- The sound for *dge*
- Oral and silent reading comprehension
- Context clues

Secondary emphasis
- Distinguishing among similar words
- Classifying words
- Reviewing factual information
- Writing and study skills

Word Chart

1. Sounds for *c* introduced:
   - *c* followed by *a, o,* or *u* sounds like /k/
   - *c* followed by *e* or *i* sounds like /s/

2. Sounds for *g* introduced:
   - *g* followed by *a, u,* and sometimes *i* sounds like /g/
   - *g* at the end of a word sounds like /g/
   - *g* followed by *e* or *i* often sounds like /j/

3. *dge* at the end of a word sounds like /j/

4. Special note: There are many common exceptions to the soft *g* rule such as *get, give, gift, giggle,* and *girl.*

Pre-reading Activities

Ask or say:

1. Review the story in Lesson 17 briefly.

2. Have you ever made plans to do something, only to find you didn't have enough money to do it? What did you do?

3. Bob has no money. He must call June about their date. What do you think will happen?

Post-reading Activities

Ask or say:

1. Tell the story in your own words. Start with why Bob didn't have any money (from Lesson 17).

2. Do you think it was difficult for Bob to ask Aunt Louise for money? Find a place in the story that supports your answer.

3. Was Aunt Louise the only person Bob considered borrowing money from for his date? How do you know?

4. Do you think Aunt Louise wanted to help Bob by lending him money? Why?

5. Aunt Louise didn't give Bob money. What did she give him? Was it valuable to Bob?

6. How did Aunt Louise and June know something was wrong when Bob called them?

7. What would you have done in Bob's place?

Language Experience or Writing Activities

1. Tell about something you have done that didn't cost much money but was fun.

2. Both women in the story knew something was wrong because of Bob's voice on the phone. What are some other ways you can tell how someone is feeling?

3. List recreational activities in your community that are inexpensive; for example, going to parades, parks, nature centers, street festivals, and community centers.

Exercises

1 **Read and Write** (word sounds)

Explain that for some items students will use all the choices, while for other items they will choose only one word depending on the number of blanks in the sentences.

2 **Read and Write** (classifying words)

Review the procedures for Exercise 2 in Lesson 17 if necessary.

3 **Twelve Questions**

This exercise is primarily for word review. Students are not expected to know all the answers. Explain that if students don't know an answer, they should make an intelligent guess. If reference materials are available, they could work in pairs and look up answers. During the homework review, take some time to explain items students didn't know.

Note: Either *true* or *false* is correct for item 4. According to some sources, both deer and bears can run at a speed of 30 miles per hour. Other sources claim that deer can run 40 miles per hour.

Summarizing the Lesson

Since this is the final lesson in *Challenger 1*, spend some time discussing what students have learned from working in this book.

First Review and Second Review

These reviews give students an opportunity to work with many of the words and concepts they have studied in this book one more time before beginning Book 2. An accuracy rate of 85 per cent or better indicates that a student is ready to go on to Book 2.

The reviews can either be completed in class or assigned as homework. Preview the exercises as you have been doing for the lesson work. For the sake of variety and exposure to new formats, three new types of exercises appear in the reviews: multiple choice questions, analogies, and word pairs. Preview these exercises as follows:

1 **Read and Write** (multiple choice, pages 101 and 105)

Explain that students should select from the four choices the word that best fits in the sentence and write the word in the blank.

3 **Read and Write** (analogies, page 107)

Have students read the example and explain why *father* is the correct choice. Then students should read item 2 and explain the relationship between *shirt* and *blouse*. Ask them which word choice has the same relationship to *pants* that *blouse* has to *shirt*. If necessary, do item 3 together also.

4 **Word Pairs** (page 108)

Explain that words in the column on the left often are paired with words in the column on the right. Have students read item 1 and the word pair *salt* and *pepper*. Then have them read item 2 and fill in *bride* and *groom,* checking off the words as they use them. Remind students to use the process of elimination.

After going over the second review, some sort of celebration is in order. Take some time to discuss what students have accomplished. Provide a treat, if possible. They've earned it, and so have you!

Challenger 2 Introduction and Lesson Notes

Challenger 2 is generally used by students who have completed *Challenger 1*. The primary purpose of Book 2 is to reinforce phonics skills, vocabulary, and reasoning skills introduced in Book 1. Book 2 differs from Book 1 in several respects. The 20 lessons in Book 2 contain brief nonfiction reading selections on a wide variety of topics, rather than short fiction as appears in Book 1. First readings of the selections are usually silent and done as homework to develop reading independence. Written comprehension questions follow each reading selection.

Book 2 is an appropriate starting place for students who can read at the 2.0–3.0 reading levels and need the skills practice that this book provides. Book 2 is also an appropriate starting place for students who test at level 2 on the *Challenger Placement Tool* and who prefer reading nonfiction to fiction.

Few new words are introduced in Book 2 in order to give students an opportunity to review thoroughly vocabulary they have learned so far. In addition, there are reviews after every five lessons in Book 2 that provide additional opportunities to review words and reinforce concepts. The word indexes at the end of each review can be used when planning reinforcement activities.

Scheduling Considerations

One-hour sessions are appropriate for students in Book 2. This time frame allows students to do some oral reading, discuss the reading selection, go over the homework exercises, work on writing and/or reinforcement activities, and preview the next lesson.

Book 2 works well in three types of instructional settings. All types have both advantages and disadvantages that you should consider in preparing the lessons.

One-to-One Tutorial Setting

The advantage of working with only one student is that you can offer him your undivided attention. The student usually progresses rapidly because you can pace the work and plan reinforcement activities exclusively tailored to his needs.

The disadvantage is that the student is deprived of the support and stimulation that can best be provided by other students. For example, the discussions about the reading passages are more interesting when other students participate.

Classroom Setting

The advantage of this setting is that students receive support and stimulation from one another, making learning a more enjoyable activity. You can divide a larger class into small groups to work on specific activities. More-advanced students can assume much of the responsibility for giving explanations and leading reinforcement activities. This, in turn, reinforces their own skills. Less-advanced students usually benefit from peer instruction, provided you are available for any clarifications that need to be made.

The disadvantage of this setting is that you cannot usually be so thorough in addressing each student's needs as you could be working one-to-one.

Group Tutorial Setting

In this setting, each student works at his own pace. Students working at the same level can often team up. More-advanced students can help those having trouble with the material. This type of learning environment suits students who don't work well in groups on a consistent basis.

One disadvantage of this setting can be that some students begin to see the lessons more as a competition than as an opportunity to improve their reading. You may have to remind students that they are competing with their own past performance, rather than competing with each other.

A second disadvantage is that this type of setting makes incredible demands on you. Not only must you be familiar with many lessons simultaneously, but also you must be able to sustain a high level of concentration and stamina in order to work individually with several students during each session.

Suggestions for Teaching the Lessons

It is important for you to read the material in the first five chapters of this manual if you have not already done so. These chapters discuss concepts and procedures upon which *Challenger* is based and give general suggestions for using the series. The following are specific suggestions applicable to Book 2.

Words for Study

Words that appear for the first time in this controlled-vocabulary series are listed before the reading passage in each lesson. Words appear in the same form in which they initially appear in the reading selection or exercises. This gives students additional practice in reading word endings. Many students, especially those who start their reading program in Book 2, can sight-read most of these words. Have students sound out any words they don't know with as little help from you as possible. After students have read all the words, do a brief random review.

The following are some suggestions to help students sound out unfamiliar words. The examples used are all from Lesson 1.

- Have students sound out one-syllable words according to the methods used in Book 1. For students starting this series in Book 2, teach any sounds they do not know in the unfamiliar word. The material on pages 8–11, Common Phonics Elements and Principles in English Words, may be helpful.

- Students working in Book 2 may have difficulty sounding out words of more than one syllable. Have them sound out such words as *recorded* one syllable at a time. Begin by covering every syllable except *re.* After they sound out *re,* have them uncover and sound out *cord,* and then say *record.* Then have them sound out *ed* and say *recorded.*

- Key words and vowel markings also help students to sound out unfamiliar words. If a student working on the word *Clark* has forgotten the sound for *ar,* write *car* in the margin and underline *ar.* Also, most students have no difficulty sounding out *touch* if you draw a line through the *o* to indicate that it is silent.

- Combining phonics methods with verbal and context clues can help students remember new words. For example, after a student has sounded out *Pin* in *Pinocchio,* he may be able to complete the word if you ask, "Have you heard the story of the little boy whose nose grew longer every time he told a lie?" If he knows the name, point out the unusual *cch* spelling for the /k/ sound and explain that it comes from Italian. If students don't know the story of Pinocchio, briefly summarize it for them. Be alert to these opportunities to broaden students' background knowledge.

The Reading Selections

Pre-reading and post-reading activities are discussed in Chapter 2. Specific suggestions are given in individual lesson notes. Explain to students that the selections in Book 2 are not stories; they are brief articles about a variety of subjects. The following ideas may be helpful in your planning.

- After Lesson 1, first readings should be done for homework, so students can develop silent reading skills. Have students read the passage orally during the homework review. For students starting in Book 2, see suggestions for developing oral reading skills in the Introduction to Book 1 on page 49.

- Follow-up discussions of the reading selections help students to understand and enjoy the readings. For suggestions on conducting these discussions, see Chapter 2. Some questions for discussion are given in the individual lesson notes.

- You may need to remind students that they do not have to agree with the point of view presented in any selection. Many beginning readers have a tendency to believe that because something is in print, it is necessarily "true." Discuss students' opinions and points of view freely and objectively.

The Exercises

Preview the exercises during the class session and have students complete them for homework. Make sure students know how to do each exercise. Book 2 students should be able to read the directions themselves. A few deliberately difficult items are included in most of the exercises to challenge the students' reasoning abilities. Keep the following points in mind as you work with students on the exercises.

- Exercise 1 is always a reading comprehension exercise. Encourage students to refer to the reading selection when necessary. Some students consider this "cheating." Point out that even experienced readers often have to read some things more than once.

- Explain that a long line beneath a question indicates that the answer should be written as a complete sentence. Review sentence capitalization and punctuation if necessary.

- Remind students to answer all questions. Explain that they should make intelligent guesses if they don't know an answer. Show them how the use of context clues and the process of elimination can be strategies for selecting correct answers. Remind students also that mistakes are valuable because they can learn from them.

- Students should correct all exercises during the homework review. Any grading required should be done on corrected work. Consider an overall average of 80 per cent or better an excellent score.

- Common American expressions and idioms appear in many exercises. Students often appreciate learning more about these expressions, so take a few moments to explain them whenever the situation calls for it.

Suggestions for specific exercises are given in the individual lesson notes beginning on page 79.

Writing Activities

Writing activities are discussed in Chapter 3 of this manual. Suggested topics can be found in the individual lesson notes. Use these suggestions in planning writing assignments. Students working in Book 2 should do an extended writing activity at least once a week. Personal letters and short compositions about discussion topics that interest students are

Writing Activities
(continued)

appropriate writing activities. Let students pick topics from a list of suggestions you provide. Draw from discussions about the reading selections, student comments and interests, and current issues for appropriate topics. Some activities should involve formal writing that is corrected and revised.

The Lesson Segments

After the session in which Lesson 1 is completed and Lesson 2 is previewed for homework, the procedure for each session should be as consistent as possible. Most sessions will have the following segments. You may want to vary the order to suit your particular situation.

1. **Homework Review.** Have students read aloud at least some of the reading selection in the lesson studied for homework. Have them summarize the selection, go over their answers to the comprehension questions in Exercise 1, and discuss the selection. Then, go over the rest of the exercises and have students make any necessary corrections.

2. **Writing Activity.** Students may work in groups or singly on the current writing activity, depending on what it is.

3. **Reinforcement Activity.** When time permits, focus on an area of difficulty in a way that is fun for the students. See Chapter 4 of this manual for suggestions.

4. **Homework Preview.** Preview the next lesson, which students will complete for homework. Have them read the Words for Study and title of the selection and then predict what they think the selection will be about. Do one or more pre-reading activities. Also have them read the directions for the exercises and do one item in any exercise that might be confusing.

Individual Lesson Notes

The individual lesson notes that begin on page 79 contain specific suggestions and procedures for Book 2 lessons.

Lesson 1: Sneezing

Primary emphasis
- Silent and oral reading comprehension
- Phonics skills
- New vocabulary
- Consonants, blends, and digraphs

Secondary emphasis
- Context clues
- Long and short vowel sounds
- Learning/reviewing factual information
- Homonyms
- Writing and study skills

Words for Study

1. Many of these words are not phonetically regular. Pronounce those that students don't recognize and have them repeat each word several times while looking at it.
2. When introducing *Pinocchio,* ask if students are familiar with the story of the puppet who became a real boy. Tell them that the *cch* spelling for /k/ comes from Italian.

Pre-reading Activities

1. Have students read the title of the selection and share some things they know about sneezing. Ask students what things make them sneeze. Make a list of their responses.
2. Ask students if they get a warning before they are going to sneeze and, if so, what is it? If anyone is successful at stopping sneezes, ask how they do it.

Post-reading Activities

1. Discuss the answers to the questions in Exercise 1.

Ask or say:

2. What are some things June Clark probably could not do during the six months she was sneezing?
3. How do you think people probably treated June Clark during the time she was sneezing? Consider both family members and strangers.
4. Besides "God bless you," what else might people say when someone sneezes?
5. Name some of the illnesses that people can catch from germs spread by sneezing.
6. What are some other ways germs are spread besides sneezing? Discuss some preventive measures that people can take to reduce the spread of infections.

Writing Activities

1. Complete the following sentences:

   When I am just about to sneeze I feel . . .
   After I sneeze I feel . . .

2. Discuss and then write about some things people can do to maintain good health.

Exercises

1 About the Reading

During the homework preview, point out that a long line under a question indicates that the answer there should be a complete sentence. Explain that answers to "What do you think?" questions are not found in the passage and students should write their own opinions.

2 Word Sounds

During the homework preview, have students read the directions aloud. Have them read the example (sentence 1) and explain what they are to do.

Have students do the second item. Tell them to read the entire sentence in order to fill in the blank correctly. Then tell them to reread the sentence after the blank has been filled in to make sure the sentence makes sense.

Students may prefer to write the three words in the left column first.

4 Marking the *e's*

After students have read the directions, review the vowel markings, the long and short *e* sounds, and the function of the silent *e* (to make the preceding vowel long).

5 Words That Sound the Same

Have students read the two words to be used in the first sentence. Then have them read the sentence filling in the words orally. Point out that while the words sound the same, they are spelled differently and have different meanings. The correct spelling of the word depends on its meaning in the sentence.

Lesson 2: Cats

Primary emphasis
- Silent and oral reading comprehension
- Phonics skills
- New vocabulary
- Consonants, blends, and digraphs
- Classifying information

Secondary emphasis
- Context clues
- Word sounds
- Homonyms
- Writing and study skills

Words for Study

Make sure students know why *United States* is capitalized.

Pre-reading Activities

1. Show students pictures of cats and ask what students have observed about cats.

2. Ask: Have you ever seen a cat's eyes shine in the dark? (Part of a cat's eye reflects light to help the cat see when light is dim.)

3. Say: As you read this article, look for the answer to the question "Why does it take more time to train a cat than a dog?"

4. Read a poem about cats or play one or more of the songs from the musical *Cats* by Andrew Lloyd Webber, based on poems by T. S. Eliot.

Post-reading Activities

1. Discuss the answers to the questions in Exercise 1.

Ask or say:

2. Why does the author say it takes more time to train a cat than a dog? Do you agree? Why?

3. How do you feel about the man on the West Coast leaving $415,000 to his cats?

4. What information from the article shows that cats are well suited to hunt at night? What are some other animals that see well at night? What is the reason some cats and other animals are equipped to see well at night?

5. What are some other kinds of cats besides house cats?

6. Discuss cats. What are some characteristics and behaviors common to members of the cat family?

Writing Activities

1. Complete one of the following sentences:

   I like cats because . . .

   I do not like cats because . . .

2. Write about a pet cat you have now or had in the past. If you never had a cat as a pet, write about one in your neighborhood.

3. Write one new thing you learned about cats from reading this selection.

Additional Activities

1. Find one or more comic strips with a cat character. Cut the comic into story sections and use it to help students practice putting events in correct sequence.

2. Show an interesting picture of a cat. Write a group story by asking each person to contribute one sentence.

3. Students may need help reading large numbers such as $415,000. If students want help in learning how to read large numbers, explain place values and the use of commas.

4. Learn about some of the endangered cats of the world.

Additional Vocabulary Practice

carnivorous – referring to animals that eat meat

domestic – having to do with the home

endangered – in danger of becoming extinct

fact – something done, real, or true. Ask students to find a fact in this article.

Exercises

2 Word Sounds

During the homework preview, remind students that they did a similar exercise in Lesson 1. If students find this exercise confusing, suggest that they write the three word choices on the lines provided before deciding which word completes the sentence.

4 Words That Sound the Same

Remind students that the correct spelling depends upon the meaning of the word in the sentence.

Lesson 3: The Number Seven

Primary emphasis
- Silent and oral reading comprehension
- Phonics skills
- New vocabulary
- Consonants, blends, and digraphs

Secondary emphasis
- Context clues
- Contrasting word sounds
- Number words
- Writing and study skills

Words for Study

Students may need definitions for *Rome, renewed, tailor,* and *scroll.* Help students find Rome on a map or globe. Point out that *Rome* and *Bible* are capitalized and ask why.

Pre-reading Activities

1. Write the number seven in different ways, for example 7, VII, seven, 1+6, 8–1. Introduce the lesson by saying there are many ways to represent the number 7. Ask for additional suggestions.

2. Ask if students can think of anything significant about the number seven.

3. Ask: Do you have a lucky number? What is it? How did you decide on it? How do you use it?

Post-reading Activities

1. Discuss the answers to the questions in Exercise 1.

Ask or say:

2. What does "sail the seven seas" mean? What is another way to say the same thing?

3. Tell how the number seven is considered lucky for some people and unlucky for others. What is another number that some people consider unlucky?

4. Explain the meaning of the sentence "Seven years is how long it takes for every cell in the human body to be renewed."

5. How do you think the woman figured out how much money she saved on cigarettes?

Writing Activities

1. List the seven days of the week and their abbreviations and ask students to practice writing them. Point out that days of the week and months of the year are always capitalized. Suggest that students write the day of the week on their journal entries for spelling practice.

2. Complete one of the following sentences:

   People who are lucky . . .

   People who are unlucky . . .

3. Have you ever tried to stop smoking? Write about the experience. If you did stop smoking, write about why you quit. If you never smoked, write about why you never did.

Additional Activities

1. Ask students to write one sentence every day for the next seven days. The sentence should tell something about the day and each should be different. Give students an opportunity to share what they wrote the following week.

2. Help students to use an encyclopedia to look up the "Seven Wonders of the World."

3. Discuss the "seven deadly sins" (anger, covetousness, envy, pride, lust, gluttony, and sloth).

4. Help students to locate the world's oceans on a globe or map. Some students may not know the names of the oceans and continents and may want to learn them.

Exercises

3 Word Sounds

During the homework preview, make sure students understand how to do this exercise. Have students read aloud the list of words and then decide together where to write *blow* and *clown.*

4 Number Words

Explain that the answers to the "Do you know?" questions are different in different states. Encourage students to try to find out the correct answers if they don't already know them or to make an "intelligent guess." Students usually enjoy seeing if their "intelligent guesses" come close to the correct answers.

Lesson 4: A Few Facts about Beer

Primary emphasis
- Silent and oral reading comprehension
- Phonics skills
- New vocabulary
- Consonants, blends, and digraphs
- Antonyms

Secondary emphasis
- Oral reading
- Context clues
- Reviewing factual information
- Writing and study skills

Words for Study

Students may be confused about the difference between *English* and *England*. Find *Egypt* and *England* on a globe or map. Draw attention to the capitalized words.

Pre-reading Activities

Ask or say:

1. Share some things you already know about beer before reading this article.

2. In this article, you will find that the expression "mind your p's and q's," an Egyptian ruler, and the *Mayflower* all have something in common.

Post-reading Activities

1. Discuss the questions in Exercise 1.

Ask or say:

2. The title of this article is "A Few Facts about Beer." What is a fact? How is it different from an opinion?

3. What is the meaning of the expression "Mind your p's and q's"? What is another way of saying the same thing?

4. If the people sailing on the *Mayflower* had landed farther south, how might their lives have been different?

5. Why do you think some beer is bottled in dark glass?

Writing Activities

1. Write two or three facts from this article.

2. Write about beer or beer drinking. When can beer drinking be a problem?

3. Write about what you think it was like to sail on the *Mayflower*.

Additional Activities

1. Help students to locate England and Egypt on a map or globe. Ask why each country was significant in the article about beer.

2. Help students to read the numbers 3,500 and 30,000.

3. Study cups, pints, quarts, and gallons and their metric equivalents (milliliters and liters). Most dictionaries have metric equivalent tables. Bring to class any appropriate measuring cups or containers that would help students understand the conversions.

4. Trace the journey of the *Mayflower* from Plymouth, England, to Plymouth, Massachusetts, on a map or globe.

5. Discuss the long ocean voyage the pilgrims made. Point out how preventing food spoilage and carrying enough fresh water and provisions was a problem. Ask the class what some of the other problems might have been for people on the *Mayflower*.

Exercises

3 Word Sounds

During the homework preview, go over the example and tell students to read through each sentence before filling in the blanks. Read the second sentence as follows: "Dave was so *blank* of the *blank* he drew in art class that he said in a *blank* voice, 'Hey everybody, look at my picture!'" Tell students to reread the sentences after the words are filled in to make sure they make sense.

5 Word Opposites

During the homework preview, go over the example. Point out the check mark next to *clear*. Then explain the process of elimination. Tell students they don't have to do the items in order. They can do the ones they know first, skipping those they aren't sure of. Then they can go back and do the skipped ones when fewer choices remain.

BOOK 2

Lesson 5: Love Letters

Primary emphasis
- Silent and oral reading comprehension
- Phonics skills
- New vocabulary
- Consonants, blends, and digraphs

Secondary emphasis
- Context clues
- Reviewing factual information
- Long and short vowels
- Homonyms
- Writing and study skills

Pre-reading Activities

1. Ask students if they like to write letters. Tell the class that this is the story of a very strange love letter.

2. Ask students if they know what a scribe is. Tell them that in this article they will find out what one scribe had to do.

Post-reading Activities

1. Discuss the questions in Exercise 1.

2. Ask students to summarize the selection.

Ask or say:

3. Is this article about love letters or about *a* love letter? Suggest another title for the article.

4. Was the scribe paid for his work? How do you know?

5. Why do you think the painter did not write the letter himself?

6. Instead of "scribe," what are some titles for people who do similar work today? What tools do people today have that would make the work of a scribe easier?

7. What is the most boring job you ever had to do? What are some of the factors that make something interesting or boring?

Writing Activities

1. Have students write answers to these questions about the article: What is it about? Who is it about? Where did it take place? When did it happen? Why did it happen?

2. Discuss the kinds of letters or notes students need to write. Study the forms of a friendly letter and a business letter. Ask students to write a short note or letter to someone.

Additional Activities

1. Find France on a map.

2. Help students to read the number 1,875,000.

3. Do you know anyone who did something unusual to demonstrate their love?

4. Discuss the fact that in former times many people didn't know how to write, so they hired scribes when they needed to have something written.

Exercises
5 Marking Vowels

Review the marks for long, short, and silent vowel sounds introduced in Lesson 1.

Review: Lessons 1–5

Explain to students that reviews appear after every five lessons. In addition to the review, you might also have students do a research and report activity in which students select one topic from the five lessons and find out more about it. Students can work singly, in pairs, or in groups, and give oral and/or written reports.

Exercises
1 Choosing the Answer

Tell students that the process of elimination is useful for multiple choice questions. If students are not sure of the correct answer, they can eliminate the ones they know are incorrect first. Have students complete the first item during the preview so that they understand what to do.

3 Facts

If students don't recall this information, tell them to refer to Lesson 1.

Word Index

Mention to students that this list includes the words in Lessons 1 through 5 that had not been introduced in Book 1. The index can be used for word reviews, spelling checks, and reinforcement activities.

BOOK 2

Lesson 6: Wigs

Primary emphasis
- Silent and oral reading comprehension
- Phonics skills
- New vocabulary
- Consonants, blends, and digraphs

Secondary emphasis
- Context clues
- Words that rhyme
- Word associations
- Sounds for *ea*
- Compound words

Words for Study

Explain *B.C.* (before Christ) and *A.D.* (*anno Domini,* in the year of the Lord) as used in dates. Find France on a map or globe. Review the locations of Rome, England, and Egypt.

Pre-reading Activities

1. Bring in pictures of people from historical periods when wigs were popular.

Ask or say:

2. Have you ever worn a wig? What did you like or dislike about wearing a wig?

3. Read this selection about wigs to find out why some people in history wore wigs and how they kept wigs from sliding off their heads.

Post-reading Activities

1. Discuss the answers to the questions in Exercise 1.

Ask or say:

2. Have people always worn wigs just to be in fashion?

3. Name one kind of animal and one kind of insect found in Egypt in 4000 B.C.

4. How do you think the king of France got everybody to wear wigs?

5. Compare the wigs described in the reading to the wigs people wear today.

6. Why do people wear wigs today? (Examples: as theater costumes, for disguise, to cover bald spots, for fashion, after chemotherapy)

Writing Activities

1. Write a sentence using the word *bigwig*.

2. How has hair fashion changed during your lifetime?

3. What information in this article was the most interesting to you? Complete the following sentence: I thought the most interesting information about wigs was . . .

Additional Activities

1. How many years have passed since 4000 B.C.? Draw a time line to illustrate B.C. and A.D. Figure out how many years have passed since 4000 B.C. Then add A.D. 1624, 1702, and 2000 to the time line, and any other dates that students would like to add.

2. In the first paragraph it states that in Egypt, "The bigger the wig was, the more important the person was." Discuss whether people still make judgments based on size today. (Examples: judgments about big homes, big cars, paychecks)

3. Describe how you think it would feel to wear a wig made out of wool, animal hair, or gold. How heavy would it be? How would it feel on a hot summer day? Discuss other fashions that have been painful or uncomfortable. (Examples: corsets, bound feet, tight jeans, spike-heeled shoes)

Additional Vocabulary Practice

term – Look up the word *term* in the dictionary to see how many different meanings it has. Ask the students what *term* means in the first paragraph.

toupee – a man's wig designed to cover a bald spot

Exercises

3 Which Word Does Not Fit?

During the homework preview, go over the example and have students explain why *month* is the word that doesn't fit. Then have them do the second item and explain their choice.

4 Vowel Sounds

During the preview, have students read aloud the list of words to make sure they can pronounce all of the words correctly.

Lesson 7: Skunks

Primary emphasis

- Silent and oral reading comprehension
- Phonics skills
- New vocabulary
- Consonants, blends, and digraphs
- Synonyms and antonyms

Secondary emphasis

- Context clues
- Compound words
- Writing and study skills

Words for Study

Point out that *he's* is the contraction for both *he is* and *he has*. Review the word *apostrophe*.

Pre-reading Activities

Background information: Skunks have an unusual defense against danger. These black and white mammals can spray a liquid that can cause stinging and temporary blindness. Skunks can be found searching for mice, insects, eggs, and berries from sundown to sunup. They have few enemies aside from great horned owls and automobiles. Skunks are found in the Western Hemisphere from Hudson Bay, Canada, to the Strait of Magellan at the tip of South America.

1. Ask students to share any information they already know about skunks or any experiences they have had.

2. Ask if everyone is familiar with the smell of a skunk. If someone has not smelled a skunk, ask someone else to try to describe it. Discuss the difficulty of trying to describe a smell.

Post-reading Activities

1. Discuss the answers to the questions in Exercise 1.

Ask or say:

2. Does the skunk in the picture show signs of being threatened? How would the skunk look if it were about to spray?

3. What causes a skunk to spray?

4. Do you think a skunk will spray without warning? What information in the article supports your answer?

5. If a skunk is stamping its forefeet and raising its tail, will it always spray?

6. What do you think you should do if you see a skunk? What should you probably not do?

Writing Activities

1. Write one or two sentences telling something new that you learned about skunks.

2. Write about what you would do or not do if you saw a skunk.

Additional Activities

1. Skunks will follow a sequence of steps when threatened. On slips of paper, write each of these steps. Ask students to work in pairs or individually to put them in correct order. When they are finished, have students check their work against the article.

2. Some skunks are striped and some are spotted, but they all are black and white. Ask students if a skunk's defense depends on hiding and escaping notice. Ask the class to list some animals that defend themselves by hiding. Pictures of animals that are camouflaged would illustrate this.

3. Make a list of animals and discuss how they react to danger. Compare these responses to what skunks do. (Skunks usually move slowly and do not run if chased.) Next, discuss the terms *predator* and *prey,* and classify the listed animals accordingly.

Exercises

2 Words That Mean the Same and 3 Word Opposites

After students have read the directions and studied the examples, have them complete one item in each exercise during the homework preview. Remind them to use the process of elimination in completing these exercises.

5 Silly Verses

Students may be interested to know that the name of this verse form is *limerick*. Both the rhyme scheme and the rhythm distinguish limericks from other verse forms. Ask if students have heard any other limericks.

BOOK 2

Lesson 8: Eggs

Primary emphasis
- Silent and oral reading comprehension
- Phonics skills
- New vocabulary
- Context clues
- Word analogies

Secondary emphasis
- Compound words
- Writing and study skills

Words for Study

If students ask what *clutch* means, tell them they will find that out when they read the selection. Ask why *Easter* is capitalized.

Pre-reading Activities

1. Have students look at the picture, and ask how it is possible to tell which chicks in the picture have been out of the shell the longest. (Their feathers have dried and look fluffy.) If any students have seen baby chicks hatching, ask them to tell about it.

2. Say: Which came first, the chicken or the egg? This article does not answer the question, but it will give you something to think about the next time you crack an egg.

Post-reading Activities

1. Discuss the answers to the questions in Exercise 1.

Ask or say:

2. Beginning about two days before they hatch, tell what happens to the eggs.

3. Do chicks grow fast? What information from the article supports your answer?

4. Why is it necessary for the eggs to "talk" to one another? Explain what would happen if the eggs hatched at very different times.

5. What information can a person who raises chickens learn just by listening?

6. What does the word *fought* probably mean in the paragraph containing the question "Which came first, the chicken or the egg?" Are people really discussing the origins of life when they discuss this question?

Writing Activities

1. Write about whether you think the chicken or the egg came first and why you think so.

2. Eggs have a lot of food value but also a lot of cholesterol. Write something you know about cholesterol.

3. Did the information about "talking eggs" surprise you? Write about something that has surprised you.

Additional Activities

1. This article begins with a question. Ask students what purpose the author may have had in starting the article with a question. Study the question itself. Is it stated in a way that causes the reader to be curious enough to read further? Ask students if they think this is an effective way of capturing interest.

2. Help students to research information that answers the following questions:
   - What kind of birds lay the largest and smallest eggs? (ostrich: 7" x 5"; hummingbird: size of a pea)
   - What other creatures besides birds lay eggs? (turtles, snakes, fish, insects, etc.)

Exercises

2 Word Sounds

Discuss any information here that students are unfamiliar with.

3 Which Word Fits Best?

- Have students read the directions and the example and then explain why *glass* is the correct answer.

- Have students read the second item and explain the relationship between *ship* and *sea*. Then have them read the four choices and decide which choice goes with *plane* in the same way that *sea* goes with *ship*.

- Remind students that the process of elimination is helpful in selecting the correct answer.

5 Word Sounds (the *oo* vowel combination)

During the homework preview, have students read aloud the list of words to be sure they can pronounce them correctly.

Lesson 9: Gold

Primary emphasis
- Silent and oral reading comprehension
- Phonics skills
- Context clues
- New vocabulary
- Consonants, blends, and digraphs

Secondary emphasis
- Vowel sounds
- Matching definitions
- Writing and study skills

Words for Study

If students ask for the definitions of any of these words, encourage them to figure out the meanings in the context of the lesson. Point out that *isn't* is the contraction for *is not*.

Pre-reading Activities

1. Ask students how gold is used. (Examples: for jewelry, coins, repairing teeth, and manufacturing)

2. Tell students that gold has been considered valuable worldwide since ancient times. It is beautiful, scarce, and very easily worked. Gold can be melted, drawn into fine wires, or pounded to be very thin (gold foil and gold leaf).

3. Explain the process of panning for gold: swirl a mixture of water and sediment from a river bottom in a pan rapidly enough to carry the water and most of the gravel and sand over the edge. Because gold weighs more than rock, any gold there is will remain on the bottom of the pan.

Post-reading Activities

1. Discuss the answers to the questions in Exercise 1.

Ask or say:

2. Why didn't John Sutter want people to know gold had been found on his land?

3. Explain what "made a strike" means in the article. What can "a strike" mean in other contexts? (Examples: in bowling, baseball, labor disputes)

4. Do you think streets were really "knee-deep in mud" when the rains came? Can you think of other common expressions that are not meant to be taken literally?

5. What do you think became of mining camps when the gold ran out? (Some mining camps became ghost towns while others grew into cities.)

6. Discuss the difference between "a lot of money" in 1848 and "a lot of money" now. Ask if students know how much such things as movie tickets and food items cost 20 or 30 years ago.

Writing Activity

Think of advantages and disadvantages of living during the period of the gold rush. Decide in which time you would rather live and then complete one of the following sentences:

I would rather live during the gold rush because . . .

I would rather live today because . . .

Additional Activities

1. Ask students how they think people traveled to northern California. Follow the three routes that forty-niners took from the eastern United States:
   - by boat to Panama, across Panama, and then by boat to San Francisco (the closest port)
   - by boat around Cape Horn, South America
   - overland across the country

2. People also came to California from China, Australia, Latin America, and Europe. Find these places on a globe or map and trace possible routes to California.

3. Students who are interested in learning more about the California gold rush may enjoy reading *Along the Gold Rush Trail* published by New Readers Press.

Exercises

2 Word Sounds

Discuss any information here that is unfamiliar to students. Ask if they know another way to state the Golden Rule in item 7. ("Do unto others as you would have them do unto you.")

Lesson 10: Mother Goose

Primary emphasis
- Silent and oral reading comprehension
- Phonics skills
- Context clues
- New vocabulary
- Consonants, blends, and digraphs

Secondary emphasis
- Word associations
- Silent letters
- Homonyms
- Writing and study skills

Pre-reading Activities

1. Ask if students are familiar with Mother Goose rhymes. Recite or have students recite one or two.

2. Ask if students recognize the rhyme depicted in the illustration. If not, tell them that they will find out about the picture by reading the article.

3. Bring in a variety of Mother Goose books and invite students who have young children to bring in books to share. Read aloud some of the rhymes. Ask which books people like the best and why.

Post-reading Activities

1. Discuss the answers to the questions in Exercise 1.

Ask or say:

2. If there never was a real person named Mother Goose, who created these rhymes? (Like folk songs and folktales, they came from the people and were passed down orally.)

3. If many of these rhymes had been around for hundreds of years before 1760, where do you think they came from? (The colonists brought them from Europe.)

4. Do you think people who do not know the story behind "Hey diddle diddle" still enjoy the rhyme? Why?

5. Why did the queen never eat her soup without having one of her ladies-in-waiting taste it first? (Royalty often had servants taste food and drink to detect poisoning.)

Writing Activities

1. Visit a library and select a number of children's books from a variety of cultures and countries. Look for books at the appropriate reading levels for your students. Read one or two stories aloud in class. Ask each student to choose a book, write about why a child might like it, and share it with the group. To help students begin writing, ask questions about what made their book interesting or why they think children would like their book.

2. Interested students could write a children's poem. Students with artistic ability could illustrate the poems. The poems and art could then be compiled into a student book.

Additional Activities

Ask or say:

1. Figure out how many years have passed since 1760.

2. Compare Mother Goose rhymes to folk songs and stories. Explain that passing on information, stories, poems, and songs orally was common in days when few people could read or write.

3. Discuss and list reasons why students think it is important for adults to read to children often.

Exercises

2 Word Sounds

During the homework review, students might enjoy reading the rhymes these lines came from.

4 Silent Letters

During the preview, have students explain what was done in the example and complete the next item to make sure they understand what to do. Then have them read the 12 words to make sure they can decode them.

Review: Lessons 1–10

Encourage students to select one topic from Lessons 6 through 10 to research and report on. Students can work singly, in pairs, or in groups, and give oral and/or written reports.

BOOK 2

Lesson 11: Sleeping

Primary emphasis
- Silent and oral reading comprehension
- Phonics skills
- Context clues
- New vocabulary
- Consonants, blends, and digraphs

Secondary emphasis
- The sound for *aw*
- Long and short vowels
- Reordering words into sentences
- Writing and study skills

Words for Study

Students may need the definition for *pawns.* If students confuse *dawn* with *dusk,* clarify the meanings of these times of day.

Pre-reading Activities

Ask or say:

1. Have you ever watched a child, cat, or dog while they were sleeping? What are some of the things you observed? Do you think you could tell when they were dreaming? How?

2. Do you think you or someone you know "sleeps like a log"? As you read this article about sleep, think about how much activity really occurs during the time people sleep.

Post-reading Activities

1. Discuss the answers to the questions in Exercise 1.

Ask or say:

2. When people fall asleep, what are some changes in the body that can be measured?

3. Do you think sleep is necessary for good health? Why?

4. What happens when people do not get enough sleep? (A lack of sleep affects both physical and mental processes.)

5. What are some other needs that all humans have in common? (Examples: air, food, water, and shelter)

6. Name some jobs where it is very important that the workers have enough rest to do the job safely.

Writing Activities

Ask or say:

1. Write about a dream you remember.

2. About one-third of a person's life is spent in sleep. Write about what you would do with this extra time in your life if you did not have to spend it sleeping.

3. Discuss factors that affect sleep such as crossing time zones, working different shifts, stress, and uncomfortable surroundings. Ask students to choose one of these factors and write about their experience with it.

Additional Activities

1. Discuss how a paragraph is a series of sentences developing one idea or topic. As a group or in pairs, have students write brief topic headings for each paragraph in this article. (Examples: yawning, body changes, sleep stages, REM, and movement)

2. Read about Charles Lindbergh, who flew across the Atlantic alone, or someone else who went for a long time without sleep. Find out what the person did to stay awake.

Additional Vocabulary Practice

REM – Rapid Eye Movement sleep is a stage of sleep when the eyes move rapidly even though eyelids are closed.

Exercises

2 **Word Sounds**

During the homework review, ask students to read these sentence pairs as couplets (two-line verses), emphasizing both the rhymes and the rhythms.

3 **Long and Short Vowels**

Have students pronounce the words in the column at the left during the preview. Review the silent *e* rule that makes the preceding vowel sound long.

4 **Putting Words in Order**

During the preview, remind students to capitalize the first word of each sentence and to use end punctuation. Note that there is more than one correct order for item 5: "The next day he was fired for sleeping on the job." "He was fired the next day for sleeping on the job." "He was fired for sleeping on the job the next day."

BOOK 2

Lesson 12: Honeybees

Primary emphasis
- Silent and oral reading comprehension
- Phonics skills
- Context clues
- New vocabulary
- Consonants, blends, and digraphs

Secondary emphasis
- The endings -*y* and -*ly*
- Common sayings
- Writing and study skills

Words for Study

If students ask for any definitions, tell them to try to figure out the meanings from reading the selection. Tell them that the ability to figure out the meaning of a word from context clues is a skill proficient readers use regularly.

Pre-reading Activities

1. Tell students that this is an article with many interesting facts about bees. Ask the class what they already know about bees. Make a list and add to it during the lesson. Review this list at the end of the class session.

2. Ask students if they like the taste of honey and if they use it in cooking.

3. Ask if anyone has ever been stung by a bee. If so, ask them to tell about it.

Post-reading Activities

1. Discuss the answers to the questions in Exercise 1.

Ask or say:

2. Is it possible to pick out a queen bee just by looking at it? Find the place in the article that supports your answer.

3. Is one of the three kinds of bees more important than the others? Why?

4. How long is the life of a drone?

5. Are bees important for other reasons besides making honey? (They aid in pollination.)

6. In the bee colony, which is more important, the welfare of each bee or the colony? In a community of people, which do you think are more important, the rights of the individual or the interests of the group? Why do you think so?

Writing Activity

Write a paragraph to complete one of the following:

I would rather be a worker bee than a drone because . . .

I would rather be a drone than a worker bee because . . .

Additional Activity

Help students find other facts about bees and honey. For instance, bees are insects that live throughout the world except near the North and South Poles. Honey differs in flavor and color, depending on the source of the nectar (e.g., clover, wildflower, buckwheat). Bees' enemies include weed sprays, insecticides, bears, and skunks.

Additional Vocabulary Practice

pollinate – to fertilize plants by spreading pollen from one to another

beeline – the shortest route. It comes from worker bees taking the shortest route back to the hive after they have gathered food.

Exercises

3 **Words That End in -*y***

Review the rules for adding endings that start with a vowel, and have students state the rule that applies to each column of words.

- For column 1 words, add -*y* to the base word.

- For column 2 words, drop the silent *e* before adding -*y*.

- For column 3 words, double the final consonant before adding -*y*.

If students don't know or remember the rules, ask, "Have any letters been added, dropped, or changed in the examples when -*y* was added?"

5 **Common Sayings**

Students may not be familiar with all of these sayings. Encourage them to use the process of elimination and then make intelligent guesses for the ones they don't know.

Lesson 13: Handwriting

Primary emphasis
- Silent and oral reading comprehension
- Phonics skills
- Context clues
- New vocabulary
- Consonants, blends, and digraphs

Secondary emphasis
- Synonyms and antonyms
- *r*-controlled vowel sounds
- Writing and study skills

Pre-reading Activities

Ask or say:

1. Do you know that some people study the handwriting of others? Do you know why?

2. Read the following article to find out if people can learn anything about you by studying your handwriting. What kinds of things do you think they can learn?

Post-reading Activities

1. Discuss the answers to the questions in Exercise 1.

2. The first sentence in the article states, "Everything we do tells other people something about who we are." Ask students if they agree or disagree and to give examples.

Ask or say:

3. Do handwriting specialists look at many aspects of a person's handwriting or can a single feature give them enough information? How do you know?

4. What does "ruled by his head" mean? What would "ruled by his heart" mean?

5. What does "roll with the punches" mean? Do you think it is healthy to be able to do this? Why?

6. Studying handwriting is one way some people can learn about a person. What are other ways people can learn about each other?

7. Each person forms letters and words differently. What other distinctions or characteristics prove no two people are exactly alike? (Examples: fingerprints, voice, facial characteristics, genetic makeup)

8. In what kinds of police cases would a handwriting expert be called upon? (Examples: to examine a sample of writing and tell if it was written by a particular person; to tell something about the type of person who left a handwritten ransom note or warning)

Writing Activities

1. This lesson on handwriting provides a good opportunity to remind students to continue to write in their journals or to begin a journal. Say, "Each person's handwriting is unique. Each person is different and special. In your journal today, consider writing about something that is special about you."

2. Is "going by the rules" important in a community of people? Explain your answer. What can be done if a person disagrees with a rule?

Additional Activities

1. Make a list of the kinds of messages students might write by hand. (Examples: school notes, shopping lists, telephone messages, personal notes, letters) Briefly discuss each kind of message and ask for suggestions, writing tips, or ideas from class members.

2. Discuss the importance of a signature in a court of law. Remind students never to sign a contract they do not fully understand or one that contains blank spaces. Stress that students should not allow themselves to be pressured into signing anything without carefully reading the entire document or getting help from someone they trust.

Exercises

4 Vowel Sounds

After students have read the directions and the words at the left, have them fill in the first item for both the second and third columns (*bear* and *beer*). Point out that it is the vowel sound and not the spelling of the word that determines in which column each word belongs. During the review, point out the various spellings for each sound. You may want to use these words in a reinforcement activity or spelling quiz.

Lesson 14: To Be a Slave

Primary emphasis
- Silent and oral reading comprehension
- Phonics skills
- Context clues
- New vocabulary
- Consonants, blends, and digraphs

Secondary emphasis
- Determining categories
- Adding -er to words
- Words that end in -er
- Sequencing events
- Writing and study skills

Words for Study

Point out the prefix ex- in ex-slave and make sure students know it means former.

Pre-reading Activities

Background information: During the Civil War, ending slavery became a war goal with the passage of the Emancipation Proclamation on January 1, 1863. This proclamation provided for the abolition of slavery only in the Confederate states. Slavery officially ended in the United States with the passage of the Thirteenth Amendment to the Constitution on December 18, 1865.

1. Discuss slavery. Ask students what they already know about the subject.

2. Ask students how they think people become slaves. (Examples: in payment of debt, as punishment, by being captured during war, being kidnapped, or being born into slavery)

3. What do you think it would be like to be a slave? (Slaves have no social or legal rights. Slaves are considered property to be used or sold.) As you read this article, think about how difficult it would be to start a new life after being a slave.

Post-reading Activities

1. Discuss the answers to the questions in Exercise 1.

Ask or say:

2. What is another name for the War Between the States?

3. Were slaves religious people? What details in the reading make you think so?

4. What kinds of things do you think this ex-slave and others like her needed before they could love being free?

5. Why do you think the slaves did not know what to do with freedom when they got it?

6. What do you think the ex-slave wanted the people who read her story to understand?

7. What is one way that people today can learn what it was like to be a slave?

8. How can learning about the lives of slaves help us to understand what it means to be free?

Writing Activities

1. Write about something you learned from reading the words of the ex-slave.

2. Write what you think about slavery.

3. Write what you think it would be like to be a slave.

4. Write about what freedom means to you.

Additional Activities

1. Read excerpts from *Roots* by Alex Haley to the class.

2. Bring in recordings of some well-known spirituals. (Examples: "Swing Low, Sweet Chariot," "Go Down, Moses," "Deep River," "Nobody Knows the Trouble I've Seen") Discuss what the slaves' music tells us about the experience of slavery.

Exercises

3 Words That End in -er

During the preview, have students state the spelling rule illustrated in each of the three examples.

5 Putting Sentences in Order

During the preview, tell students that these sentences have been taken from the book that the reading selection came from. When placed in the correct order, the sentences tell about an incident in another ex-slave's life. Tell students to read the five sentences and then number them in the correct order before writing them on the lines.

BOOK 2

Lesson 15: A Very Strange Hobby

Primary emphasis
- Silent and oral reading comprehension
- Phonics skills
- Context clues
- New vocabulary
- Consonants, blends, and digraphs

Secondary emphasis
- Sequencing events
- Collective nouns
- Writing and study skills

Pre-reading Activities

Background information: During the time the western plains of the United States were being settled, conflicts arose between cattlemen and farmers over land rights. Many farmers needed fences to protect their fields from grazing sheep and cattle. Some cattlemen also wanted to build fences, while others continued allowing their cattle to graze on open range. Wood and stone, fencing materials used in the East, were scarce in the West. The invention of barbed wire provided a means of fencing, but the fences resulted in range wars.

1. Ask students if they have seen barbed wire where they live. If so, for what purpose was it used? What two purposes is barbed wire used for in the pictures on page 81?

2. Say: As you read the article, look for reasons people collect barbed wire and find out some interesting things they do with it.

Post-reading Activities

1. Discuss the answers to the questions in Exercise 1.

Ask or say:

2. What does a "link to this country's past" mean in the first paragraph on page 82?

3. Has a relative or friend ever given you something old and valued as a link to the past?

4. What are some other hobbies that are "links to this country's past?" (Examples: coins, stamps, antique furniture, antique cars, model trains)

5. Why is it difficult for people to get a piece of each kind of barbed wire?

6. In what part of the United States would people most likely find old barbed wire?

7. What do you suppose the people of 1867 thought about barbed wire? Was it valued then for the same reasons that collectors value it today?

8. What kind of problems do you think the farmers were trying to avoid by fencing their property?

9. Why do you think people have hobbies?

Writing Activities

1. If you have been saving something old, write about what it is and why you are saving it.

2. Write about your hobby or one you would like to have.

3. Write about any strange hobbies you have heard about.

Additional Activities

1. Read an excerpt from *Shane* or some other western literature that illustrates the conflict between the homesteaders and ranchers.

2. What does "won the West" mean in the first paragraph on page 82? What do you think "won the West" means from the viewpoint of a Native American?

Exercises

3 How Do You Say It?

During the preview, have students read the words at the left and complete one or two items on the right. Remind them to use the process of elimination and to make intelligent guesses for unfamiliar phrases.

Review: Lessons 1–15

During the preview, make sure students understand how to do Exercise 4. You may want them to complete one or two items in class.

Encourage students to select one topic from Lessons 11 through 15 to research and report on. They can work singly, in pairs, or in groups, and give oral and/or written reports.

Lesson 16: Whales

Primary emphasis
- Silent and oral reading comprehension
- Context clues
- New vocabulary
- Consonants, blends, and digraphs
- Analogies

Secondary emphasis
- Phonics skills
- Change *y* to *i*
- Distinguishing similar words
- Writing and study skills

Pre-reading Activities

Background information: Whales can be found in all oceans of the world. Although they are mammals, whales have only a few bristles on their heads or are hairless. Some whales have teeth and some do not. The largest whales, including the blue whale in the picture on page 92, do not have teeth. They take in large amounts of water containing tiny animals and plants. Then they push the water out through their whalebone (baleen), which acts like a filter, and swallow the food that is left. Whales need to breathe air, but they can stay under water as long as 50 minutes. Many species of whales are endangered. Efforts to ban whaling worldwide have only been partially successful.

1. Point out the two scuba divers in the picture and compare their sizes to the size of the whale. Find additional pictures of whales to share with the class.

2. Ask students to tell what they already know about whales. Some students may be aware that whales are endangered.

3. Say: As you read the article, compare fish and whales. Think about how they are similar and how they are different.

Post-reading Activities

1. Discuss the answers to the questions in Exercise 1.

Ask or say:

2. Are the largest whales bigger than dinosaurs? How do you know?

3. What part of a whale's body do scientists use as proof that ancestors of whales lived on land?

4. What do whales have in common with other mammals? (They breathe air, are warm-blooded, and bear live young.)

5. Does a larger whale usually have a bigger baby than a smaller whale?

6. Why do people kill whales? (Whales are hunted primarily for oil. Today there are substitutes for all whale products.)

7. One method whalers have used to catch an adult female whale is to kill her baby first. What information in the reading explains why this is an effective way to catch the mother whale?

Writing Activities

1. What new information did you learn about whales from the reading? What information did you find to be the most interesting?

2. Whales are in danger of becoming extinct. What other animals are endangered? What can be done to save them?

Additional Activities

1. Bring to class information on international efforts to ban whaling. Discuss why some nations have opposed the ban.

2. Do you think the author of this article thinks whales are valuable and worth saving? If a whale hunter wrote an article about whales, in what ways might the article be different? In what ways might the article be the same?

Exercises

2 **Changing the *y* to *i***

During the preview, have students study the example and ask, "What happens to the *y* when -*er* and -*est* are added?" During the review, state or have students state the spelling rule:

- When a word ends with a consonant plus *y,* change the *y* to *i* before adding any ending that doesn't start with *i.*

5 **Which Word Fits Best?**

Remind students that they did a similar exercise in Lesson 8. Review the steps students should follow.

Lesson 17: Black Bart

Primary emphasis
- Silent and oral reading comp...
- Phonics skills
- Context clues
- New vocabulary
- Synonyms and antonyms

S...

...and digraphs

...ills

Student
Try to figure out
the meaning as
the word is used
in context in
the lesson.

Words for Study

- Point out that *he'd* is the contr... *he would* and *he had.* In this ar... for *he would.*
- Draw attention to the hyphens ... and *middle-aged.* Tell students ... part of the correct spelling of th...

Pre-reading Activities

Background information: This art... a clever outlaw who called himself Black Bart the PO8 (poet). Here is a poem he left at the scene of a robbery:

"here I lay me down to Sleep,
to wait the coming Morrow,
perhaps Success perhaps defeat,
And everlasting Sorrow,
let come what will Ill try it on,
My condition can't be worse,
And if theres money in that Box,
Tis Munny in by purse"

Black Bart was an educated man. The spelling and punctuation mistakes were intentional.

1. Ask students to study the picture on page 98 and read the caption. If they have seen any movies with stagecoach robberies, have them describe a typical stagecoach robbery.
2. Tell students that Black Bart was an unusual outlaw. As a mask, he often wore a flour sack over his head with eye holes cut out. Ask students to look as they read the article for other ways Black Bart was different.

Post-reading Activities

1. Discuss the answers to the questions in Exercise 1.

Ask or say:

2. According to this article, why did Black Bart first break the law? What was his reason for continuing?
3. Do you think Black Bart considered robbing stages serious business? Why or why not?

... Black Bart was differ-... ber.

...ent man? What infor-... upports your answer?

...gun" mean?

...ck Bart left a verse ... a stage? Do you think ... es of being caught?

Writing Activities

1. Write a class poem about Black Bart.
2. Write a class story using the picture at the top of page 98. Decide where the story will take place, what year, who the people are, and what happened next.
3. Write several reasons why people break the law and turn to a life of crime.

Additional Activities

1. It is thought that "PO8" was Black Bart's spelling of *poet.* Ask students for their interpretation of the PO8 signature.
2. Students may be interested to know that Black Bart lived in San Francisco, California. He was finally caught by tracing a laundry mark on a handkerchief he dropped during a holdup.
3. Suggest other stories about the Old West as supplementary reading for students who show a particular interest in this article.

Exercises

4 The Ending *-ful*

Remind students to read the entire sentence before selecting the word that fits in the blank. During the review, discuss the meaning of the suffix *-ful.*

5 A Verse from Black Bart

During the homework review, help students to read this verse aloud. The meter is not regular and may be difficult for them at first.

BOOK 2

Lesson 18: One Idea about How the Earth Was Formed

Primary emphasis
- Silent and oral reading comprehension
- Phonics skills
- Context clues
- New vocabulary
- Consonants, blends, and digraphs

Secondary emphasis
- Sequencing events accurately
- The ending -*less*
- Reviewing *same* and *opposite*
- Spelling scrambled words
- Writing and study skills

Pre-reading Activities

1. To stimulate interest, show one or more pictures of the earth taken from outer space.

2. Ask students if they have thought about how the earth was formed. If they have seen any television shows about the subject, have students tell about them.

3. The title of this article is "One Idea about How the Earth Was Formed." Ask students why they think the author chose this title instead of "How the Earth Was Formed." As students read the article, ask them to compare this idea about how the earth was formed with others they have heard.

Post-reading Activities

1. Discuss the answers to the questions in Exercise 1.

Ask or say:

2. Compare this idea of how the earth was formed with others you have heard.

3. What method of determining the age of the earth was mentioned in the article?

4. How does the temperature near the center of the earth compare with that at the surface?

5. Why did the earth have to cool before rain could fall? What form was the water in when it was very hot?

6. What is meant by "the stream of life"?

7. What life forms may have come after the seaweed and starfish?

8. Ask students if they think studying about other planets and stars helps people understand the earth

Note: Rocks older than 2.3 billion years are continually being found. As of 1993, the oldest rocks discovered are 4.3 billion years old. You may want to point this out and have students look up in reference books the most recent figures.

Writing Activity

Show students pictures of the earth taken from space. Read the words of one of the astronauts who viewed the earth from the moon. Ask students to write about how these words make them feel.

Additional Activities

1. Show students pictures from an encyclopedia or book that illustrate the structure and composition of the layers of the earth.

2. Compare and contrast the account of the earth's beginnings in Genesis Chapter 1 with the account in this selection.

3. Use a globe to illustrate that 70 per cent of the earth's surface is covered by water.

4. Students may be interested in exploring more about the earth, the moon, the stars, the solar system, and the universe. Help them to find appropriate resources.

Exercises

2 Word Sounds

The consonant blends emphasized in this exercise can be difficult. Have students read the words on the left during the preview. Point out that items 1 and 3 have more than one sentence. Remind students to read an entire item before filling in the blanks.

3 The Ending -*less*

During the review, discuss the meaning of the suffix -*less* and contrast it with -*ful* (in Lesson 17).

4 Same or Opposite?

During the homework preview, make sure students understand the difference between *same* and *opposite*.

5 Spelling Check

Treat this as a game or puzzle rather than just another exercise. Remind students that it may help to cross out letters as they use them.

Lesson 19: Jails on the High Seas

Primary emphasis
- Silent and oral reading comprehension
- Phonics skills
- Context clues
- New vocabulary
- Consonants, blends, and digraphs

Secondary emphasis
- Homonyms
- Choosing the unrelated word
- Words that begin with *un-*
- Common sayings
- Writing and study skills

Pre-reading Activities

1. Tell students that the picture (silhouette) on page 109 is of a galley. Ask them to tell you anything they can about galleys from the picture. Prompt with such questions as: Does it look like a modern ship? What are some parts of the ship?

2. Read the title. Ask: Can you think of reasons why there would be jails at sea? Read the article to find a reason.

Post-reading Activities

1. Discuss the answers to the questions in Exercise 1.

Ask or say:

2. What is meant by "the coming of steam" in the first sentence?

3. What do you think "inland sea" refers to? (the Mediterranean Sea)

4. Did the author say that a convict "was like an oar" or that a convict "was an oar"? Which is the more powerful statement? Why?

5. Do you think convicts preferred to be at sea or in port? Explain. Why do you think there were jails on the high seas?

6. Galleys were propelled by oars and sails. What advantages would there be to having two methods? What conditions may have determined which method was used? Would there be times when using both sails and oars would be necessary? (Galleys were used for war as well as trade.)

7. What do you think happened to galleys after steam was used to propel ships?

8. What do you think is the main idea of this article? What do you think the author really wants the reader to understand?

9. Besides steamships, what other forms of transportation used steam? (Examples: trains, cars, tractors)

Writing Activities

1. Summarize this article in two or three sentences.

2. Why would the speed of a ship be especially important during a war?

3. Compare the life of a convict today with that of a convict on a galley.

4. What is the difference between a convict and a slave? Do you think the convicts in this reading were really slaves? Why or why not?

5. What do you think is the most powerful statement in this article? Why?

Additional Activities

1. Find France and the Mediterranean Sea on a world map or globe. Ask students what countries today border the Mediterranean Sea. Ask what continents border it.

2. Help interested students find information on the development of steamships and their impact on world trade.

Exercises

2 Words That Sound the Same

Remind students that it is the meaning of the word in context that determines the correct spelling of homonyms.

3 Which Word Does Not Fit?

All the words in most of these groups have some relationship to each other. Students will have to find the word that relates differently from the other words. You may want to have students do the first item during the preview.

4 Words That Begin with *un-*

Discuss the meaning of *un-* during the homework review.

5 Common Sayings

Discuss these sayings with students during the review. Explain any unfamiliar ones. Students may enjoy writing about what one of the sayings means or where they think it came from.

BOOK 2

Lesson 20: The Father of Our Country

Primary emphasis
- Silent and oral reading comprehension
- Phonics skills
- Context clues
- New vocabulary
- Consonants, blends, and digraphs

Secondary emphasis
- Vowel sounds
- The ending -ly
- Compound words
- Common sayings
- Writing and study skills

Pre-reading Activities

Ask or say:

1. Why do you think George Washington is known as "the Father of Our Country?" Think about this question as you read.

2. Study the picture on page 114. Is this a photograph from life or is it a painting? How do you know? What seems to be happening in the picture? Why do you think Washington is shown in a military uniform?

Post-reading Activities

1. Discuss the answers to the questions in Exercise 1.

Ask or say:

2. What is George Washington known for besides being the first president? (He commanded the Continental Army in the Revolutionary War, and he was president of the convention that wrote the Constitution.)

3. What is the difference between *vice* as in *vice-president* and *vice* as it is used in paragraph 3?

4. George Washington was against swearing, yet he allowed himself to be sworn in as first president. What is the difference?

5. Was George Washington a religious person? Why do you think so?

6. What is the difference between a king and a president? Why do you suppose George Washington became upset when someone suggested he should be king?

7. Was Washington well liked and respected by everyone? Find information in the article to support your answer.

Writing Activities

1. Write one new thing you learned about George Washington.

2. During Washington's time, few people went to school. Washington went to school only until he was 14 or 15. Write about whether or not you feel people need more education today than in Washington's time and why.

3. Do you think public executions "serve as a warning to others?" Why or why not?

Additional Activities

1. Students who enjoyed this article about Washington may enjoy biographies about other presidents such as Lincoln.

2. Read to the class excerpts from the Constitution and discuss them.

3. Since this is the last lesson in *Challenger 2*, ask students what were their favorite reading selections and why. You might guide students to supplementary reading books on similar subjects.

Exercises

4 Compound Words

During the homework review, have students give the definition for *compound word*. Point out that when compound words are formed, the spelling and pronunciation of the two base words usually does not change.

5 More Common Sayings

Discuss these sayings and encourage students to pick one to write about. They may enjoy making up a story about how a given saying came to be.

Review: Lessons 1–20

Tell students to refer to the lessons for any of the items in "Twenty Questions" that they don't remember. Students who complete this review with a score of 85 per cent or more are ready to begin Book 3.

After going over the review, discuss what students have learned and accomplished while working in *Challenger 2*. Students may want to plan and prepare a celebration as well.

Challenger 3   Introduction and Lesson Notes

The format of *Challenger 3* corresponds to that of *Challenger 1*. Each of the 20 lessons begins with a word chart in which specific phonics principles are emphasized. The readings are short fictional pieces about a group of young adults. Comprehension and skill-building exercises provide opportunities to develop vocabulary, to use words in various contexts, and to improve analytical and reasoning skills.

Students who completed the final review in Book 2 with 85 per cent or better accuracy should be ready to go on to Book 3. In addition, Book 3 is an appropriate starting place for students who test at levels 3 or 4 on the *Challenger Placement Tool* and for students who test at levels 3.0–4.5 on standardized reading inventories.

Students working in Book 3 should be able to sound out or sight-read words on the word chart. They should also be able to read the stories and answer comprehension questions by themselves. They should, however, read all or most of the stories aloud when going over the homework.

Scheduling Considerations

One-hour sessions are appropriate for students in Book 3. This time frame allows students to do some oral reading, discuss the reading selection, go over the homework exercises, work on writing and/or reinforcement activities, and preview the next lesson.

Book 3 works well with students in a classroom setting or in a one-to-one or group tutorial setting, as described in the Introduction to *Challenger 2* on pages 75–76 of this manual. It is unlikely that students in Book 3 will need extensive individual tutoring. You should, however, allow some time to work with individual students on a regular basis.

Suggestions for Teaching the Lessons

It is important for you to read the material in the first five chapters of ← this manual if you have not already done so. These chapters discuss the concepts and procedures upon which *Challenger* is based and give general suggestions for using the series. The following are specific suggestions for Book 3.

The Word Chart

chart words done 10/17

Book 3, like Book 1, uses common phonics principles to organize the introduction of new words. This helps students to recognize better the many regular patterns in English, which contributes to reading development. Have students read at least some of the chart words either during the lesson preview or the homework review. When appropriate, review the phonics principles involved. (See pages 8–11 for a listing of common phonics elements and principles.) How much emphasis you place on the phonics principles depends upon the needs of your students.

- Students who started in Books 1 and 2 but who still need practice on word attack skills should continue sounding out unfamiliar chart words according to methods they used in the earlier books.
- Students who start in Book 3 usually have a good sight vocabulary but often have difficulties arising from careless habits. It is often enough for you to pronounce an unfamiliar word and point out a specific phonics element, such as a double vowel that represents a long

vowel sound. These students can often correct a misread word themselves if you say, "Look at it again."

- Plan to incorporate troublesome words into reinforcement activities.

Words for Study

This section, which precedes the story in each lesson, lists words that appear in the story and exercises for the first time in the series. The words appear in the same form in which they initially appear in the lesson, often giving students practice in reading word endings.

The Story

Make sure students understand that the readings in Book 3 are stories rather than articles such as those in Book 2. The terms *fiction* and *nonfiction* can be introduced. The following ideas may be helpful in your planning.

- The initial reading should be done for homework following one or more pre-reading activities during the homework preview. Suggestions for these activities are given in the individual lesson notes.
- As students move through the book, review with them what they already know about the characters from stories in earlier lessons.
- As often as possible, have students read the stories aloud before discussing them during the homework review.
- The lesson notes give suggestions for inferential- and applied-level questions to stimulate discussion and allow you to assess comprehension.

The Exercises

Students should preview the exercises to be done for homework following procedures established in Books 1 and 2. Encourage students to develop the habit of reading directions carefully.

The wide variety of exercises helps students to develop recall and reasoning abilities. Keep the following points in mind when working on the exercises.

- Encourage students to refer to the reading selection when answering the comprehension questions in Exercise 1. Remind them that a long line under a question indicates that the answer should be a complete sentence.
- Remind students to answer all questions. If they aren't sure of an answer, they should use such strategies as intelligent guessing, the process of elimination, and using context clues. Remind them also that they can learn from their mistakes. A fundamental premise of this series is that mistakes can be valuable sources of learning. If students have a problem with an exercise, help them to recognize what went wrong. Point out also what they did well.
- Students should correct all exercises during the homework review. Any grading that is required should be done on corrected work. Consider an average of 80 per cent or better an excellent score.

Writing Activities

Student writing is discussed in Chapter 3 of this manual. Use those suggestions to help plan appropriate writing activities. Students in Book 3 should have weekly opportunities for extended writing, including projects that involve formal writing. For these projects, students can work together in pairs or small groups, helping each other to generate and organize ideas, reacting to each other's drafts, and helping each other to polish and edit pieces of writing.

CV. 10/24

Discuss ✓

Writing Activities
(continued)

Students should pick their own topics for writing activities. Topics related to the lessons are suggested in the lesson notes. Personal hobbies and interests and current issues can also provide appropriate topics for writing assignments.

The Lesson Segments

After the session in which Lesson 1 is completed and Lesson 2 is previewed for homework, the procedure for each session should be as consistent as possible. You may want to vary the order of the following segments to suit your particular situation.

1. **Homework Review.** Have students read aloud at least some of the story in the lesson studied for homework. Have them summarize the story, go over their answers to the comprehension questions in Exercise 1, and discuss the story. Then, go over the rest of the exercises and have students make any necessary corrections.

2. **Writing Activity.** Students may work in groups or singly on the current writing activity, depending on what it is.

3. **Reinforcement Activity.** When time permits, focus on an area of difficulty in a way that is fun for the students. See Chapter 4 of this manual for suggestions.

4. **Homework Preview.** Preview the next lesson, which students will complete for homework. Have students read some of the words in the word chart either now or during the homework review. Have them read the Words for Study and the title of the story and predict what they think it will be about. Do one or more pre-reading activities. Have students read the directions for the exercises and do one item in any exercise that might be confusing.

Individual Lesson Notes

The individual lesson notes that begin on page 102 contain specific suggestions and procedures for Book 3 lessons.

Lesson 1: Review of Long and Short Vowels

Primary emphasis
- Comprehension and literary understanding
- Long and short vowels
- Phonics, word analysis, and context clues
- New vocabulary
- Writing and study skills

Secondary emphasis
- Oral reading skills
- Spelling (adding -*ing*)
- The -*er* ending
- Compound words

Word Chart

1. Long vowel patterns reviewed:
   - the silent *e* (**VCe**): *ape, eve, vine, owe, Luke*
   - the open syllable (**V**): *ivy*
2. Short vowel patterns reviewed:
   - closed syllables (**VC, CVC, CVCC**): *ad, van, raft*
3. Point out the apostrophes in *she's* and *she'd* and make sure students recognize these contractions.

Words for Study

Tell students that these are words that appear in this lesson for the first time in the *Challenger* series. Point out the contractions *they're, we'll,* and *how's.*

Pre-reading Activities

1. Introduce the terms *fiction* and *nonfiction*, giving examples of each. Tell students that the reading selections in *Challenger 3* are short fiction pieces about a group of young adults.
2. After reading the title, ask what it means to "take advice." Tell students to think about how Steven is persuaded to take his sister's advice. Have students read the story aloud. Assign a second reading for homework.

Post-reading Activities

1. Discuss the questions in Exercise 1.

Ask or say:

2. Did Steven see a need to exercise at the beginning of the story? At the end of the story, why did he change his mind?
3. Do you think Ruth often gives Steven advice? What clues in the story support your answer?
4. Find the place in the story where Ruth manages to turn an argument into a challenge.
5. In your opinion, did Ruth give Steven good advice? Explain your answer.

6. Do you think Steven and Ruth care about each other? Explain.
7. If this story continued, what do you think would happen next?

Writing Activities

1. Write about your favorite form of exercise.
2. Explain why exercise is important.

Additional Activities

1. Do you ever feel your life is in a rut? What are some things you can do to get out of a rut?
2. Is exercise a good way to relieve tension? What are some other benefits of exercise?

Exercises

1 About the Story

During the homework preview, tell students to answer the questions in complete sentences. Explain that the answers to "What do you think?" questions should reflect students' own opinions.

2 The Ending -*ing*

During the homework preview, study the examples and ask, "Were any letters added, dropped, or changed when -*ing* was added?" Review the three rules for adding endings that start with a vowel:

- For column 1 words, add -*ing* to the base word.
- For column 2 words, drop the silent *e* before adding -*ing*.
- For column 3 words, double the final consonant before adding -*ing*.

3 How Do These People Earn a Living?

During the homework preview, review the process of elimination. Tell students they don't have to do items in order. They should do the ones they know first. Then they can go back and do any skipped ones when fewer choices remain.

Lesson 2: Review of Consonant Blends and Digraphs: Part 1

Primary emphasis
- Comprehension and literary understanding
- Consonant blends and digraphs *ch, sh, st*
- Phonics, word analysis, and context clues
- New vocabulary
- Writing and study skills

Secondary emphasis
- Oral reading skills
- Spelling (adding *-est*)
- Identifying terms
- Compound words

Word Chart

1. Have students pronounce the digraphs and blend before reading the words.
2. Special notes:
   - The *l* in *chalk* is silent.
   - *Shove* and *breast* have short vowel sounds although they have long vowel spelling patterns (**VCe** and **VV**).

Words for Study

If students ask for definitions of any of these words, encourage them to try to figure out the meanings from the story.

Pre-reading Activities

1. Briefly review the story in Lesson 1 in which Steven was introduced. What did students learn about Steven? What did Steven decide to do at the end of the story?
2. The title of this story is "Meet Jerome." A character named Jerome is introduced in this story. Ask students to list things that make a good impression on them when they meet a person for the first time.
3. Say: In this story, Steven has begun his class at the Y.M.C.A. He is practicing his exercises when his friend Jerome arrives. Read to find out what kind of exercise class Steven is taking and why.

Note: From this lesson on, the first reading can be done for homework. Oral reading practice is important, however. Have some or all of the story read aloud during the homework review whenever time allows.

Post-reading Activities

1. Ask students to summarize the story.
2. Discuss the questions in Exercise 1.

Ask or say:

3. The title of the story is "Meet Jerome." What things did you learn about Jerome from this first meeting?

4. Why was Jerome shouting his questions about yoga to Steven?
5. Did Steven consider the cost of the class?
6. What was Steven concerned about when he noticed Jerome shaking his head? What did he think Jerome was going to say?
7. Is this class helping Steven relax? What information supports your answer?
8. Do you think Steven was sorry he ended up in the yoga class, or do you think it worked out in his best interest? Explain.

Writing Activities

1. Write about your favorite way to relax.
2. Have you ever wandered into the wrong place? Write about your experience.

Additional Activities

1. Ask students to underline or highlight in color the conversation between Steven and Jerome. Discuss quotation marks, if necessary. Ask for volunteers to read the parts of Steven and Jerome and for a narrator to read the non-dialogue parts.
2. In this story, students meet Jerome. Discuss the skills involved in meeting new people. Make a list of suggestions for starting conversations and keeping them going. Ask for volunteers to role-play helping a new person feel welcome in class.
3. Ask if anyone is interested in reading about yoga and telling the class more about it. Have a book or article available if possible.

Exercises

2 **Adding *-est* to Words**

During the homework preview, have students state the spelling rule for each example.

3 **How Do These People Earn a Living?**

Review the process of elimination and remind students to make intelligent guesses when they are unsure of an answer.

Lesson 3: Review of Consonant Blends: Part 2

Primary emphasis
- Comprehension and literary understanding
- Consonant blends *bl, br, cl, cr, fl, fr*
- Phonics, word analysis, and context clues
- New vocabulary
- Writing and study skills

Secondary emphasis
- Oral reading skills
- Spelling (adding -*y*)
- Identifying terms
- Compound words

Word Chart

Have students pronounce the consonant blends before reading the chart words.

Pre-reading Activities

Ask or say:

1. Is there a type of place, such as a bank, hospital, or government office, that you dread going into? Do you know why you dread it? Is it linked to a bad or embarrassing experience you had?

2. Have you ever revisited a place after many years? Was it the way you remembered it, or had it changed?

3. Review what you learned about Jerome in the story in Lesson 2. The story in this lesson starts shortly after that one ended. Read this story to find out why Jerome goes to the library for the first time in 12 years.

Post-reading Activities

1. Ask students to summarize the story.
2. Discuss the questions in Exercise 1.

Ask or say:

3. How did Jerome form his opinion about yogurt? Do you think the television ad did what it was intended to do?

4. Do you think Mrs. Harvey handled well the problem of Jerome flirting with girls in the library? Why or why not? What do you think she might have done differently?

5. Why did Jerome want to talk Steven out of going to the yoga class?

6. Did Jerome feel more comfortable after he had been in the library awhile? What details in the story support your answer?

7. A *phobia* is an extreme fear of something. Do you think Jerome has a phobia about libraries? Explain your answer.

Writing Activities

1. Write about a time when you or someone you know had a bad experience in a public place.

2. Write about a phobia you or someone you know has or had. Is it possible to overcome a phobia? Do you know someone who has done so?

3. If you haven't already done so, introduce journal writing and encourage students to write in their journals every day. Journal writing is described in Chapter 3 of this manual.

Additional Activities

1. Say: Jerome "braced himself" before going into the library. What does "braced himself" mean? What are some things people do when they expect something bad to happen to them?

2. Find out what services libraries offer in your area. Library-card application forms could be filled out in class. The class could meet at a local library for a tour.

3. Have students look through magazines for advertisements and read them. After reading each ad, ask students how the advertiser probably wants readers to react. Ask if the ad has caused that reaction in them.

Exercises

2 **Adding -*y* to Words**

Review the spelling rule for each example during the homework preview. Note that *wool* is an exception to the pattern. Generally, the final consonant is not doubled for words with double vowels.

3 **Who Uses What?**

During the homework preview, tell students to read through each sentence before filling in the blank. Read the first sentence as follows: "A Boy Scout uses a *blank* to see in the dark on a camping trip." Tell students to reread the sentences after the words are filled in to be sure they make sense.

Lesson 4: Review of Consonant Blends: Part 3

Primary emphasis
- Comprehension and literary understanding
- Consonant blends *gl, gr, pl, pr, sl, str*
- Phonics, word analysis, and context clues
- New vocabulary
- Writing and study skills

Secondary emphasis
- Oral reading skills
- Spelling (changing *y* to *i*)
- Identifying terms
- Compound words

Word Chart

Have students pronounce the blends before reading the words. The three-letter blend *str* is difficult for some people to pronounce.

Pre-reading Activities

Ask or say:

1. How do you react if you are interrupted by a phone call when you are busy or concentrating? Do you find it hard to be polite?

2. Review how the story in Lesson 3 ended and what you have learned about Jerome.

3. This story takes place shortly after the story in Lesson 3 ended. What do you think Jerome is doing at the beginning of this story?

Post-reading Activities

1. Discuss the questions in Exercise 1.

2. Ask volunteers to read this story aloud as a dialogue between Jerome and Ginger. Suggest that they underline or highlight the lines they will be reading. Point out that a new paragraph begins whenever a different person speaks. Encourage them to express the emotions felt by the two characters.

Ask or say:

3. Why do you think Jerome let the phone ring eight times before he answered it?

4. Describe Jerome's mood when the phone rang. What was Ginger's mood when she called? Compare their moods at the beginning and at the end of the story.

5. How well do you think Ginger and Jerome know each other? What information from the story supports your answer?

6. In your opinion, who is more responsible for the argument, Ginger or Jerome? Why?

7. In your opinion, at what point in the story did trouble begin between Ginger and Jerome?

8. One of the benefits of yoga is that it helps people relax. How relaxed do you think Jerome

was? Compare his reaction to being interrupted with Steven's reaction in Lesson 2.

9. What do you think will happen next?

Writing Activities

1. Think about what might have happened next if Ginger hadn't hung up. Write three or four more lines of dialogue.

2. Remind students to continue to write in their journals.

Additional Activities

1. Discuss why good phone skills are important.

2. Discuss ideas for dealing with difficult people or people in a bad mood.

3. Practice phone skills. Ask students what kinds of phone calls they make. Then write a variety of telephone calling situations on slips of paper. Ask pairs of students to draw a slip, and then to plan and role-play the various telephone conversations.

4. Suggested topics for a discussion on phone etiquette: phone calls at meal times, taking messages, answering machines, wrong numbers, and children and phones.

Exercises

2 **Changing the *y* to *i***

During the homework preview, have students state the spelling rule for the *y* to *i* conversion. Point out that the *y* is changed to *i* before adding endings that begin with consonants, as well as endings that begin with vowels.

3 **More Work with the Ending -*y***

During the preview, tell students to write out the words in the left column before using them in the sentences.

5 **Compound Words**

As a reinforcement activity, you might dictate 20 words that are parts of 10 compound words and then have students match them.

Lesson 5: Review of Consonant Blends: Part 4

Primary emphasis
- Comprehension and literary understanding
- Consonant blends *dr, tr, thr, sc, sk, sw*
- Phonics, word analysis, and context clues
- New vocabulary
- Writing and study skills

Secondary emphasis
- Oral reading skills
- The ending *-ly*
- Synonyms
- Compound words

Word Chart

1. The blend *thr* is difficult for some people to pronounce.
2. In these words, *sc* and *sk* sound alike.

Words for Study

Make sure students know that *etc.* stands for *et cetera,* a Latin term meaning *and so forth.* If necessary, review the term *abbreviation.*

Pre-reading Activities

1. Review what was learned about Ginger from the story in Lesson 4.

Say:

2. In this story, we find out more about Ginger, including what she does for a living and how she met Jerome.
3. As you read, find out who influenced Ginger as a small girl and what information she privately keeps from her mother and from Jerome.

Post-reading Activities

1. Discuss the questions in Exercise 1.

Ask or say:

2. The title of this story is "Who Is Ginger?" What things did you learn about Ginger from reading the story?
3. Had Ginger made up her mind about how she felt about Jerome?
4. What does the sentence "As for Jerome—well, who knew what went on in his mind?" tell you about Jerome?
5. What does the saying "A penny saved is a penny earned" mean?
6. Do you think Ginger's grandmother would approve of how Ginger manages her money? Why or why not?
7. What information in the story indicates that Ginger is a talented and creative person?
8. Why do you think Ginger was not truthful with her mother?
9. If you were Ginger, would you spend some of your money to furnish your apartment? Why or why not?

Writing Activities

1. What lesson did Ginger's grandmother teach her? Write about how an older relative or friend influenced your life.
2. If you had money to invest, write about how you would invest it.

Additional Activities

1. Discuss in pairs or small groups the role of grandparents in raising children. Consider special circumstances such as divorce or families separated by distance. How may either of these situations change the grandparent's role? In what ways can the role of a grandparent be different from that of a parent?
2. Help students to understand financial transactions such as reading bills, writing checks, opening and using a checking account, applying for a safe deposit box, completing credit/loan applications, and other banking services.

Exercises

2 The Ending *-ly*

During the preview, point out that no letters are added, dropped, or changed when *-ly* is added to these words. Note that *shyly* is an exception to the *y* to *i* conversion rule introduced in Lesson 4. Remind students to write the words in the left column before using them in the sentences.

3 Words That Mean the Same

Remind students to use the process of elimination in this matching exercise.

BOOK 3

Lesson 6: Review of Consonant Blends and Digraphs: Part 5

Primary emphasis
- Comprehension and literary understanding
- Consonant blends and digraphs *sm, sn, sp, scr, th, wh*
- Phonics, word analysis, and context clues
- New vocabulary

Secondary emphasis
- Oral reading skills
- The ending *-ly*
- Antonyms
- Compound words

Word Chart

1. The *th* is unvoiced, or soft, in these *th* words.
2. Some people pronounce the *wh* sound as /hw/; others pronounce it /w/. Either pronunciation is acceptable.

Pre-reading Activities

1. After reading the title, discuss the word *fate*. Ask what it means and what "a strange twist of fate" means.
2. Review what students know about Jerome and Ginger, including what they know about Jerome's job.
3. Tell students to read the story to find out how Jerome got himself into trouble at work.

Post-reading Activities

1. Discuss the questions in Exercise 1.

Ask or say:

2. Describe how Jerome got into trouble at work. What is the "twist of fate" in this story?
3. Did Jerome care for Ginger? What information from the story supports your answer?
4. Compare how Jerome and Ginger think apartments should be furnished and kept.
5. Is entertaining friends more important to Jerome or to Ginger? Explain.
6. If Jerome gave Ginger a can of paint, do you think he would be giving her something she really wants? Why or why not?
7. What kind of a friend is Tony?
8. Why was Jerome concerned about telling his boss what happened? Do you think Jerome planned on telling his boss the whole truth?
9. Do you think Jerome should pay for the spilled paint? Why or why not?

Writing Activities

1. In Lesson 4, Ginger thinks of Jerome as "a jerk." After reading this story, do you agree or disagree? Write about why you think Jerome is or isn't a jerk.
2. Did you ever have to clean up a mess like Jerome's paint spill? Write about a situation you remember.
3. Write about a "twist of fate" in your life or someone else's life.

Additional Activities

1. Say: The first sentence in the story states that Jerome was not a thief, but he did enjoy having sneaky ideas now and then. What is the difference?
2. Ask: If you were in Jerome's situation, what would you tell the boss?
3. Tony spent seven hours helping his friend Jerome clean up. Ask students to think about a time they helped a friend with a problem or a friend helped them. Invite volunteers to share their stories with the class.
4. Discuss the problem of employees who steal. Ask such questions as: How serious is this problem? Is it common? What can be done about it?
5. List some of the words for colors such as emerald, vermilion, burgundy, ruby, and amber. Ask students to match the colors to the common names green, red, yellow, etc.

Exercises

2 More Work with the Ending *-ly*

Remind students to write all the words with *-ly* added first and to use the process of elimination when putting the words in the sentences.

3 Word Opposites

During the homework preview, make sure students understand the concept of opposite meanings.

BOOK 3

Lesson 7: Review of Silent Letters

Primary emphasis
- Comprehension and literary understanding
- Silent letters *kn, wr, gn, tch, dge, gh, ght*
- Phonics, word analysis, and context clues
- New vocabulary
- Writing and study skills

Secondary emphasis
- Oral reading skills
- The endings *-ful* and *-less*
- Synonyms and antonyms
- Compound words

Word Chart

Have students identify the silent letters before reading the words. Students may want to cross out the silent letters in troublesome words.

Words for Study

Ask students what two words are contracted to form *you've.*

Pre-reading Activities

1. Review what was learned about Steven in Lessons 1 and 2.

Ask or say:

2. Think about the things that cause stress in your life. What can you do to help relieve or avoid stressful situations?

3. In this story, Steven learns that there is a lot more to yoga than he thought. Read to find out what is important besides the exercising.

Post-reading Activities

1. Discuss the questions in Exercise 1.

2. Ask for volunteers to read the parts of Holly and Steven, beginning with paragraph 4.

Ask or say:

3. Did Steven seem to enjoy the yoga classes? What information in the story supports your answer?

4. How successful was Steven at learning the yoga exercises? What information in the story supports your answer?

5. After class, Steven's cold seemed to come back. Why did Steven notice his cold more before and after class than during it?

6. What things did you learn about Holly from this story?

7. What is important in yoga besides excercising?

8. Why does Holly suggest Steven should not eat chocolate cake?

9. Do you agree with what Holly's book says about sugar? Why or why not?

Writing Activities

1. Write two things you learned about yoga from reading this story.

2. Have you ever changed your diet to improve your health? Explain.

3. Write about a time when you got involved with something and found out there was more to it than you thought.

Additional Activities

1. Have students work in pairs or small groups to read a magazine or newspaper article on a health topic. Have them summarize what they read for the entire group.

2. Working in pairs or small groups, students can write down and report to the class on one or both of the following questions:
   - What are some things people can do to try to prevent illness?
   - What are some things people can do to help themselves get better when they are sick?

Exercises

2 **The Endings *-ful* and *-less***

During the homework preview, point out that no letters are added, changed, or dropped when *-ful* and *-less* are added to these words. Tell students to form the words indicated in Part A and then match those words to the definitions in Part B. During the homework review, ask students to explain what *-ful* and *-less* mean.

3 **Same or Opposite?**

Occasionally students have trouble grasping the difference between *same* and *opposite* when they are combined in an exercise. For those students, use one or two pairs in sentences. For instance:

- He put the newspaper on the *floor.*
  He put the newspaper on the *ceiling.*

- You had a good *idea.*
  You had a good *thought.*

Lesson 8: Review of Vowel Combinations: Part 1

Primary emphasis
- Comprehension and literary understanding
- Vowel combinations *ai, ee, ēa, ĕa, ui*
- Phonics, word analysis, and context clues
- New vocabulary
- Writing and study skills

Secondary emphasis
- Oral reading skills
- Long and short vowel sounds
- The endings *-ful* and *-less*
- Synonyms and antonyms
- Compound words

Word Chart

Four of these combinations spell long vowel sounds. Note that *ea* also spells a short vowel sound. Point out the long and short vowel markings in the chart. If students have trouble remembering the pronunciation of a troublesome word, suggest that they mark the vowel with the appropriate mark until they have learned the word.

Words for Study

Point out that *who's* is the contraction for both *who is* and *who has*. It is not the possessive form of *who*. Contrast *whose* and *who's*.

Pre-reading Activities

Ask or say:

1. In most families, parents and children sometimes disagree. What are things that cause conflicts between parents and children?

2. In the following story, Ginger helps her friend Gail begin to resolve her family problems. As you read, decide if Ginger is a good listener. Think about the kinds of questions Ginger asked Gail.

Post-reading Activities

1. Discuss the questions in Exercise 1.

2. Ask for volunteers to read the lines for Ginger and Gail as a dialogue.

Ask or say:

3. Describe how Gail looked when Ginger opened the door.

4. Did Gail assume Ginger would let her stay? What information supports your answer?

5. Find a place in the story that shows Gail's father cares for her.

6. Ginger asked Gail questions to find out what had happened. Which questions helped Gail to see things in a different light?

7. Was Ginger a good listener? Explain.

8. What did Gail want from her parents? What did Gail's parents want from her? Did Gail understand? Did Ginger understand?

9. Compare how Gail feels about her father at the beginning and at the end of the story.

Writing Activities

1. Write one sentence about Ginger and one sentence about Gail.

2. Suggest a different title for this story and explain why you think it would be a good one.

3. Gail shared her difficulties with her friend, Ginger. In your opinion, is it a good idea for people to talk to friends and share their problems? Explain.

Additional Activities

1. Discuss what students think Ginger would advise Gail to do if the story continued.

2. Ask pairs or groups of students to discuss the following questions: When someone has a problem and asks for help, is it better to give advice or listen and ask questions? Why? Ask each pair or group to report to the class.

3. Say: Think about times you had arguments. Did you try to see the other viewpoint? Do you think it is a good idea to do this? Why?

Exercises

2 More Work with the Endings *-ful* and *-less*

Remind students to form the words indicated in Part A and then to match those words with the descriptions in Part B.

4 Compound Words

During the preview, tell students to read the description on the right first and then to form a compound word that matches the description by using a word from List A and adding a word from List B. You may want students to complete item 2 in class to make sure they understand how to do this exercise.

Lesson 9: Review of Vowel Combinations: Part 2

Primary emphasis
- Comprehension and literary understanding
- Vowel combinations *oa, oo, ou, oi, oy*
- Phonics, word analysis, and context clues
- New vocabulary
- Writing and study skills

Secondary emphasis
- Oral reading skills
- The ending *-en*
- Choosing the unrelated word

Word Chart

1. Point out the two pronunciations for *oo*.
2. Note that *oy* is usually at the end of a word or syllable, while *oi* is usually in the middle. *Joyce* is an exception.

Words for Study

Point out that *how's* is the contraction for both *how is* and *how has*. Ask students what letters the apostrophe stands for in *you'll*.

Pre-reading Activities

1. Review with students what they have learned about Jerome and Ginger and about Steven and Holly.

Say:

2. As you read the following story, try to re-member times when you wanted to make up with someone after an argument.
3. As you read, think about Jerome and why he is having trouble getting along with his friends.

Post-reading Activities

1. Discuss the questions in Exercise 1.
2. Ask volunteers to read the story as a dialogue between Jerome and Steven beginning with paragraph 3.

Ask or say:

3. What was Jerome going to do at the begin-ning of the story to help himself feel better? Do you think it would have helped? Why or why not?
4. When the phone rang, Jerome thought it was Ginger. How do you think Jerome would have spoken to Ginger if it had been her? Explain.
5. Was Steven familiar with Jerome's problem? What in the story supports your answer?
6. Jerome apologized to Steven when he offended him. Do you think he should also apologize to Ginger? Why or why not?

7. Why do you think Jerome is having trouble getting along with his friends?
8. How is pride involved in this story? Have you heard the expression "swallow your pride"? What do you think it means? What do you think Jerome would do if he could swallow his pride?

Writing Activities

1. Complete the following sentences:
   - I think Jerome should . . .
   - I think Jerome should not . . .
2. Suggest another title for this story and explain why you think it would be a good one.
3. Jerome offended Ginger and Steven. Think about what Jerome is doing or saying that is causing the trouble. What advice would you give Jerome?

Additional Activities

1. Discuss the sentence "Of course, he could have called her up, but that would have been against his rules on how to treat women." What do you think some of Jerome's rules were?
2. Jerome had considered two ideas at the beginning of the story to cheer himself up: having a drink and reading. Ask students what they do to cheer themselves up. Share ideas as a group.
3. Jerome told Steven that he thought Ginger had "no sense of loyalty." Ask: What does this mean? Do you agree or disagree with Jerome? Why?

Exercises

3 Which Word Does Not Fit?

Have students do the first item during the preview so that they understand what to do. Ask students to explain the difference between *buddy* (a friend) and the other words (relatives).

Lesson 10: The Sound for *au*

Primary emphasis
- Comprehension and literary understanding
- The sound for *au*
- Phonics, word analysis, and context clues
- New vocabulary
- Writing and study skills

Secondary emphasis
- Oral reading skills
- The ending *-en*
- Choosing the unrelated word
- Spelling scrambled words

Word Chart

The *au* sound may be difficult for students, and many of these chart words are difficult as well. If students have trouble with this chart, plan reinforcement activities for these words.

Words for Study

Contrast the sounds for *ch* in *search* and *machine.* Tell interested students that the /sh/ sound for *ch* occurs mostly in words of French origin.

Pre-reading Activities

1. Review what students already know about Jerome and Holly.
2. Ask students if they ever go to a laundromat. Ask how they feel about going to the laundromat. Tell them this is a story that takes place in a laundromat. Ask students to compare how they feel about laundromats with how Jerome feels.
3. Say: As you read the following story, decide if you agree more with Holly or with Jerome.

Post-reading Activities

1. Ask students to summarize the story.
2. Discuss the questions in Exercise 1.

Ask or say:

3. What was Jerome's attitude toward doing the laundry?
4. Do you think Holly was being honest with Jerome? Why or why not?
5. Do you think Holly was interested in helping Jerome solve his problem? Explain.
6. What kind of person is Holly? What words would you use to describe her?
7. What did Jerome mean when he told Holly, "You women. You stick together like glue"?
8. Do you agree more with Holly or Jerome? Explain your answer.

9. What do you think will happen next? Do you think Jerome will call Ginger? Why or why not?

Writing Activities

1. Write one sentence about Jerome and one sentence about Holly.
2. Write about what you like to do on rainy days.
3. What household task do you dislike the most? Explain.

Additional Activities

1. Holly thought for a moment before she answered Jerome. Why is thinking for a minute before speaking often a good idea?
2. Laundromats frustrated Jerome. What kinds of things frustrate you? Why? What are some ways to deal with frustration?
3. In the laundromat, Holly writes two "Out of Order" signs. Ask students how they use their reading and writing skills in everyday places outside the classroom.

Exercises

3 Which Word Does Not Fit?

If students had trouble with this type of exercise in Lesson 9, have them do the first item during the homework preview and explain the difference between *newspaper* (a thing) and the other words (people).

4 Spelling Check

During the preview, have students do the first item so that they understand what to do. Suggest that they cross out letters as they use them to be sure the words are spelled correctly. Treat this exercise like a puzzle or game.

Lesson 11: Review of the *r*-Controlled Vowel

Primary emphasis
- Comprehension and literary understanding
- The *r*-controlled vowels *ar, er, ir, or, ur*
- Phonics, word analysis, and context clues
- New vocabulary
- Writing and study skills

Secondary emphasis
- Oral reading skills
- The prefix *re-*
- Synonyms
- Classifying words

Word Chart

Remind students that when *r* follows a vowel, the sound of the vowel is somewhat affected. Point out that *er, ir,* and *ur* sound alike.

Pre-reading Activities

1. After reading the title, ask students if they have ever been camping. Ask if they enjoy outdoor activities. Have them share their experiences.

2. Say: In this story Ginger goes camping alone. Read to find out what causes Ginger's camping trip to end suddenly.

Post-reading Activities

1. Discuss the questions in Exercise 1.

Ask or say:

2. Why did Ginger have her phone taken out? Do you think Ginger was going to extremes since she had plenty of money? Why or why not?

3. Do you think Ginger was as concerned as Jerome about getting together again? Why or why not?

4. Is Ginger an experienced camper? What details in the story support your answer?

5. What made this story interesting or uninteresting for you?

6. If you thought you heard growling while eating lunch alone in the woods, would you react the same way that Ginger did? If not, what would you do differently?

7. Do you think the fishermen helped Ginger? What might they have done to help?

8. Do you think Ginger did the things she said she would do when she got back to the city? Why or why not?

Writing Activities

1. Write another title for this story and explain why you think it would be a good one.

2. Write about a camping trip or some other outdoor activity that you or someone you know took part in.

3. Ask class members to imagine their favorite outdoor place. Next, ask each student to write a story or poem about that place. Help students get started by asking them questions. Share the poems and stories in class, or compile them in a book.

Additional Activities

1. Beginning after paragraph 3, where Ginger is eating her lunch, ask each student to contribute one or two sentences and create a different ending to the story.

2. Use catalogs from camping supply stores to practice filling out forms.

3. Read a short story or article about an outdoor adventure to the class. Ask students to summarize and react to what you read.

4. Help interested students find appropriate supplementary reading material on such subjects as outdoor adventure, nature, or high adventure nonfiction.

Exercises

2 Words That Begin with *re-*

During the homework review, have students read the words in the left column. Most of these are new words. Encourage students to try to complete the exercise using the process of elimination. Discuss any words the students have questions about during the homework review.

4 and 5 What Is Where?

During the preview, explain that students should list each word at the left under the heading that tells where the item would most likely be found. Point out that there will be three words under each heading, so students can use the process of elimination if they are unsure about some of the words.

BOOK 3

Lesson 12: Review of Vowels Followed by the Letter l

Primary emphasis
- Comprehension and literary understanding
- Vowels followed by *l*: *al, el, il, ol, ul*
- Phonics, word analysis, and context clues
- New vocabulary
- Writing and study skills

Secondary emphasis
- Oral reading skills
- The prefix *re-*
- Antonyms
- Compound words

Word Chart

1. Point out that the sound of *a* in *palm* is different from the *a* sound in the other words because the *l* in *palm* is usually silent.

2. Point out the double *l* spelling pattern for one-syllable short vowel words: *gall, mall, dill, sill, pill,* and *gull*.

Words for Study

Ask students to predict a song that might be included in the story based on the words *spangled* and *banner*.

Pre-reading Activities

1. Ask students if they enjoy football. Ask those who do to describe the sport briefly. See if they prefer to watch high school, college, or pro football, if they have favorite teams, etc.

2. Say: In this story, Steven takes Holly to her first football game. As you read, think about a time when you had to ask a lot of questions to learn about something you did not understand.

Post-reading Activities

1. Ask students to summarize the story.
2. Discuss the questions in Exercise 1.
3. Ask for volunteers to read the story aloud as a dialogue between Holly and Steven, beginning with Holly's line: "Steven, don't be sulky. The game is starting."

Ask or say:

4. What clue did Steven have that it was going to be a strange afternoon?
5. What things upset Steven before the game started? Did those same things bother Holly? How do you know?
6. Do you think Steven will ask Holly to another football game? Why or why not?
7. Why did Steven compare yoga to football?
8. Do you know what the phrase "a flag on the play" means? If so, please explain.

9. Imagine the rest of Steven's afternoon. What do you think will happen next? Continue the story.

Writing Activities

1. Write about a sport you enjoy and tell why you like it.
2. Write a thank you note from Steven to his boss, thanking him for the free passes to the football game.
3. If you could play any sport and be good at it, which sport would you choose? Why?

Additional Activities

1. Help students who are interested in sports to find stories at an appropriate reading level. New Readers Press publishes nonfiction books about football, baseball, basketball, and boxing titled *3rd and Goal, Bases Loaded, Fast Break,* and *Lights Out* written at low reading levels.

2. Read to the class a sports story, article, or an excerpt from a biography or autobiography of a famous sports personality.

3. Bring the sports section of a newspaper to class. Help students find examples of statistics, human interest stories, editorials, and straight news stories in the sports section.

Exercises

2 **More Work with Words That Begin with *re-***

During the homework preview, have students read the words on the left. Many of these words are new. Encourage students to use the process of elimination and make intelligent guesses when filling in the blanks in the sentences.

4 **Compound Words**

Remind students that they did a similar exercise in Lesson 8.

BOOK 3

Lesson 13: Review of the Hard and Soft *c* and *g*

Primary emphasis
- Comprehension and literary understanding
- The hard and soft *c* and *g*
- Phonics, word analysis, and context clues
- New vocabulary
- Writing and study skills

Secondary emphasis
- Oral reading skills
- The prefix *in-*
- Analogies
- Dividing words into syllables

Word Chart

1. Sounds for *c* reviewed:
   - *c* followed by *a, o,* or *u* sounds like /k/
   - *c* followed by *e, i,* or *y* sounds like /s/

2. Sounds for *g* reviewed:
   - *g* followed by *a, o,* or *u* and sometimes *e* or *i* sounds like /g/
   - *g* at the end of a word sounds like /g/
   - *g* followed by *e* or *i* often sounds like /j/

Words for Study

Point out the /sk/ sound in *scheme.* Tell interested students that this spelling for /sk/ is usually found in words from Greek.

Pre-reading Activities

1. After reading the story title and Words for Study, discuss the meaning of the word *scheme.* Ask students what they think Jerome's scheme might be in this story.

2. Say: Jerome really wants to see Ginger, but he is too proud to call her. In this story, he figures out a scheme to get back together again. Read the story to find out if his scheme is successful.

Post-reading Activities

1. Ask students to summarize this story in two or three sentences.

2. Discuss the questions in Exercise 1.

Ask or say:

3. Why didn't Jerome invite Ginger to the party himself?

4. What do you think Ginger would say if she found out about the scheme?

5. Why do you think most people do not like to be the first guests to arrive at a party?

6. Did Jerome's guests seem to be enjoying themselves? What information from the story supports your answer?

7. Did Jerome blame Tony for his own unhappiness at the party? How do you know?

8. Compare how Jerome felt before and after the party. Did Jerome's scheme turn out the way he thought it would? Did it turn out the way you thought it would?

Writing Activities

1. Write about why you do or don't like parties.

2. Write a different ending to this story.

3. Describe the best or worst party you remember.

4. Write what you would need to do to prepare for giving a party.

Additional Activity

Celebrate the progress your students are making toward their goals by having a class party. Begin by discussing what kind of party to have and when and where to have it. Decide if there will be games or entertainment, what kind of food to have, and if anyone else will be invited. Help students to plan and organize the party.

Exercises

3 **Which Word Fits Best?**

During the homework preview, have students:
- read the first sentence saying "blank" where the blank occurs.
- explain the relationship between *bark* and *dog.*
- read the four answer choices and decide which choice goes with *bird* in the same way that *bark* goes with *dog.*
- write *chirp* on the blank and read the complete sentence.

4 **Consonants**

In this exercise, students discover that when words have a double consonant in the middle, the syllable break usually comes between the consonants, creating a closed first syllable. During the homework review, make sure students do not pronounce the double consonants twice. They should say /gŭt er/ not /gŭt ter/.

Lesson 14: The *gh* and *ght* Words

Primary emphasis
- Comprehension and literary understanding
- Words with *gh* and *ght*
- Phonics, word analysis, and context clues
- New vocabulary
- Writing and study skills

Secondary emphasis
- Oral reading skills
- Synonyms and antonyms
- Dividing words into syllables

Word Chart

1. Point out that *igh* is a common spelling for long *i* and that *eigh* is a less common spelling for long *a*.
2. Note that *gh* is pronounced /f/ in *laugh, laughter, tough, rough, enough,* and *cough.*
3. Note different pronunciations used for *ough* (*bought, tough, cough, dough*). You may want to review *though, thought,* and *through,* which are commonly confused.

Pre-reading Activities

1. Ask students to tell in their own words what happened in the story in Lesson 13.
2. After reading the title of this story, ask students to think about what might have happened to Tony and Ginger. Ask them to write down their ideas and then share them.

Post-reading Activities

1. Discuss the questions in Exercise 1.

Ask or say:

2. When Tony first moved into the neighborhood, he got along with Mrs. Darkpill. What clue was there that trouble might lie ahead? What other clues suggest that Mrs. Darkpill was difficult to get along with?
3. Did Mr. Darkpill care about his children? Find a sentence in the story that supports your answer.
4. What do you think it would be like to grow up in the Darkpill home? How do the Darkpill children behave? What clues in the story support your answer?
5. Find the place in the story where Tony recognizes he is going to have trouble with Mrs. Darkpill.
6. Tony's deed to the property proved he owned the tree. If you were Tony, what would you do to stop Mrs. Darkpill from sawing branches off your tree?

7. What do you think happened that led Tony and Ginger to end up at police headquarters?
8. How does the title create interest in reading the story?
9. What unanswered question is raised at the end of this story? What additional questions do you want answered?

Writing Activities

1. Write one sentence about Tony and one sentence about Mrs. Darkpill.
2. Write some advice for Tony about dealing with Mrs. Darkpill.
3. Write about a person you consider difficult to get along with.

Additional Activities

1. Ask: When Mrs. Darkpill started to saw branches off Tony's tree, what did he do to persuade her to stop? Did it work? Do you think talking to someone who offends you is a good first step in getting a problem solved? What suggestions do you have for a second step?
2. Discuss what Mrs. Darkpill did to Tony. Ask someone to explain the position of the police. Do police have to uphold the law even if they disagree with what the law says at times? Why or why not?
3. Mr. and Mrs. Darkpill never fought in front of their children. Discuss whether or not students think this is a good idea.

Exercises

4 **More Work with Double Consonants**

This exercise reviews the decoding strategy introduced in Lesson 13 for words with double consonants.

Lesson 15: Review of *r*-Controlled Vowel Combinations

Primary emphasis
- Comprehension and literary understanding
- Combinations *air, ear, eer, oar, oor, our*
- Phonics, word analysis, and context clues
- New vocabulary
- Writing and study skills

Secondary emphasis
- Oral reading skills
- Syllables
- Identifying terms

Word Chart

As with single vowels, when *r* follows a vowel combination the vowel sound is somewhat affected. Have students pronounce the vowel combinations before reading the words.

Pre-reading Activities

1. Before reading this story, ask students what they already know about Tony and Ginger. Ask what plans they had for the evening.

2. Tony and Ginger did not leave for the party immediately after Ginger stopped to pick up Tony. If they had left right away, the evening may have turned out very differently. Ask students to read the story to find out what the delay cost Tony and Ginger.

Post-reading Activities

1. Discuss the questions in Exercise 1.

Ask or say:

2. Why do you think Tony had not told Ginger where they were going? Do you think Ginger would have agreed to go to Jerome's party if she knew that's where Tony planned to take her?

3. Do you agree with Tony that Mrs. Darkpill was looking for a fight? Why or why not?

4. What do you think would have happened if Ginger had not gotten involved in the argument?

5. What was Tony's attitude toward Mrs. Darkpill? What was Ginger's attitude toward Mrs. Darkpill? What was Mrs. Darkpill's attitude toward them?

6. Did Mrs. Darkpill have a right to be angry about where Ginger had parked? How could she have persuaded Ginger to move her car without offending Ginger and Tony?

7. Did Tony's neighbors do the right thing in calling the police? Why or why not?

8. Is trying to get along well with neighbors a good policy? Explain.

9. What do you think will happen next? What do you think Jerome will say when he hears what happened to Tony and Ginger?

Writing Activities

1. Write one sentence each about Ginger, Tony, and Mrs. Darkpill.

2. List some of the ways Mrs. Darkpill offended other people.

3. Write about a good or bad experience you had with a neighbor.

Additional Activities

1. What were some of the mistakes made by people in the story? List them and then rank them by importance.

2. Ask students to think about experiences in their lives where people have lost their temper and were out of control. What are some ways of dealing with such people? What are some things not to do or say? What helps? Discuss in pairs and have each pair report to the group.

Exercises

2 The *ea* and *ear* Words

Have students read the words in the left column during the homework preview. Make sure they are reading them correctly and not confusing words such as *head, heart,* and *heard*.

3 Syllables

During the preview, explain that a syllable is a unit of sound and that each syllable has one vowel sound. Go over the first example and point out that *board* is spelled with two vowels, but there is only one vowel sound. Some students have difficulty hearing syllables in words. Have students read the words orally, pausing briefly between syllables.

Lesson 16: Common Word Beginnings: Part 1

Primary emphasis
- Comprehension and literary understanding
- Common prefixes *de-, ex-, mis-, com-, con-*
- Phonics, word analysis, and context clues
- New vocabulary
- Writing and study skills

Secondary emphasis
- Oral reading skills
- Defining words containing *ow*
- Combining syllables to form words
- Reviewing factual information

Word Chart

Interested students might like to look up the meanings of these prefixes in a dictionary. The concept that a word part can have a meaning of its own may be new to students.

Pre-reading Activities

1. Ask students if they like to try new foods. Do they like to try out new recipes? Ask them to share experiences with trying new foods.

2. Tell students that in this story, Steven and Holly discuss Jerome. Read the story to find out what each one thinks about Jerome.

Post-reading Activities

1. Discuss the questions in Exercise 1.

2. This story is a dialogue between two people. Have volunteers read the two parts aloud.

Ask or say:

3. This story has two different parts in which two different subjects are discussed. What are they? Find the place where the subject changes.

4. Does Holly agree with Steven's opinion of the prune whip? How do you know?

5. What kind of cookbook is Holly writing? (See Lesson 9.)

6. In the story, Holly asks if Jerome still thinks the world's giving him a raw deal. What does she mean by a "raw deal"?

7. Does Steven think Ginger had a good excuse for not coming to the party? Does Steven think Jerome should call Ginger? Why do you think so?

8. What do you think Steven meant when he said that Jerome was a very complex person? Do you agree?

9. Discuss the relationship between Steven and Holly. What words would you use to describe their relationship?

Writing Activities

1. Write about a good or bad experience you had when trying a new food. Your story could begin, "The first time I tried . . ."

2. Write a story about trying to cook or otherwise make something that did not turn out right.

3. Think of something you know how to cook or make. List the ingredients or materials needed and write the steps in the process.

Additional Activities

1. Make a list of common cooking abbreviations and terms. Some cookbooks provide such a list. Help students with any terms or abbreviations they need to have explained. Read several recipes together and clarify the terms used.

2. Ask students to bring to class copies of their favorite recipes. The recipes could be exchanged or compiled into a class cookbook. Volunteers might gather the ingredients and prepare one of the recipes.

Exercises

3 More Work with Syllables

After students have read the directions and studied the example during the preview, have them do one item in class. Tell students to read the sentences and pick one they know the answer to. Explain that the process of elimination is important in this exercise. Remind them to cross out the syllables in the box as they use them.

4 Brain Benders

During the preview, emphasize that students should make a good guess even if they don't know the answer. Tell students that newspapers and magazines often have self-quizzes similar to this.

BOOK 3

Lesson 17: Common Word Beginnings: Part 2

Primary emphasis
- Comprehension and literary understanding
- Common prefixes *de-, ex-, com-, con-, un-*
- Phonics, word analysis, and context clues
- New vocabulary
- Writing and study skills

Secondary emphasis
- Oral reading skills
- Compound words with *ow*
- Choosing the unrelated word
- Syllables

Word Chart

Students probably know the meaning of *un-*. If they don't, have them figure it out by reading the base words without *un-*.

Pre-reading Activities

Ask or say:

1. What do you like to do in your free time or on your days off?
2. Do you know someone who got a day off by calling in sick when he or she wasn't sick?
3. As you read this story find out why Tony gets more than he bargained for at a clothing sale.

Post-reading Activities

1. Discuss the questions in Exercise 1.

Ask or say:

2. Had Tony planned to call in sick the morning of the story? How do you know?
3. Based on his manner on the telephone, what kind of boss do you think Mr. Dennis was?
4. Where did Tony expect Mr. Dennis to be? Where did Mr. Dennis expect Tony to be?
5. What did Mr. Dennis mean when he told Tony he had "all the time in the world"?
6. Do you think Tony regretted telling his boss he was sick so that he could have the day off? How did he feel when he hung up the phone? When do you think he regretted it?
7. In your opinion, did Tony deserve to get fired? Why or why not?
8. Did this story turn out the way you thought it would? Did it turn out the way Tony thought it would? Explain.
9. If you were Tony, what would you do next?

Writing Activities

1. Write one sentence about Tony and one about Mr. Dennis.

2. Imagine the perfect day off. If you could do anything you wanted, what would it be? Write about it.

Additional Activities

1. Discuss what Tony might have done differently. What might Mr. Dennis have done differently?
2. Tony found the clothing sale by reading an advertisement in the newspaper. Bring some newspaper ads to class and discuss them. What store is advertising? Where is it located? When is the store open? What is being advertised?
3. Discuss good phone manners. Tony's boss answered the phone in an extremely unfriendly manner. Do you think this was his usual way to answer the phone? Why or why not? Name businesses that depend on having a good relationship with telephone customers. List some suggestions for good telephone manners.
4. Copy key action sentences from this story, and cut them apart. Rearrange the sequence. Have students put the sentences in the correct sequence.

Exercises

3 Which Word Does Not Fit?

During the homework review, discuss the relationships among the words in any group that caused students trouble.

4 More Work with Syllables

During the preview, point out that the number of blanks for each word indicates the number of syllables in the word. If necessary, have students do item 4 in class.

Lesson 18: Common Word Beginnings: Part 3

Primary emphasis
- Comprehension and literary understanding
- Common prefixes *ex-, dis-, un-, im-, in-*
- Phonics, word analysis, and context clues
- New vocabulary
- Writing and study skills

Secondary emphasis
- Oral reading skills
- Classifying words
- Spelling scrambled words

Word Chart

Interested students might look in a dictionary to see how many words start with these prefixes.

Words for Study

Point out that *you'd* is the contraction for both *you had* and *you would*.

Pre-reading Activities

1. Review what students have learned about why Ginger didn't come to Jerome's party. Then tell students that when this story takes place, Jerome and Ginger still haven't spoken.

Ask or say:

2. Who do you think has a talk with Jerome? What do you think the talk will be about?

3. As you read the story, decide if you think Jerome gets some good advice.

Post-reading Activities

1. Discuss the questions in Exercise 1.
2. Ask for volunteers to read the story as a dialogue. You might also make an audio tape of the reading after students have had an opportunity to rehearse their lines.

Ask or say:

3. What was Steven trying to persuade Jerome to do?
4. Did Ginger ever find out where Tony intended to take her the evening they spent at the police station?
5. Why do you think Steven felt like he was talking to a child?
6. Find the place in the story where Steven feels like giving up on Jerome. Why do you think he continues to try to help Jerome?
7. Did Steven's talk with Jerome do any good? Why do you think Jerome finally decided to call Ginger?
8. What do you think will happen when Jerome calls Ginger?

Writing Activities

1. What might Jerome say to Ginger when he calls her? How might she respond? Write the first few lines of their conversation.

2. Do you agree with Steven that you have to do something to get what you want out of life? Write about something you want in life and what it will take to get it.

Additional Activities

1. In this story, Steven gives Jerome his opinion. Sometimes it is hard to know when to get involved and when not to get involved in someone else's business. Discuss what is helpful to people when they have a problem and what is not helpful.

2. Steven told Jerome that he should forget about what other people should do. He told Jerome to think about what he should be doing for himself. Do you consider this good advice? How does this relate to what Holly said about Jerome in Lesson 16?

3. Does someone you know have trouble admitting mistakes? Why do you think it is so difficult? What do you think about people who do admit their mistakes? Do you admire them? Why or why not?

Exercises

2 Short Stories

Review the words in the left column during the homework preview. Point out that there are three paragraphs on separate topics, each with five missing words. Students should read a whole paragraph before filling in the blanks. Remind them to reread the paragraphs with the words filled in to be sure they make sense.

4 Spelling Check

Remind students to cross out the letters in each group as they are used.

BOOK 3

Lesson 19: Up-, Down-, Out-, Over-, and Under-

Primary emphasis
- Comprehension and literary understanding
- Words with *up-, down-, out-, over-, under-*
- Phonics, word analysis, and context clues
- New vocabulary
- Writing and study skills

Secondary emphasis
- Oral reading skills
- Reviewing calendar information
- Classifying terms
- Identifying terms

Word Chart

Be sure students recognize the individual words that make up these compound words. Remind students that when compound words are formed, the pronunciation and the spelling of the individual words stay the same.

Pre-reading Activities

1. After they have read the story title and Words for Study, ask students to predict what this story will be about.

2. Ask: Do you think Jerome and Ginger will finally make up, or do you think they'll have another fight?

Post-reading Activities

1. Discuss the questions in Exercise 1.

2. Ask a student to summarize the first three paragraphs and then ask for volunteers to read the rest of the story as a dialogue. You might audio tape the dialogue after students have had a chance to rehearse their lines.

Ask or say:

3. How did you feel after reading the first sentence in the story? Were you disappointed that Jerome had decided not to call Ginger? Jerome decided to go to see her in person. Do you think this was a good idea? Why or why not?

4. When Jerome saw Ginger at the nightclub, do you think he was sorry he waited so long to see her? Why or why not?

5. When Ginger walked over to Jerome's table, what do you think she wanted Jerome to say?

6. Why do you think Jerome lied to Ginger about why he had come to see her? What does "beating around the bush" mean? Why did Ginger accuse Jerome of beating around the bush? Why did Ginger insist that Jerome be honest with her?

7. Did Ginger forgive Jerome? Find information in the story to support your answer.

8. Do you think Ginger and Jerome will get along with each other in the future? Why or why not?

9. Did the story turn out the way you thought it would? Were there any surprises in the story? What were they?

Writing Activities

1. Write two sentences about Ginger and two sentences about Jerome.

2. Find a picture of a music-related activity in a magazine or newspaper. Ask students to write one or two statements about the picture.

3. If any students are interested in music, ask them to write about their interest.

Additional Activities

1. Ginger was a singer in a band that played in clubs around the city. Ask students to describe the kind of band they imagine Ginger sang with. What instruments would probably be in the band? What type of music would they play? Why do you think so?

2. When Jerome decided to act, he no longer felt downhearted. Think about a time in your life when you had a difficult decision to make. How did you feel before you made the decision? How did you feel afterward?

Exercises

3 The Four Seasons

Students will have to use the process of elimination to do this exercise. Tell them to fill in the items they are sure of first, and then to make intelligent guesses for the rest of the items. Students who live in a warm climate may well question which season *flowers blooming* and *beach* belong to. All students will probably wonder, "Which All-Star game?" Treat this exercise as a game to avoid confusion or frustration.

Lesson 20: More Work with Compound Words

Primary emphasis
- Comprehension and literary understanding
- Compound words
- Phonics, word analysis, and context clues
- New vocabulary
- Writing and study skills

Secondary emphasis
- Oral reading skills
- Identifying terms
- Synonyms and antonyms

Word Chart

Most of these compound words are fairly long. Remind students that each word is made up of two shorter words. If they have trouble decoding any of the compound words, they should identify the two shorter words and read them first.

Pre-reading Activities

1. Say: This is the last story in the book. Before reading it, write down a few of your own ideas about how you would like the book to end.

2. After reading the title of the story, ask students what they think this story will be about. Does knowing that it is the last story in the book influence their thinking? Do they expect a happy ending? What unanswered questions do they have about the group of friends in this book?

Post-reading Activities

1. Discuss the questions in Exercise 1.

Ask or say:

2. Compare your ideas about how you wanted the book to end with the story the author wrote. Were you surprised? Pleased? Disappointed? Satisfied?

3. How did Holly thank Steven for testing her recipes?

4. What was Jerome concerned about when he called Holly? In what ways was Jerome helpful when he called?

5. Does Jerome expect some trouble in his future? What else does he expect? Support your answer with information from the story.

6. Why did Holly make prune whip? What did Steven mean when he said, "Now I know why they call a gag a gag"?

7. Did Ginger show a strong interest in yoga? What information from the story supports your answer?

8. Recall Jerome's attitude at the beginning of the book. In what ways did he change?

9. Think about Steven's life at the beginning of the book. Is he better off now for having taken his sister's advice? Explain.

Writing Activities

1. Write a one- or two-sentence description of each of the following characters: Steven, Jerome, Ginger, Holly, and Mrs. Darkpill.

2. In the last paragraph of the story, Jerome says, "One minute you're down, and the next minute you're up. You just never know what's going to happen next!" Do you agree? Explain.

3. Have you experienced situations or feelings similar to those of the characters in this book? Write about them.

4. Write down some of the ways you are using reading in your life. Review and update your reading goals.

Additional Activities

1. Plan a class party to celebrate the progress students have made in *Challenger 3*. Help students to organize, plan, and divide up the tasks.

2. For each student, compare a writing sample done at the beginning of the book with one done near the end of the book to show the progress they have made.

Exercises

2 **More Work with Compound Words**

Some of the word choices are new compound words. Remind students to identify the two shorter words in any compound they have trouble decoding.

5 **Feelings**

After students have read the directions, have them do the first item in class so they understand what to do. Make sure they understand that their answers should be appropriate responses to the situations described and that their sentences should explain their choices.

Review: Lessons 1–20

The purpose of this review is to give students one more opportunity to work with many of the words and concepts emphasized in *Challenger 3*. Preview each exercise and, if necessary, have students complete an item during the review.

The following exercises include new material for students and may require a bit of extra time during the preview.

1 Word Study

No new words are introduced in this exercise, but the format is new. Tell students to select the answer choice that best defines the italicized word and to write the letter for their choice on the line provided.

6 Spelling Check

During the preview, make sure students understand that they are to use the first letter of each answer word to spell the name of the dessert at the bottom of the page.

After going over the review, discuss what students have learned and accomplished while working in *Challenger 3*.

Challenger 4 Introduction and Lesson Notes

The format of *Challenger 4* corresponds to that of *Challenger 2*. The 20 lessons in Book 4 reinforce vocabulary, reasoning skills, and phonics principles introduced in earlier books and continue to develop reading comprehension skills. Relatively few new words are introduced in Book 4 in order to give students an opportunity to review thoroughly what they have learned so far.

Book 4 contains brief, nonfiction selections on a wide variety of subjects. Written comprehension questions follow each reading selection. After every five lessons are reviews that provide additional opportunities to review words and reinforce concepts. Each review is followed by a word index listing the words introduced in lessons up to that point.

Book 4 is generally used by students who have completed *Challenger 3*. Book 4 is also an appropriate starting place for students who test at level 4 on the *Challenger Placement Tool,* and those who read at levels 4.0–5.0 as determined by standardized reading tests.

Scheduling Considerations

One-hour sessions are appropriate for students in Book 4. This allows time for students to do some oral reading, discuss the reading selection, go over the homework exercises, work on writing and/or reinforcement activities, and preview the next lesson.

Book 4 works well with students either working together in a classroom setting or working independently in a tutorial setting. Students working in Book 4 usually do not need intensive skill development and are often able to assist each other, requiring less supervision from you. A more detailed description of these instructional settings can be found in the Introduction to *Challenger 2* on pages 75–76 of this manual.

Suggestions for Teaching the Lessons

It is important for you to read the material in the first five chapters of this manual if you have not already done so. These chapters discuss the concepts and procedures upon which *Challenger* is based and give general suggestions for using the series. The following are specific suggestions for Book 4.

Words for Study

This section, which precedes the story in each lesson, lists words that appear in the reading and exercises for the first time in the series. The words appear in the same form in which they initially appear in the lesson, often providing practice in reading word endings.

The Reading Selections

Tell students that the readings in Book 4 are articles containing information about a variety of subjects. Review the terms *fiction* and *nonfiction*. Students whose long-range goal is to pass the high school equivalency examination are particularly motivated when they learn that brief readings in science and social studies are included in those tests. The following ideas may be helpful in your planning.

- With the exception of the first lesson, the initial readings should be done for homework, following pre-reading activities during the homework preview. Pre-reading suggestions are given in the individual lesson notes.

Suggestions for Teaching the Lessons (continued)

- Oral reading of the selections should be done as often as possible during the homework review, before discussing the selection. Inferential- and applied-level comprehension questions, suggested in the lesson notes, stimulate discussion and help students to develop their reasoning skills.

The Exercises

Preview the exercises during the class session and have students complete them for homework. Make sure students know how to do each exercise. The wide variety of exercises helps students to develop recall and reasoning abilities. Keep the following points in mind.

- Encourage students to refer to the reading selection when answering comprehension questions in Exercise 1. Remind them that a long line under a question signals that the answer should be a complete sentence.
- Remind students to answer all questions. If they aren't sure of an answer, they should use such strategies as intelligent guessing, the process of elimination, and using context clues. Remind them also that they can learn from their mistakes. If students have a problem with an exercise, help them to recognize what went wrong. Point out also what they did well.
- Students should correct all exercises during the homework review. Any grading that is required should be done on corrected work. Consider an average of 80 per cent or better an excellent score.

Writing Activities

Student writing is discussed in Chapter 3 of this manual. Use those suggestions to help plan appropriate writing activities. Book 4 students should have extended writing opportunities at least weekly. For formal writing projects, students can work together in pairs or small groups to generate ideas, plan the organization and development of the theme, give feedback to each other's drafts, and help each other to polish and edit pieces of writing.

Students should pick their own topics for writing activities. Topics related to the lessons are suggested in the lesson notes. Personal interests, hobbies, and current issues and events can also provide appropriate topics for writing assignments.

The Lesson Segments

After the first session, the procedure for each session should be as consistent as possible. You may want to vary the order of the following segments to suit your particular situation.

1. **Homework Review.** Have students read aloud at least some of the reading selection studied for homework. Have them summarize the selection and go over their answers to the questions in Exercise 1. Discuss the selection, using some of the inferential- and applied-level questions suggested in the lesson notes. Then, go over the rest of the exercises and have students make any necessary corrections.
2. **Writing Activity.** Students may work in groups or singly on the current writing activity, depending on what it is.
3. **Reinforcement Activity.** When time permits, focus on an area of difficulty in a way that is fun for the students. See Chapter 4 of this manual for suggestions.
4. **Homework Preview.** Preview the next lesson, which students will complete for homework. Have students read the Words for Study and the title of the selection and predict what they think the selection will

be about. Do one or more pre-reading activities. Have students read the directions for the exercises to be sure they know what is required for each of them.

Individual Lesson Notes

The individual lesson notes that begin on page 126 contain specific suggestions and procedures for Book 4 lessons.

Lesson 1: The Heart

Primary emphasis
- Literal/inferential/applied comprehension
- Phonics, word analysis, and context clues
- New vocabulary
- Writing and study skills
- Common expressions

Secondary emphasis
- Oral reading and listening skills
- Spelling (adding -er)
- Syllabication
- Identifying vowel sounds

Words for Study

These words appear in this lesson for the first time in the *Challenger* series. Have students read the words that they recognize. Pronounce any word that students don't recognize and have them repeat the word several times while looking at it.

Pre-reading Activities

1. The reading passages in Book 4 are nonfiction. Discuss *fiction* and *nonfiction*.

2. Have students study the diagram on page 6. List the information they find in the diagram.

3. Say: Where is your heart located? What is the size of a heart? What does the heart do? This article will help answer these questions.

4. For this first lesson, have students read the article aloud in class. Assign a second reading for homework.

Post-reading Activities

1. Discuss the questions in Exercise 1.

Ask or say:

2. Does a heart weigh more than a pound?

3. How and where does blood get oxygen? Is oxygen necessary for our bodies?

4. What do veins and arteries do? How are they similar? How are they different?

5. Is the heart in a protected location in the body? How do you know?

Writing Activities

1. Write something you learned about hearts from this lesson.

2. Write about one thing you do that is good for your heart and one thing you do that is not good for your heart.

Additional Activities

1. Bring to class additional diagrams and pictures showing the circulatory system. Help

students trace the route blood takes through the heart, to the lungs, back to the heart, and out to the rest of the body. Explain why the blood flows to the lungs.

2. Ask students to share information they have heard about how to keep hearts healthy. What types of food and exercise are good for the heart? What types are not good?

3. Ask if anyone has ever donated blood. Discuss how and why it is done.

Exercises

1 About the Reading

During the homework preview, tell students that a long line under a question indicates that the answer should be a complete sentence. Explain that in answer to "What do you think?" questions, students should write their own opinions.

2 The Human Body

During the homework preview, review the process of elimination. Tell students to do the items they know first, skipping the ones they aren't sure of. Then they can go back and do the skipped ones when fewer choices remain.

3 The Ending -er

During the preview, study the examples and ask, "Have any letters been added, dropped, or changed in the examples when -er was added?" Then review the three rules for adding endings that start with a vowel.

- For column 1 words, add -er to the base word.
- For column 2 words, drop the silent e before adding -er.
- For column 3 words, double the final consonant before adding -er.

4 Syllables

During the preview, remind students that each syllable will have one vowel sound, although there may be more than one vowel letter in the syllable.

Lesson 2: Babe Ruth

Primary emphasis
- Literal/inferential/applied comprehension
- Phonics, word analysis, and context clues
- Writing and study skills
- Choosing the unrelated word
- Synonyms and antonyms

Secondary emphasis
- Oral reading and listening skills
- New vocabulary
- Spelling (adding -er)
- Syllabication
- Identifying vowel sounds

Words for Study

Encourage students to figure out the meanings of unfamiliar words from the context of the lesson. Plan reinforcement activities for any words that cause difficulty.

Pre-reading Activities

Ask or say:

1. Do you have a hero? If so, who is it and why is this person special to you?

2. Do you like learning about the lives of famous people? Do you like baseball? What do you already know about Babe Ruth? List the things students mention.

Post-reading Activities

1. Discuss the questions in Exercise 1.

2. Ask students to summarize the article.

Ask or say:

3. What does *scheme* mean in the sentence, "The scheme paid off"?

4. Explain in your own words how Yankee Stadium came to be called "The House That Ruth Built."

5. Babe Ruth "didn't live the way many people thought heroes should live." Is this also true of some of today's sports heroes? Do you think sports heroes should live their private lives according to people's expectations? Why or why not?

Writing Activities

1. Babe Ruth had many nicknames. Write about how you were named or how you got a nickname.

2. Write about why you think people need heroes.

3. Write a class letter to the National Baseball Hall of Fame and Museum, Inc., P.O. Box 590, Cooperstown, NY 13326. Ask for a brochure about the Hall of Fame and/or information on Babe Ruth or another baseball star. Send a self-addressed, stamped envelope with your request.

Additional Activities

1. Explore the sports section of a newspaper with students. Help them to read any charts and graphs. Read a sports article with them.

2. Locate on a map the places where Babe Ruth lived.

3. Read to the class an article or an excerpt from a book about another well-known sports figure, or have students read one together.

4. Help interested students to find other sports hero stories to read for pleasure. New Readers Press publishes nonfiction books about football, baseball, basketball, and boxing titled *3rd and Goal, Bases Loaded, Fast Break,* and *Lights Out,* all written at low reading levels.

Exercises

2 Games and Sports

During the preview, encourage students to ask friends or fellow class members for help if they don't know about some of these games or sports.

3 Words That Mean the Same and **4** Word Opposites

During the homework preview, suggest that students use a dictionary to check on any words here they don't know. Make sure that students know how to use a dictionary efficiently.

6 Syllables

Point out the following general principles on where syllable breaks occur:

- between double letters in the middle of words (items 3, 6, 8, 9)
- between the smaller words in compound words (items 1 and 7)
- between prefixes, roots, and suffixes (items 2, 4, 5, 10)

Lesson 3: Time

Primary emphasis
- Literal/inferential/applied comprehension
- Phonics, word analysis, and context clues
- New vocabulary
- Writing and study skills
- Reviewing factual information

Secondary emphasis
- Oral reading and listening skills
- Spelling (adding -*y*)
- Syllabication
- Identifying vowel sounds

Words for Study

Review the capitalization of proper nouns with *Asia, Pueblo, Indians,* and *Southwest.* Point out that *Southwest* is capitalized only when it refers to a section of the country. When it is used as a direction, as in "Drive southwest for three miles," it is lowercased.

Pre-reading Activities

1. Bring to class several devices that measure time, for example, a sandglass, a digital watch, an analog watch, a clock. Ask students to think of other ways of telling time. (Examples: water clocks, sundials, calendars, the phases of the moon)

Ask or say:

2. What is your definition of "a long time"? What does "a short time" mean to you? What does it mean to have time drag? To have time fly?

3. This article is about time and how concepts of time are different around the world. As you read, look for three different ways people in different cultures view time.

Post-reading Activities

1. Discuss the questions in Exercise 1.

Ask or say:

2. Do you call your friends at 2:00 A.M. just to chat? Why or why not?

3. What does "the time is ripe" mean? Why don't most people in the United State show up for work when "the time is ripe"?

4. Does one hour of time always seem the same to you? When does an hour seem like a long time? When does an hour go by quickly?

5. When are you very aware of time in your life? When is time a problem in your life?

6. Do you think it is good to learn about people from other cultures? Why or why not?

Writing Activities

1. If you were given a gift of two extra hours in each day, what would you do during this time?

2. If time travel were possible, which year would you choose to visit? Why?

Additional Activities

1. Have students make a list of words that refer to time, such as *now, tomorrow, before, after, never, yesterday, sometimes, always.* Write the headings Past, Present, Future, and Ongoing on the board. Help students to classify as many words as possible under the headings.

2. Help students to locate South Asia and the Southwestern United States on a map or globe.

3. Discuss time zones with students. Use maps or a globe to illustrate them.

4. Give a copy of a bus or train schedule to each student. Help students to read the schedule. Ask questions such as: What bus would you need to take to get downtown at 1:00 P.M.?

5. If anyone has lived in another country or culture, ask if they can think of examples of how people in different places have different concepts about things.

Exercises

2 Time

During the homework preview, discuss putting terms in logical order according to time, size, or quantity. You may want to have students do item 2 during the preview to be sure they understand the process.

3 More about Time

This exercise contains some common expressions about time. Remind students to use the process of elimination and context clues to complete it.

Lesson 4: Insects

Primary emphasis
- Literal/inferential/applied comprehension
- Phonics, word analysis, and context clues
- Writing and study skills
- Reviewing factual information
- Analogies

Secondary emphasis
- Oral reading and listening skills
- New vocabulary
- Spelling (adding -*y*)
- Syllabication

Pre-reading Activities

1. Before reading the article, have students take the quiz at the top of page 22. After they have checked their answers, ask them what criteria they used to determine if something was an insect. Tell them there is information in the reading that explains how to define an insect. Ask them to locate it as they read.

2. Have the class list ways we benefit from insect life. Then list problems caused by insects. Add new information to both lists after reading the article.

3. Say: Read the following article to find out what important jobs insects perform on earth. Think about what problems would result if insects disappeared from earth.

Post-reading Activities

1. Discuss the questions in Exercise 1.

Ask or say:

2. Name some creatures that depend on insects as a source of food.

3. Do you think that in the future people will learn new information about insects, or is the study of insects finished? Explain.

4. What are some things that all insects have in common? Why isn't a spider an insect?

5. Name some places on earth that are likely to have large insect populations.

6. What are some sheltered places where insects might live during the winter?

7. Why would it be useful for people who study forest management to study insects?

8. Do you think the author was trying to persuade readers to like insects? Explain.

9. If there were no insects, what would some of the resulting problems be?

Writing Activities

1. Write about an experience you have had that involved an insect or insects.

2. Write what you like and what you don't like about insects.

3. After reading the article in this lesson, did your opinion about insects change in any way? Explain.

Additional Activities

1. With students, contrast cold- and warm-blooded animals and give examples of each.

2. Ask students if they have seen caterpillars. Then ask: Do insects look the same in all stages of their lives? Show pictures of the stages in an insect's life: egg, nymph or larva, pupa, adult.

3. Read information to students about the journey of the monarch butterfly. Using a colored text, share with students the beauty of butterflies and moths. Ask students if they recognize any of the moths or butterflies.

4. What are insecticides? What are some of the problems caused by overuse or improper use of insecticides? Are there other ways to control insect populations?

Exercises

2 Name That Insect or Bug

Encourage students to use a dictionary or encyclopedia to complete this exercise.

3 Which Word Fits Best?

During the homework preview, have students:

- read the first sentence saying "blank" where the blank occurs.
- explain the relationship between *termite* and *wood*. (Termites feed on wood.)
- read the four answer choices and decide which choice goes with *blood* in the same way that *termite* goes with *wood*.
- write *tick* in the blank and read the complete sentence.

Have students complete item 2 if they seem confused.

Lesson 5: The Brain Sees All

Primary emphasis
- Literal/inferential/applied comprehension
- Phonics, word analysis, and context clues
- Writing and study skills
- Sequencing events
- Categorizing

Secondary emphasis
- Oral reading and listening skills
- New vocabulary
- Syllabication

Words for Study

Point out the hyphens in *one-third* and *one-fourth*. Explain that hyphens are used to spell fractions.

Pre-reading Activities

Ask or say:

1. Have you ever thought about what makes up the pictures on a TV screen? This article gives some information about television and moving pictures.

2. Do you think it is possible to get people to buy things they don't normally buy? Think about this question as you read, and be ready to discuss your ideas and opinions.

Post-reading Activities

1. Discuss the questions in Exercise 1.

2. Ask students to summarize the article.

Ask or say:

3. Can you think of any good uses for ads of a type similar to the "eat popcorn" ad?

4. How do you think the people in the study would've felt if they'd found out why they wanted to buy popcorn?

5. Scientists don't agree on the extent to which subliminal messages can influence people's behavior. Discuss with students the dangers involved in basing conclusions on a single example.

Writing Activities

1. Have you ever been affected by watching TV or a movie? Write about it.

2. Some people think that viewers are not affected by seeing violence on TV and in movies. Do you agree? Why or why not?

3. Describe an ad that made you want to buy or do something.

Additional Activities

1. Ask students what kinds of ads they like and dislike. Pass around magazines and ask pairs of students to choose an advertisement to talk about. List questions for students to consider such as: What group of people do you think this ad is aimed at? How does the ad make the product seem desirable? What else would you like to know about the product?

2. "Use it or lose it" seems to be the way our brains work. Frequent review helps people remember. Another way to remember information is to put what you heard or read into your own words. How does this information apply to improving reading skills?

Exercises

2 Putting Sentences in Order

During the homework preview, recommend that students number the sentences in a sensible order before writing them on the lines. The only guideline is that the sequence must make sense.

4 Working with Headings

During the preview, have students explain why "Spending Time with Friends" is the best heading for the words in the example. If necessary, have students do the next item as a group.

Review: Lessons 1–5

Explain that reviews appear after every five lessons. Tell students that they may refer to previous lessons or a dictionary to review factual information.

In addition to the review, you might also have students do a research-and-report activity in which they select one topic from the five lessons and find out more about it. Students can work singly, in pairs, or in groups, and give oral and/or written reports.

Explain that the word index after this review lists words introduced in Lessons 1–5.

Lesson 6: The Sun

Primary emphasis
- Literal/inferential/applied comprehension
- Phonics, word analysis, and context clues
- Writing and study skills
- Classifying
- Definitions

Secondary emphasis
- Oral reading and listening skills
- New vocabulary
- Spelling (adding -*ing*)
- Distinguishing between similar words

Pre-reading Activities

1. Bring in books with illustrations and pictures of the sun, stars, and moon to build interest and help students understand the lesson.

2. Ask: What do you know about the sun? Is the sun a star? What is the difference between a star and a planet? Why does life on earth depend on the sun? How long do you think life would last without the sun?

Post-reading Activities

1. Discuss the questions in Exercise 1.

Ask or say:

2. Explain in your own words the connection between the sun and the earth's food chain.

3. Have people understood the importance of the sun for a long time?

4. Why do you think ancient people worshipped the sun? What does it mean to call someone a "sun worshiper" today?

5. Is there more than one sun? Explain.

6. Find a place in the article where the author uses an example to help readers understand information. As a class, draw the example (the skyscraper, the man, and the dog).

7. Does the earth receive most of the sun's light and heat? Explain.

8. How have scientists learned about the possibilities for the future of the sun?

9. How long do you think life on earth would last without the sun? Explain.

Writing Activities

1. What are some ways the sun is a friend of the earth? What are some problems related to the sun?

2. Do you think there is life on planets in other solar systems? Why or why not?

3. What does "powered by solar energy" mean? Write about something you have heard about or seen that is powered by solar energy.

Additional Activities

1. From what direction does the sun rise in the morning? In what direction does it set in the evening? Can north and south be determined from seeing a sunrise? Give other examples of how this information can be useful.

2. Use a globe and a light to demonstrate night, day, moonlight, and eclipses. Follow up with questions: Where does moonlight come from? When it is day where you live, where is it night? What is an eclipse?

3. If students are interested in this article, they may want to learn more about the solar system and the universe. Help them to find materials at an appropriate reading level.

Exercises

2 Working with Headings

During the homework preview, make sure students understand that solids, liquids, and gases are the three states of matter. Ask students to give examples of each. Remind them to use the process of elimination to do this exercise.

3 Compound Words

During the homework preview, remind students that compound words are made up of two or more smaller words. During the review, have students say the two words that make up each compound word.

4 The Ending -*ing*

Have students state the spelling rules for adding endings that start with a vowel.

5 Some Confusing -*ing* Words

During the preview, have students read the pairs of -*ing* words. Remind them that doubling the final consonant keeps the preceding vowel short.

Lesson 7: Thomas Edison

Primary emphasis
- Literal/inferential/applied comprehension
- Phonics, word analysis, and context clues
- New vocabulary
- Writing and study skills
- Analogies

Secondary emphasis
- Oral reading and listening skills
- Forming and defining compound words
- Syllabication

Words for Study

Point out the -or ending on *inspector, conductor,* and *inventor,* and ask students what they think -or means in these words (someone who does something).

Pre-reading Activities

Ask or say:

1. What do you know about Thomas Edison? Look at the picture at the top of the page. What can you tell about Thomas Edison by looking at the picture? When do you think he lived? What do you think he is doing? Describe the expression on his face.

2. As you read the following article, find some things about Edison's early life that show he was an intelligent child. Find one person who understood that he had great promise.

Post-reading Activities

1. Discuss the questions in Exercise 1.

Ask or say:

2. Do you think Edison was an unusual child? Why or why not?

3. What do you think was more important to Edison, being careful or satisfying his curiosity?

4. Why do you think the teacher thought Edison was crazy? Are people who are different, for whatever reason, often considered crazy? Why or why not?

5. Mrs. Edison thought learning could be fun. This was unusual for her time. Do you agree or disagree with her belief? Explain.

6. How would your life be different if Edison hadn't invented the light bulb?

7. How have items invented by Edison changed over the years (in particular, light bulbs, movies, and records)? What do you think might happen to them in the future?

8. Which of Edison's inventions listed at the beginning of the article do you consider the most important? Why?

Writing Activities

1. If you could invent something, what would you invent? Why?

2. Edison is quoted as saying "Genius is 99 per cent perspiration and 1 per cent inspiration." Explain what this means in your own words.

Additional Activities

1. Sometimes adults are so busy they do not take time to answer children's questions. Why is it important for adults to listen to children and answer their questions?

2. Edison conducted 10,000 experiments on a storage battery that failed. Failure did not seem to discourage Edison. Why is the ability to overcome failure important in an inventor? Why is the ability to overcome failure important to people in their everyday lives?

3. Students who enjoyed this article may be interested in learning about other inventors such as Robert Fulton, Alexander Graham Bell, Samuel Morse, and the Wright brothers.

Exercises

2 More Work with Compound Words

After students have read the directions and studied the example, suggest that they do one item together in class. If they have trouble with item 2, have them read the descriptions until they come to one they know. Remind them to check off the words in both columns as they use them.

3 Which Word Fits Best?

If students had trouble with this type of exercise in Lesson 4, review the process for determining the relationships between the word pairs.

Lesson 8: Knives, Forks, and Spoons

Primary emphasis
- Literal/inferential/applied comprehension
- Phonics, word analysis, and context clues
- Writing and study skills
- Reviewing factual information
- Singular and plural words

Secondary emphasis
- Oral reading and listening skills
- New vocabulary
- Spelling (changing *f* to *v*)

Pre-reading Activities

1. As students read the article, ask them to compare how the early humans ate with how we eat today. Ask them to think about how culture changes as life becomes less difficult.

2. Bring into class a pair of chopsticks and ask students what they are, what they are used for, and in what countries they are used.

3. Say: This article gives some advice about what to do in situations in which you are uncertain about what behavior is correct. Look for this advice as you read.

Post-reading Activities

1. Discuss the questions in Exercise 1. Make sure students understand the meaning of *key* as it is used in question 5.

Ask or say:

2. Compare how the early humans ate with how people eat today.

3. What do you think the early humans' spoons were made from? Explain.

4. Why do you think the early humans ate only enough food to stay alive? Do you think it was difficult for them to get food?

5. People use forks in many places around the world today. How and why do you think their popularity spread?

6. Why do you think spoons and knives were invented before forks?

7. What happens to cultures of people when life becomes less difficult? What are some changes that take place?

8. What advice does the author give to people who are uncertain about what to do in a given situation? Think of another situation in which this advice can be useful.

Writing Activities

1. What foods do you find difficult to eat even with a knife, fork, and spoon? Write about what it's like to eat them.

2. Eating habits have changed since the time of early humans. Write about something else that has changed.

3. Write about a situation in which you did not know what was the correct thing to do.

Additional Activities

1. Bring kitchen gadgets to class. Ask students about the intended uses, and brainstorm additional uses for them.

2. Each historical time and culture is different, and rules constantly change. Discuss the fairness of judging other people by their behavior when they may have been raised under different circumstances.

3. How do you think people today know how early humans ate? Some people make their living by studying ancient humans and cultures. Would you like this type of job? Why or why not?

Exercises

4 Singular and Plural Words

During the preview, make sure students understand the concepts *singular* and *plural.* Point out that the most common way to form plurals in English is to add *-s* to a word but that some plurals, such as *men,* take a different form.

5 One Knife/Two Knives

During the preview, state this spelling rule: Change *f* to *v* and add *-es.* Then have students write the five plural words. Point out that they will use both the singular and the plural words in the sentences.

Lesson 9: Manners

Primary emphasis
- Literal/inferential/applied comprehension
- Phonics, word analysis, and context clues
- Writing and study skills
- Choosing the unrelated word
- Sequencing

Secondary emphasis
- Oral reading and listening skills
- New vocabulary
- General information (manners)
- Singular and plural words

Pre-reading Activities

1. This selection is taken from the book *How to Eat Like a Child.* As you read, decide if it was written for children or adults. Try to remember times when you have seen children eating in these ways.

2. Say: As you read, think of a time in your life when eating was really fun.

Post-reading Activities

1. Discuss the questions in Exercise 1.

Ask or say:

2. Do you think this article was written for adults or for children?

3. What does the writer want readers to do? Did you think the article was funny? Why or why not?

4. Do you consider manners important? Explain. What are some manners or rules of behavior that are important to you?

5. Are there any eating habits that bother you? What are they?

6. Where did you learn about manners and who taught you? Do you think you know enough about manners or would you like to know more?

7. Besides eating, what are some other situations that require manners?

8. Do you think people should be judged by their manners? Why or why not?

Writing Activities

1. Suggest another title for this article and write why you think it would be a good one.

2. Write about an incident you remember that involved good or bad manners.

3. Write a funny article about how children do something.

Additional Activities

1. Examine how this article is organized. How many people wrote this article? (two) Who were they? (Delia Ephron and Corea Murphy) Where do you find who the authors are? Find the place in the article where the change from one author to another occurs.

2. Bring in newspaper columns that deal with manners. In pairs or small groups, have students read and discuss the columns. Then have each group report to the class.

3. Are manners the same in different countries and cultures? If you were going to visit another country, do you think it would be important to find out about what is considered "good manners" in that country? Why? What are some ways to learn about the manners of a particular group?

Exercises

2 Which Word Does Not Fit?

The format of this exercise may seem new to students, but the process used is the same as in Lesson 2, Exercise 2. If students seem unsure of what to do after studying the example, have them do item 2 during the homework preview.

3 Recipes

Suggest that students number the sentences in a sensible order before writing the sentences on the lines.

4 Singular and Plural Words

During the homework preview, review the meanings of *singular* and *plural* and the fact that many plurals are formed by adding -s or -es.

5 More about Manners

During the preview, mention that this exercise is similar to brief quizzes that sometimes appear in newspapers and magazines. Tell students that it is just for fun and that rules about manners change depending on time and circumstances.

Lesson 10: Flying Saucers

Primary emphasis
- Literal/inferential/applied comprehension
- Phonics, word analysis, and context clues
- Writing and study skills
- Inferring meanings from context clues
- Choosing the related word

Secondary emphasis
- Oral reading and listening skills
- New vocabulary
- Multiple meanings and pronunciations

Pre-reading Activities

1. Have students look at the pictures and read the captions. Then ask if they have seen any of the movies pictured. If so, what do they remember? What seems to be happening in each picture?

2. Ask what reports and stories students have heard about unidentified flying objects (UFOs) and flying saucers.

Post-reading Activities

1. Discuss the questions in Exercise 1.

Ask or say:

2. Compare the baker's flying saucer story to the pilot's story. What is similar? What is different?

3. Do you believe life exists only on earth? Why or why not?

4. Do you want to believe there are flying saucers? Why or why not?

5. What would be necessary to prove to you that flying saucers exist?

6. Do you think it would take courage to report seeing a flying saucer? Would you report seeing one? Why or why not?

Writing Activities

1. Look at the top picture on page 57. Write what you think the person from the flying saucer might be saying.

2. Which of the three movies pictured would you prefer to see? Why?

3. Write a group story about a flying saucer visit to earth.

Additional Activities

1. If you could communicate with beings from another planet, what questions would you ask?

2. Do you think it is likely that there could be life on other planets in our solar system? Do any other planets have conditions that could support life as we know it? Which planets are too hot? Which are too cold?

3. Read a science fiction story to the class.

Exercises

2 More about Meteors

During the preview, have students read the list of words to be filled in. Suggest that they read the whole passage first, saying "blank" for each missing word. Next, they should fill in the words they are sure of and check them off. Then they can fill in the rest of the words when they have fewer choices.

3 Choosing the Right Word

During the homework review, have students tell whether each correct answer means the same thing or is an example of the first word. Some students confuse examples with synonyms, and this exercise provides an opportunity to help them clear up this confusion.

Review: Lessons 1–10

During the preview, remind students to refer to previous lessons or a dictionary to review factual information.

5 Syllables

During the preview, stress that the process of elimination is very important in this exercise. Suggest that students read the sentences and do the ones they know the answers to first. Remind them to cross out the syllables in the box as they use them.

Encourage students to select one topic from Lessons 6–10 to research and report on. Students can work singly, in pairs, or in groups, and give oral and/or written reports.

BOOK 4

Lesson 11: Accepting Who You Are

Primary emphasis
- Literal/inferential/applied comprehension
- Phonics, word analysis, and context clues
- New vocabulary
- Writing and study skills

Secondary emphasis
- Oral reading and listening skills
- Spelling (changing *y* to *i* and puzzle)
- Word endings
- Silent letters

Words for Study

Make sure students know that M.D., which follows the author's name, stands for Doctor of Medicine. (M.D. is from the Latin *Medicinae Doctor.*)

Pre-reading Activities

Ask or say:

1. What does it mean to accept who you are? What information would you expect an article with this title to have?

2. Read the credit line on page 67. Does knowing the title of the book this article came from help you predict what it will be about?

3. As you read this article, watch for the author's main points and notice how he supports them with examples.

Post-reading Activities

1. Discuss the questions in Exercise 1.

Ask or say:

2. Discuss fact and opinion. Find examples of facts and opinions in this article.

3. Discuss the major thesis of this article. Then ask students to find one of the main ideas and supporting examples of that main idea.

4. Reread the first paragraph. How can what we choose not to do send messages to other people? Think of something you chose not to do. What does that say about you?

5. Which comes first, being an open and friendly person or being a person who accepts herself or himself?

6. What can we do to help other people, especially children, to accept who they are?

Writing Activities

1. What information in this article was useful to you? Write about something you would like to remember.

2. Is there something about yourself that you have tried to change? Write about it.

Additional Vocabulary Practice

self-esteem – having confidence in yourself; accepting and respecting yourself

Additional Activities

1. Discuss self-esteem. What are some signs that a person has high self-esteem? What are some signs of low self-esteem?

2. Discuss how students' accomplishments and progress in improving reading skills relate to self-esteem.

Exercises

2 Changing the *y* to *i*

During the preview, tell students to add the endings *-er, -est,* and *-ness* to each word after changing the *y* to *i*. Point out that *y* is changed to *i* before endings that start with consonants as well as endings that start with vowels. Note that *y* is not changed if the ending starts with *i.*

3 Word Endings

During the homework preview, have students read the words on the left. Tell them to read each sentence through before selecting the word to write in the blank.

4 Silent Letters

During the preview, have students read the words to be sure they are pronouncing them correctly.

5 Happiness

If students have never done this type of puzzle, have them do two or three items during the preview. Tell them to fill in the letters in the quotation as they answer each item. Tell them to work back and forth between the clues and the quotation, using context clues in the quotation to complete partially filled-in words.

Lesson 12: Anne Frank: Part I

Primary emphasis
- Literal/inferential/applied comprehension
- Phonics, word analysis, and context clues
- New vocabulary
- Writing and study skills
- Synonyms and antonyms

Secondary emphasis
- Oral reading and listening skills
- Word beginnings
- Hard and soft *g*

Words for Study

Use these words to introduce background information on World War II.

Pre-reading Activities

1. Find out how much students already know about Hitler, World War II, and Anne Frank. What were some countries that fought on the same side as Germany? What were some countries that fought against Germany and Japan? Who was Hitler? What did he want to do? Discuss Hitler's attempt to destroy Europe's Jewish population during the war.

2. Bring in pictures, maps, and books about World War II to enhance understanding and create interest in the lesson. Find Germany and Holland on a globe or world map.

3. Say: As you read the article about Anne Frank, think about how hard it would be to live hiding in an attic for two years.

Post-reading Activities

1. Discuss the questions in Exercise 1.

Ask or say:

2. Anne Frank lived from 1929–1945. How old was she when she died?

3. What do you think would happen to a Jewish person who carried a suitcase in a country occupied by Nazis?

4. Did Anne think Germany had changed since Hitler became powerful? What did Anne mean when she wrote, "Hitler took away our country long ago"?

5. How do you think the people hiding in the attic were able to get the supplies and food they needed? (Many people in Holland risked their own lives to hide and help Jewish people.)

6. What do you think would be the most difficult part of hiding in an attic for two years?

7. Do you think discrimination and racism still exist today? Give examples. Have you experienced discrimination? Discuss.

8. Is reading a diary an interesting way to learn about history? Would you prefer to read a diary or a history book to learn about events in the past? Why?

Writing Activities

1. Write what you are feeling and thinking after reading parts of Anne Frank's diary.

2. Write a few sentences or a poem about Anne Frank.

3. What are some things you would try to take with you if you were forced into hiding?

4. Point out that journals are like diaries. Remind students to write in their journals.

Additional Activities

1. During the year 1933, Anne Frank's family moved to the Netherlands (Holland) from Germany to avoid trouble following Hitler's rise to power. Find these places on a map.

2. How do you think it was possible for a person such as Hitler to become so powerful? Do such people continue to reach positions of power in the world today? Discuss.

3. Anne wrote, "I want to go on living after my death." Things a person writes are often read years after the writer has died. Think of examples of other people who have died but whose writings are still read. Do you consider their work a means for them to be "living after death"?

Exercises
2 Word Beginnings

Information in the reading and background information about World War II should help students to answer these questions.

Lesson 13: Anne Frank: Part II

Primary emphasis
- Literal/inferential/applied comprehension
- Phonics, word analysis, and context clues
- Writing and study skills
- Inferring meanings from context clues
- Classifying

Secondary emphasis
- Oral reading and listening skills
- New vocabulary
- Word endings

Words for Study

Find the places listed in the fourth column on a world map.

Pre-reading Activities

1. Review the selection in Lesson 12.

Ask or say:

2. What would you miss the most if you had to live in an attic for two years? List the things you would miss. After completing the reading, compare your ideas with the list of things in Anne's diary.

3. As you continue to read about Anne Frank, find something that Anne was hopeful about.

Post-reading Activities

1. Discuss the questions in Exercise 1.

Ask or say:

2. Describe how you picture the hiding place.

3. Why do you think Anne feels she cannot show her rage?

4. Did Anne have any contact with friends her age? Would it be especially difficult for a teenager to live in those conditions? Explain.

5. Did the people living in hiding wish for expensive things or simple things? Explain.

6. Did you find Anne's diary interesting? If so, what did you find interesting about it? Do you think Anne's diary helped her survive the two years in hiding? Explain.

7. Did Anne think she would survive? Find a sentence that supports your answer.

8. Think about a time when you were very afraid. Imagine what it must have been like to live year after year in fear of losing your life. Imagine having to be quiet at all times and often go hungry. Discuss the problems of living with a group of eight people who are under great stress and in fear.

Writing Activities

1. Write about what you would miss the most if you had to live under the circumstances that Anne's family did.

2. If you had been hiding in an attic for two years and were suddenly freed, what would you want to do first?

3. What can each of us do in our lives to work toward a better world?

Additional Activities

1. Students may have questions about how Anne Frank's story ended. Germany was defeated in 1945. Anne died in a concentration camp less than two months before the end of the war. Anne's father, Otto, was the only survivor among the eight people in the attic. After the war, he visited the people who had hidden his family. They had found Anne's diary, and they gave it to him.

2. Read other excerpts from *Anne Frank: The Diary of a Young Girl* if the class is interested. Many books written about Anne Frank have pictures of Anne and the secret hiding place. Some students may want to read the entire diary.

3. Watch a movie or film about Anne Frank and have students discuss it or write a review.

4. Think about the article "Accepting Who You Are" in Lesson 11. Do you think Anne Frank accepted who she was? Find details from her diary that support your answer.

Exercises

2 World War II

Suggest that students read the entire passage before filling in the missing words.

3 Cities, States, and Countries

Tell students that they can find this information in most dictionaries. During the homework review, have maps of the United States and the world available to help students locate all these places.

Lesson 14: The Ship of the Desert

Primary emphasis
- Literal/inferential/applied comprehension
- Phonics, word analysis, and context clues
- New vocabulary
- Writing and study skills
- Forming and defining compound words

Secondary emphasis
- Oral reading and listening skills
- Word endings
- Syllabication
- Identifying vowel sounds

Pre-reading Activities

1. After looking at the pictures, ask students if they have ever seen camels at a zoo. Ask them to describe what they saw. Find out why they think camels are called "ships of the desert."

2. Ask if students have seen a desert. If so, have them describe it. If no one has been to a desert, ask students to imagine what one is like.

3. Find the deserts of Asia and Africa on a map.

Post-reading Activities

1. Discuss the questions in Exercise 1.

Ask or say:

2. What are Asia and Africa? What are the other continents? Find them on a map.

3. Is it always hot in a desert? (Nights are often cold.) Are all deserts hot? (No.) Are all deserts dry? (Yes.)

4. How is a camel's body well suited to life in the desert? Why is fat stored in the hump? (Fat provides energy when food is scarce.)

5. Do people have to be careful around camels? Explain.

6. Find a place in the article where the author expresses a personal opinion about camels. Does this article contain more facts or more opinions?

7. Compare horses and camels. What are the similarities? What are the differences? Consider such things as how their bodies are built, how they are used by people, and the parts of the world where they are found.

8. Would you like to ride a camel? Why or why not?

Writing Activities

1. According to an old joke, a camel is a horse that was designed by a committee. Write what you think the joke means.

2. Just for fun, design an animal that would be useful to you. Write a description or draw a picture of your animal.

3. Write a humorous short poem about a camel.

Additional Activities

1. How do you think camels came by the name "ships of the desert"? One explanation for the name is found in the article. Another explanation is that when a camel paces, both legs on the same side of its body move up and down together. This causes it to sway and pitch like a ship on waves. The swaying motion sometimes makes riders "seasick."

2. Some camels grow thick, long hair under certain conditions. What do you think those conditions are? (in winter or in cold regions)

3. Some camels can tolerate water loss of up to 25 per cent of their body weight. Humans die at water losses of only 12 per cent. Figure out how much you would weigh if you lost 25 per cent of your body weight.

4. Help interested students find information on the two types of camels, those with one hump (Arabian) and those with two (Bactrian). Look for pictures of the two types.

5. Find pictures of other animals that illustrate how their bodies are especially suited to their habitat. (Examples: anteaters, armadillos, giraffes, mountain goats, sharks)

Exercises

2 Compound Words

Students may want to use the dictionary to do this exercise.

BOOK 4

Lesson 15: Some Facts about Southpaws

Primary emphasis
- Literal/inferential/applied comprehension
- Phonics, word analysis, and context clues
- New vocabulary
- Writing and study skills
- Common expressions

Secondary emphasis
- Oral reading and listening skills
- Singular and plural words

Pre-reading Activities

1. After reading the title, ask: What is a fact? What is a southpaw? Ask students what they know about right- or left-handedness.

2. If there are left-handed students in the group, ask them to describe some of the common obstacles they face in daily life.

3. Say: As you read this article, think about the advantages and disadvantages of being right- or left-handed.

Post-reading Activities

1. Discuss the questions in Exercise 1.

Ask or say:

2. Explain the sentence "No culture has ever been left-handed."

3. Why do you think people who were left-handed were regarded as bad or crazy? Is this a form of discrimination?

4. Is there general agreement about why people are left- or right-handed?

5. Does the article's author believe left-handed people are at a disadvantage? Explain.

6. Compare right- and left-handedness. What are some advantages and disadvantages of each?

7. What are some traits children inherit from their parents?

8. Do you think there is discrimination against left-handed people today? Explain.

Writing Activities

1. Ask students to write today's journal entries using their nondominant hand.

2. Interview someone who is left-handed. Ask about problems left-handed people face. Write a report of the interview.

Additional Activities

1. Have students talk with left-handed people about common things that are problems for them. Develop a list from their findings.

2. Are most tools made for right- or left-handed people? What are some reasons that many companies do not make both kinds? What is one reason most stores do not devote shelf space to items for left-handed users? Call local stores and ask if they carry items for left-handed people. If they do not, ask why they don't.

3. Ask students if they know anyone who went to school during the period when left-handed children were forced to write with their right hands. If they do, ask them to find out what the person remembers about the experience and have them report what they learned to the rest of the class.

Exercises

2 "Handy" Sayings

Discuss the meanings of any unfamiliar expressions during the homework review.

3 "Handy" Words

Students may enjoy looking in a dictionary to see the many words that begin with *hand*.

4 Singular and Plural Words

During the homework review, have students identify the various ways these plurals are formed:

- adding *-s* or *-es*
- changing *y* to *i* and adding *-es*
- changing *f* to *v* and adding *-es*
- making no change (deer)
- making an irregular change (oxen, cattle)

Review: Lessons 1–15

During the preview, remind students to refer to previous lessons or a dictionary to review factual information.

Encourage students to select one topic from Lessons 11–15 to research and report on. Students can work singly, in pairs, or in groups, and give oral and/or written reports.

Lesson 16: Some Thoughts about Dying

Primary emphasis
- Literal/inferential/applied comprehension
- Phonics, word analysis, and context clues
- New vocabulary
- Writing and study skills
- Sequencing events

Secondary emphasis
- Oral reading and listening skills
- The ending -*ly*
- Compound words

Words for Study

If students ask for definitions for unfamiliar words, encourage them to try to figure out the meanings from the context of the reading.

Pre-reading Activities

Ask or say:

1. This article talks about dying. Briefly discuss how, when, and why living things die. Injury and the effects of old age are two common causes of death. Can you think of a third? (disease)

2. As you read, think about what the author's message is about dying. Decide if you think this article would be good for a dying person to read.

Post-reading Activities

1. Discuss the questions in Exercise 1.

Ask or say:

2. Summarize the author's message about dying. What is the main idea of the article? Would you describe the article as positive or negative? Do you agree or disagree with the author? Why?

3. Why do you think so many people have written books about death?

4. Describe the French writer's near-death experience. Why did the French writer advise letting nature control the dying process?

5. The author says "pain is useful." When is pain useful? When is it not useful?

6. Under what circumstances does the author think pain is "turned off"?

7. Do you think this would be a good article for a dying person to read? Why or why not?

Writing Activities

1. Write some of your thoughts about dying.
2. Write some of your thoughts about pain.

Additional Activities

1. The definition of death has changed because of machines that can restore and maintain vital functions. Discuss drugs, machines, and other means used to continue body functions. When should they be used? Should they always be used? What about cost? Who should have access first to limited resources? Who should make these important decisions?

2. What are "right to die" groups concerned about?

3. In years past, so many people died at home that death was viewed as a natural part of life. Many people today have not had the experience of being around a dying person. Do you think this makes it more difficult to view death as a natural part of life? Explain.

Additional Vocabulary Practice

hospice – a program that provides homelike care for dying people

living will – a will that states a person does not want to be kept alive with life-support systems in the event of a terminal illness

brain dead – the absence of brain activity for 24 hours. It is considered evidence of death in many states.

Exercises

2 **About the Reading**

Have students number the sentences in the correct sequence before they write out the sentences.

3 **The Ending -*ly***

Tell students to write the words with -*ly* added before using them to fill in the blanks in the sentences.

5 **More Work with Compound Words**

During the homework review, briefly discuss the meanings of any of the answer choices that students don't know.

BOOK 4

Lesson 17: The Number One Eater in America

Primary emphasis
- Literal/inferential/applied comprehension
- Phonics, word analysis, and context clues
- New vocabulary
- Writing and study skills
- Common expressions

Secondary emphasis
- Oral reading and listening skills
- The ending *-ful*
- Forming words with syllables

Pre-reading Activities

Ask or say:

1. Did you ever eat too much? How did you feel? This is an article about a man who ate too much every day for years.

2. List some things that can be learned about James Brady from the picture on page 106. Was the picture taken recently? How old do you think the car is? Was James Brady rich? What else can you learn from the picture?

3. List what you ate today. Then read the article to find out what Diamond Jim Brady would have eaten in the same period of time. Compare your list to what he would have eaten.

Post-reading Activities

1. Discuss the questions in Exercise 1.

Ask or say:

2. Would you like to have been a friend of Diamond Jim Brady? Why or why not?

3. Do you think Diamond Jim was a hard worker? Why or why not?

4. What kind of qualities do you think an "extremely successful salesman" has?

5. Did Jim Brady live near the ocean? What clues in the article did you use to decide?

6. What did the restaurant owner mean when he said Diamond Jim was "the best twenty-five customers we had"?

7. Was $100,000 worth more in Diamond Jim's time than it is today?

8. Discuss tone. Did the author admire Jim Brady? Was the author impressed? Would the tone change if Brady had been referred to as "The Number One Glutton"? How would the tone be different if the article were written by or for people who had gone hungry?

Writing Activities

1. If you could afford to eat any foods you wanted, write about what you would eat.

2. If you were as rich as Diamond Jim Brady, write about what you would do with your wealth.

Additional Vocabulary Practice

glutton – a person who consumes excessive amounts of food and drink

gluttony – excessive eating or drinking

Additional Activities

1. Find Atlantic City and New York on a map.

2. Diamond Jim drank a gallon of orange juice for breakfast. Bring in empty containers that hold different volumes. Make labels for each container. Ask students to match the labels to the containers. Ask about equivalent measures. For example: How many quarts are in a gallon? How many cups are in a pint? in a quart? in a gallon?

3. What health problems are associated with overeating?

4. People like Diamond Jim Brady are gluttons while many people in the world are hungry and do not get enough to eat. Do you think this is fair? Can anything be done about it?

Exercises

2 Food for Thought

During the homework review, discuss any expressions here that are unfamiliar to students.

3 The Ending *-ful*

Tell students to add *-ful* to each word listed at the top of the page before filling in the blanks in the sentences.

4 Working with Syllables

Remind students to use the process of elimination and to cross out the syllables in the box as they use them.

Lesson 18: The Great Hunger

Primary emphasis
- Literal/inferential/applied comprehension
- Phonics, word analysis, and context clues
- Inferring meanings from context clues
- Writing and study skills
- Word associations

Secondary emphasis
- Oral reading and listening skills
- New vocabulary
- The ending -less

Pre-reading Activities

1. Before reading the article, have students study the picture. Ask: Does this look like a recent photo? Why do you think the people are on the ship? Would you like to be one of the people on the ship? Why or why not? Do you think the ship is overcrowded? Do you think there are enough lifeboats? Return to these questions and compare your answers after reading the article.

2. Ask students what they know about Ireland. Does anyone have relatives or ancestors who came from Ireland? Can anyone name some Irish symbols or traditions? (Examples: St. Patrick's Day, shamrocks, leprechauns) Find Ireland on a map or globe.

Post-reading Activities

1. Discuss the questions in Exercise 1.

Ask or say:

2. List some facts given that illustrate the poverty in Ireland during the 1800s.

3. Do you think it is wise to depend on only one crop for food? Why do you think the people in Ireland did so?

4. What are two reasons why the population of Ireland decreased during the years of potato blight?

5. Why do you think people waited so long before they left the country? Why do you think some people never left?

6. Besides starvation, what are some other reasons that people immigrate to another country?

7. Contrast the famine described in this article with the feasting described in Lesson 17.

Writing Activities

1. Explain what the phrase "at the end of their rope" means.

2. Write about what you would have done if you had lived in Ireland at the time of the potato blight.

Additional Activities

1. Interested students may want to learn more about Ireland's history. Help them to find appropriate materials.

2. Did the people from Ireland speak the same language as the people in the United States? Do you think that knowing the language is an advantage to people who immigrate? What difficulties result when people move to countries where a different language is spoken?

3. Read to the class about an immigrant or immigrant family. What was it like for people to have to be separated from their relatives and friends and move to another country?

4. Some students may have ancestors or relatives who migrated to or from other countries. If any students know their family stories, ask them to share these stories with the class or to write about them.

5. Does famine exist in the world today? Find places on a world map where people have suffered from food shortages or famine in the past two years. Are there people in your community who do not have enough food? Why? What can be done to help them?

Exercises

2 More about Potatoes

Remind students to take their time and to use context clues and the process of elimination while completing this exercise. During the review, trace on a world map the path potatoes took to get from South America to North America.

3 Where Would You Find It?

General background knowledge is needed to do this exercise correctly. During the review, discuss any items that are unfamiliar to students.

BOOK 4

Lesson 19: Digestion

Primary emphasis
- Literal/inferential/applied comprehension
- Phonics, word analysis, and context clues
- New vocabulary
- Writing and study skills
- Cause-and-effect relationships

Secondary emphasis
- Oral reading and listening skills
- Factual information
- Word endings

Pre-reading Activities

Ask or say:

1. Study the diagram and read the captions aloud. What does *digestion* mean and what do you know about it? What kind of information do you expect to find in this article on digestion?

2. This article traces the path of food people eat as it goes through the body. Read to find out where food goes after you swallow it.

Post-reading Activities

1. Discuss the questions in Exercise 1.

Ask or say:

2. It takes the food you eat about 24 hours to complete the journey through your body. After swallowing, where does the food go? Trace the path through the digestive system.

3. What are two things that people must have to survive? The food we eat is used for what two purposes?

4. If a basketball player changed jobs and became a keyboard operator, would that person need to eat more or less?

5. Why do you think people need different amounts of food in different seasons? In different parts of the world?

6. Do you think it takes longer to digest steak or orange juice? Why?

7. Why is breakfast an important meal?

8. Why is food broken down into smaller and smaller parts? (It must enter the bloodstream through the intestinal walls to be carried to all parts of the body.)

9. Do you think this article has more facts or opinions? Was it written to inform or to persuade?

Writing Activities

1. Write two new things you learned about the digestive system.

2. Write about any information in this article that can be useful in your daily life.

Additional Activities

1. Ask students what other systems are in the body. Can students name any body parts that belong to the skeletal system, the respiratory system, the nervous system, and/or the circulatory system? Pictures illustrating the other systems would enhance the lesson.

2. What are "empty calories"? Why is it important to eat food that is useful to our bodies?

3. Bring in a copy of the "Food Guide Pyramid" showing the relative amounts recommended for each of the six food groups: 1) bread, cereal, rice, pasta; 2) fruit; 3) vegetables; 4) meat, poultry, fish, dry beans, eggs, nuts; 5) milk, yogurt, cheese; 6) fats, oil, sweets. List foods on slips of paper and ask students to sort them into food groups. Ask students to plan a meal using one item from each group.

Exercises

2 **More about Digestion**

During the preview, be sure students understand the two parts to this exercise. First, they are to write the four body parts in order. Then, they are to describe briefly how each aids digestion.

3 **Cause and Effect**

During the preview, explain that an effect is a result. Advise students to number each effect with the number of the corresponding cause before writing the effects on the lines provided.

Lesson 20: Nail Soup

Primary emphasis
- Literal/inferential/applied comprehension
- Phonics, word analysis, and context clues
- New vocabulary
- Writing and study skills
- Reading a menu

Secondary emphasis
- Oral reading and listening skills
- Synonyms and antonyms
- Using context clues
- Word endings

Pre-reading Activities

1. Unlike the nonfiction articles in the rest of this book, this is a well-known folktale. After reading the title, ask if anyone is familiar with the story. (There is also a version called "Stone Soup.") Discuss some of the differences between fiction and nonfiction.

2. Ask students to think of stories they have heard about a clever person living by his or her wits. There are many examples in fairy tales, fables, and folk stories. There are also examples in history and in the news today.

Post-reading Activities

1. Discuss the questions in Exercise 1.

2. Have students underline in different colors the text of this story according to speaking parts. The speaking parts are the old woman (Granny), the stranger, and the neighbor Martha. Any lines not in quotation marks can be read by a narrator. Have students practice reading the parts in groups of four students. Then have volunteers read it for the class.

Ask or say:

3. Did the story turn out the way you thought it would? What was the point of the story?

4. Was the little old lady on her guard against anyone taking advantage of her? Was she a hard worker? Why do you think so?

5. Do you think the stranger had a plan in mind before he met the old lady? Do you think it was the first or only time he made nail soup?

6. Do you think the woman would have helped the young stranger if he had told her he was hungry? Why or why not?

7. Find the place in the story where Granny begins to change her attitude.

8. Do you think the old woman understood what the stranger was doing?

9. The young man said he always earns his dinner. Do you think he earned the nail soup? Why or why not?

Writing Activities

1. Write about something someone did or said that you consider clever.

2. Write about something you do now that you didn't do when you started *Challenger 4.*

Additional Activities

1. Read another story about someone clever who lived by his or her wits. Some sources are fairy tales, fables, folk stories, and human interest news stories. New Readers Press publishes a series of such stories titled *Timeless Tales.*

2. This is the last lesson in *Challenger 4.* Review students' goals and discuss their progress. Look back at some of the writing students have done since beginning the book.

Exercises

2 May I Take Your Order?

There is no one right answer for questions 3, 4, and 5. Accept any answers that make sense.

3 Same or Opposite?

Encourage students to use a dictionary for any items that give them difficulty.

Review: Lessons 1–20

The purpose of this review is to give students one more opportunity to work with many of the concepts emphasized in Book 4. Preview each exercise as usual. Advise students to refer to the lessons for answers they don't remember.

After going over the review, discuss what students have learned and accomplished while working in *Challenger 4.* Help students to plan and prepare for some sort of celebration.

Answer Key for Book 1

Lesson 1

1 **Copying Sentences**
See student text.

2 **Word Sounds**
1. Tim, time
2. tube, tub
3. not, note
4. can, cane
5. quit, quite

Lesson 2

1 **Copying Sentences**
See student text.

2 **Word Sounds**
1. huge
2. cut
3. met
4. us
5. cope
6. rode
7. hopes
8. at

Lesson 3

1 **Word Sounds**
1. mad, mud, made
2. hot, hates, hat
3. six, sit, sip
4. cop, cope, cup
5. man, men, mine
6. us, fuse, used
7. at, as, am
8. late, dates, Kate
9. pet, pep, pen

2 **Marking the Vowels**
1. fīr¢
2. sĭp
3. cān¢
4. nīc¢
5. wōk¢
6. sŭn
7. hōl¢
8. bĕd
9. āt¢
10. ūs¢
11. mē
12. lĭd
13. jăb
14. cūt¢
15. kēep
16. rūl¢

Lesson 4

1 **Word Sounds**
1. cute
2. tub
3. rod
4. Cape
5. ripe
6. rid
7. wine
8. fad
9. hope
10. fuss
11. let
12. feel
13. hot
14. ham
15. feed

2 **Yes or No**
Answers will vary.

Lesson 5

1 **Adding -ed**
1. looked
2. lasted
3. talked
4. asked
5. messed
6. relaxed
1. faced
2. saved
3. joked
4. hired
5. lined
6. refused
1. hopped
2. sipped
3. patted
4. gunned
5. popped
6. sobbed

2 **Word Sounds**
1. phone
2. bus
3. sale
4. bed
5. pan
6. red
7. cane
8. hut
9. bone
10. hugs
11. horn
12. name
13. park
14. lap

Lesson 6

1 **Adding -ed**
1. called
2. hunted
3. landed
4. walked
5. dumped
6. mended
1. baked
2. named
3. liked
4. dated
5. tired
6. hoped
1. robbed
2. kidded
3. ripped
4. netted
5. topped
6. rammed

2 **Word Sounds**
1. sick
2. sent
3. hunt
4. damp
5. ducked
6. hand
7. kick
8. pond
9. sent
10. neck
11. end

Lesson 7

1 **Adding -ing**
1. going
2. fixing
3. singing
4. looking
5. missing
1. taking
2. having
3. baking
4. joking
5. hoping
1. running
2. sipping
3. patting
4. jabbing
5. hopping

Lesson 8

1 **Word Sounds**
1. code
2. fox
3. dam
4. pad
5. dive
6. tame
7. rate
8. dined

2 **Using a and an**
1. an
2. a
3. a
4. an
5. an
6. a
7. a
8. a
9. an
10. an

3 **Marking the Vowels**
1. fūm¢
2. lĕss
3. nĕck
4. rōb¢
5. tĭck
6. hănd
7. sŏck
8. sāf¢
9. quĭck
10. cĕnt
11. mīnd
12. rēfūs¢
13. ŭs
14. bēef
15. fēmāl¢

4 **Words That Mean the Same**
1. huge
2. keep
3. seek
4. honk
5. six
6. jab
7. fix
8. fun
9. weep
10. females

5 **Writing Sentences**
Answers will vary.

Lesson 9

1 **Adding -y to Words**
1. messy
2. fussy
3. bumpy
4. needy
5. robbery
1. icy
2. nosy
3. lacy
4. bony
5. wiry
1. funny
2. sunny
3. Mommy
4. Daddy
5. nutty

Lesson 2 (Word Sounds)

2 **Word Sounds**
1. sat
2. hen
3. pig
4. zone
5. rat
6. side
7. dot
8. nuts
9. pale
10. dump
11. file
12. pick
13. lump
14. fond
15. band

2 Words That End in -ly
1. quickly   4. friendly
2. lovely   5. weekly
3. safely

3 Words That End in -y
1. baby   6. Andy
2. candy   7. muddy
3. sixty   8. handy
4. lobby   9. forty
5. ninety   10. Bucky

4 Words That Mean the Same
1. hide   7. joke
2. behind   8. refuse
3. ten cents   9. funny
4. male   10. jack
5. not happy   11. Sunday
6. mock   12. Saturday

Lesson 10

1 Word Sounds
1. gas, pass
2. fact, acts
3. None, one, done
4. knew, few, new
5. right, lights, night
6. see, fee, knee
7. wrote, note, vote
8. heck, neck, wreck
9. dock, locked, knock
10. lay, way, day

2 Word Opposites
1. night   6. huge
2. last   7. wrong
3. back   8. play
4. bad   9. there
5. sad   10. same

3 Word Study
1. yesterday   6. females
2. friend   7. wine
3. foot   8. numb
4. ant   9. cot
5. sun   10. fit

Lesson 11

1 Adding -er to Words
1. quicker   1. finer   1. bigger
2. tighter   2. ruder   2. fatter
3. fewer   3. cuter   3. hotter
4. boxer   4. baker   4. winter
5. hunter   5. later   5. hitter
6. burner   6. diner   6. mugger

2 Words That End in -er
1. bumper   5. pepper
2. hammer   6. ruler
3. Copper   7. worker
4. summer   8. better, better

3 Changing y to i and Adding -er
handier   1. luckier
happier   2. happier
luckier   3. lovelier
lovelier   4. fussier
fussier   5. bumpier
bumpier   6. handier

4 Who Does What?
1. a hunter   5. a banker
2. a writer   6. a fighter
3. a singer   7. a player
4. a joker   8. a thinker

Lesson 12

1 Context Clues

five, work, house
eat, meat, boiled, tea, mug, fork
soap, water, night (water, soap, night)

2 Word Sounds
1. deer   8. peas   15. mouse
2. road   9. soak   16. coals
3. due   10. moon   17. main
4. far   11. pain   18. dirt
5. barn   12. foot   19. bored
6. ails   13. maid   20. hard
7. load   14. real

3 Writing Sentences
Answers will vary.

Lesson 13

1 Word Sounds
1. moon   11. meal   21. lean
2. noon   12. mean   22. lead
3. soon   13. code   23. leaf
4. mail   14. cope   24. worn
5. main   15. cone   25. horn
6. maid   16. tore   26. corn
7. carve   17. sore   27. torn
8. cart   18. wore   28. born
9. card   19. more
10. meat   20. leak

2 Words That End in -er
1. painter   4. boarder   7. helper
2. keeper   5. voter   8. teacher
3. catcher   6. diner

3 Word Study
1. head   6. air
2. year   7. food
3. pear   8. tea
4. dice   9. fake
5. oven   10. wages

4 Marking the Vowels
1. ădd   9. fūmȩ
2. bītȩ   10. rēēl
3. gātȩ   11. hīkȩ
4. dămp   12. hŭnt
5. sĕnd   13. dōzȩ
6. clŏck   14. dŭnk
7. pŏp   15. zōnȩ
8. sāmȩ   16. dĕck

Lesson 14

1 The Ending -ful
handful   1. useful
harmful   2. handful
helpful   3. helpful
careful   4. harmful
useful   5. careful
thankful   6. thankful

2 The Ending -less
harmless   1. jobless
helpless   2. careless
hopeless   3. homeless
homeless   4. harmless
careless   5. hopeless
jobless   6. helpless

3 Words That Mean the Same
1. carve   6. shout
2. ill   7. hurt
3. handy   8. bare
4. film   9. poor
5. soaked   10. dead

4 Word Opposites
1. cold   6. messy
2. start   7. others
3. day   8. false
4. worse   9. dumb
5. take   10. harmless

5 Sayings
1. told   6. hills
2. call   7. ball
3. cold   8. will
4. bell   9. fall
5. milk   10. fill

Lesson 15

1 The Ending -est
1. nearest	1. finest	1. biggest
2. cheapest	2. safest	2. hottest
3. richest	3. rudest	3. fattest
4. smartest	4. ripest	4. maddest
5. loudest	5. latest	5. reddest

2 Changing y to i and Adding -est
funniest	1. loveliest
happiest	2. fussiest
luckiest	3. luckiest
fussiest	4. happiest
loveliest	5. funniest

3 Word Sounds
1. chess	5. wall	9. Last
2. odd	6. loaf	10. well
3. sharp	7. case	
4. talked	8. vote	

4 Words That Mean the Same
1. wish	5. queer	9. two
2. drop	6. faint	10. must
3. torn	7. chair	
4. tug	8. boring	

Lesson 16

1 Word Sounds
1. mouse, house	17. bleached, beach
2. blouse	18. rage
3. coast	19. stage
4. toast	20. page
5. roast	21. plain, pain
6. flew	22. stains
7. new	23. shame, lame
8. blew	24. blamed, same
9. pale	25. rush, slush
10. stale	26. blush
11. tales	27. platter, shattered
12. slip	28. matter
13. dip	29. map
14. ship	30. clapped
15. each	31. nap, slap
16. reach	

2 Compound Words
1. downtown	6. lifeboat
2. baseball	7. weekend
3. football	8. homework
4. cupcakes	9. household
5. cookbook	10. sunshine

3 Writing Sentences
Answers will vary.

Lesson 17

1 Word Sounds
1. blow	9. chest, vests	17. clay, may
2. flow	10. pests	18. prayed, hay
3. slow, row	11. clown, gown, brown	19. drops, stopped
4. price	12. trunk	20. crops
5. pride, prizes	13. truck	21. gum, plums
6. toast	14. trust	22. drum
7. taste, tested	15. harming	
8. best	16. farm, charming	

2 Putting Words into Classes
Town	School	Farm
bus stops	classes	barn
churches	courses	cows
parks	homework	crops
stores	reading	hay
street lights	teachers	hens

3 Best and Least
Answers will vary.

Lesson 18

1 Word Sounds
1. lift	9. grilled	17. lit
2. left	10. chill	18. fibs
3. gift	11. dare	19. bib, crib
4. shift	12. fare	20. ribs
5. math, bath	13. spare	21. coach
6. path	14. flares	22. coast
7. hill	15. spit	23. coals
8. spilled	16. pit	

2 Numbers
1. eighteen	11. seven
2. twenty	12. twelve
3. fifteen	13. Answers may vary.
4. fifteen	14. four (or five counting the spare)
5. sixteen	15. Answers will vary.
6. eleven	16. Answers will vary.
7. fifteen	17. Answers will vary.
8. seven	18. Answers will vary.
9. four	19. Answers will vary.
10. thirteen	20. nine

3 Compound Words
1. armchair	6. bedroom
2. sunburn	7. checkbook
3. bathroom	8. shortstop
4. notebook	9. pancakes
5. popcorn	10. downstairs

Lesson 19

1 Word Sounds

1. list	4. math	7. spilled	10. threw
2. flops	5. egg	8. fork	11. cream
3. boss	6. other	9. wipe	12. snow

2 Colors

1. white	3. red	5. black	7. blue
2. Pink	4. green	6. brown	8. gold

3 Which Word Does Not Fit?

1. drive	4. body	7. shrimp	10. yard
2. bedroom	5. raw	8. Christmas	11. slacks
3. neck	6. whale	9. number	12. dune

4 Words That Begin with *un-*

unsafe   1. unhappy
unless   2. unless
unlucky   3. unlucky
unhappy   4. unsafe
unwrapped   5. unwrapped

5 Words That Begin with *re-*

refuse   1. return
remain   2. repaid
remind   3. refuse
repaid   4. remind
return   5. remain

Lesson 20

1 Word Sounds

1. found, ground	7. carve, starve
2. step	8. but, butter
3. marry	9. sweating, sweater
4. pity, city	10. crawl
5. steep	11. hard, hardly
6. Ms., Miss, Ms., Mrs.	12. stood, wood, hood

2 Putting Words into Classes

Breakfast	Dinner	Snacks
corn flakes	pork chops	candy bar
French toast	rice and beans	Coke
fried eggs	roast beef	ice cream cone
ham and eggs	spare ribs	popcorn
pancakes	stuffed peppers	pretzels

3 Twelve Questions

1. true	7. false
2. true	8. true
3. false	9. true
4. Either true or false	10. false
5. false	11. false
6. false	12. Answers will vary.

4 Writing Sentences

Answers will vary.

First Review

1 Choosing the Right Answer

1. bull	4. tall	7. heart	10. been
2. vase	5. Coast	8. ear	11. care
3. sick	6. close	9. anywhere	12. bless

2 Words That Mean the Same

1. scrub	5. cash	9. gleam
2. swift	6. crazy	10. patch
3. useful	7. strange	
4. mock	8. faint	

3 Word Opposites

1. tired	6. awake
2. fire	7. thick
3. answer	8. calm
4. waste	9. tame
5. huge	10. loaf

4 Using *a* and *an*

1. an	6. an
2. a	7. a
3. an	8. a
4. an	9. a
5. an	10. a

5 Putting Words in Classes

Land	Sky	Water
cities	fog	boats
farms	moon	fish
houses	rain	ships
weeds	snow	waves
woods	stars	whales

Second Review

1 Choosing the Right Answer

1. helpless	5. That's	9. unsafe
2. handful	6. I've	10. guilty
3. sadly	7. Didn't	
4. cellar	8. writer	

2 Numbers

1. twelve	6. seven
2. seven	7. sixteen
3. sixty	8. two
4. Answers will vary.	9. one
5. thirteen	10. millions

3 Which Word Fits Best?

1. father	3. pig	5. worst	7. ceiling
2. slacks	4. hushed	6. upset	8. snail

4 Word Pairs

1. salt and pepper	7. reading and writing
2. bride and groom	8. rod and reel
3. Saturday and Sunday	9. black and blue
4. knife and fork	10. cats and dogs
5. ham and eggs	11. snakes and snails
6. soap and water	12. thick and thin

5 Writing Sentences

Answers will vary.

Answer Key for Book 2

Lesson 1

1 About the Reading

1. People cover their noses when they sneeze so their germs won't go all over the room.
2. When somebody sneezes, people often say, "God bless you."
3. dust, cat hairs, weeds, black pepper, colds (any three)
4. 17 years old
5. 6 months
6. Answers will vary.

2 Word Sounds

1. cape	shape	6. blob	snob
grape		job	
shape		snob	
2. drink	think	7. blown	known
stink		grown	
think		known	
3. change	change	8. smelling	Smelling
range		spelling	
strange		swelling	
4. chew	grew	9. broke	smoke
grew		choke	
knew		smoke	
5. cries	tries	10. bluffed	stuffed
dries		puffed	
tries		stuffed	

3 Matching

1. hearing
2. seeing
3. touching
4. tasting
5. smelling

4 Marking the e's

1. thēsé
2. ĕnd
3. aloné
4. blēēd
5. harmlĕss
6. nĕxt
7. uséful
8. pancaké
9. rēmind
10. swĕat
11. closé
12. choosé

5 Words That Sound the Same

1. I, eye
2. hear, here
3. Two, to
4. Dear, deer
5. four, for
6. knows, nose

Lesson 2

1 About the Reading

1. United States
2. more than 28 million
3. $415,000
4. doctor
5. Cats can see better in dim light.
6. Answers will vary.

2 Word Sounds

1. brand	stand	6. shrill	shrill
grand		skill	
stand		spill	
2. creeps	creeps	7. brown	crown
jeeps		clown	
sleeps		crown	
3. fang	slang	8. paw	paw
sang		raw	
slang		straw	
4. bean	mean	9. cow	Now
clean		how	
mean		now	
5. clear	hear	10. sends	spends
hear		spends	
near		tends	

3 Putting Words in Classes

List A — Cats	List B — Dogs
always land on their feet	barking
climbing trees	chasing cars
nine lives	digging up bones
purring	man's best friend

4 Words That Sound the Same

1. By, buy
2. knew, new
3. ate, eight
4. Do, due
5. Our, hour

Lesson 3

1 About the Reading

1. seven years
2. Rome
3. dead
4. You will have seven years bad luck.
5. Every cell is renewed.
6. Answers will vary, depending on how heavily one smokes.

2 Word Sounds

1. blink	think	6. dated	stated
drink		plated	
think		stated	
2. brave	brave	7. bone	throne
cave		cone	
wave		throne	
3. blame	game	8. chart	part
game		part	
frame		start	
4. blink	drink	9. cheek	week
drink		peek	
stink		week	
5. dice	dice	10. chins	sins
price		grins	
spice		sins	

3 Word Sounds

Cow	Slow
clown	blow
crowd	grown
how	know
now	show
wow	snow

4 Number Words

1. twenty-four
2. thirty-one
3. thirty
4. fifty
5. forty
6. twenty-five
7. Answers will vary.
8. Answers will vary.
9. Answers will vary, depending on state law.
10. Answers will vary, depending on state law.

Lesson 4

1 About the Reading

1. pub
2. pint and quart
3. He gave away 30,000 gallons of beer as a gift to the gods.
4. They had run out of beer, which served as food, and they needed to find more food.
5. Beer left in sunlight turns cloudy and takes on a funny smell and taste.
6. People who really like beer say it should be served with a head on it.
7. "Minding your p's and q's" means being careful or watching your step.
8. 1620

2 Word Sounds

1. brewed	brewed	5. ate	ate
chewed		date	
stewed		state	
2. colds	holds	6. found	pound
folds		pound	
holds		sound	
3. change	strange	7. dunes	prunes
range		prunes	
strange		tunes	
4. beans	beans	8. cream	cream
jeans		dream	
means		stream	

3 Word Sounds

1. stairs, pair, chairs
2. proud, cloud, loud
3. brave, waves, cave
4. cried, tried, dried
5. hear, clear, near
6. range, change, strange
7. mean, beans, jeans
8. lunch, munched, bunch
9. trick, bricks, stick
10. shape, cape, grape

4 Smallest and Biggest

1. second	hour
2. day	month
3. city	country
4. hundred	million
5. shrimp	human being
6. ounce	quart
7. pint	gallon
8. light bulb	sun
9. bike	ship
10. shrimp	roast beef
11. chestnut	tree
12. Rome	world

5 Word Opposites

1. clear
2. ugly
3. anger
4. children
5. always
6. grew
7. sea
8. saved
9. change
10. brand-new

Lesson 5

1 About the Reading

1. 1875
2. scribe
3. 1,875,000
4. 1,984,000
5. Answers will vary.
6. Answers will vary. Acceptable answers include that people did not have telephones and that visiting people who lived some distance away was more difficult in the 1800s than it is today.

2 Word Sounds

1. telling
2. passed
3. mail
4. life
5. six
6. more
7. vowels
8. such
9. still
10. song

3 Who Does What?

1. cab driver
2. baseball player
3. teacher
4. doctor
5. cowboy
6. tailor
7. clown
8. painter
9. preacher
10. scribe

4 Words That Sound the Same

1. write, right
2. whole, hole
3. beat, beet
4. fare, fair
5. meet, meat
6. heard, herd
7. sale, sails
8. won, one

5 Marking Vowels

1. frām¢
2. brănd
3. ōwn
4. pīnt
5. cāv¢
6. grĭn
7. tĕnd
8. măss
9. trĭck
10. spĕnd
11. spīc¢
12. thrōn¢

Review: Lessons 1-5

1 Choosing the Answer
1. fifty
2. talk
3. sense
4. lace
5. mate
6. meant
7. blob
8. bluffing
9. renew
10. deadly

2 Number Words
1. seven
2. fifty-two
3. sixteen
4. eight
5. two
6. two
7. four
8. thirteen
9. fifty
10. seven
11. 19__-1620 = the answer.
12. One thousand

3 Facts
1. sight
2. hearing
3. taste
4. touch
5. smell

Lesson 6

1 About the Reading
1. wool, animal hair, gold
2. bee's wax
3. He began to lose his hair at an early age.
4. These wigs were huge, covering people's backs and floating down over their chests.
5. 12 years
6. Many years ago in Egypt, the bigger a person's wig was, the more important the person was.
7. Answers will vary.

2 Word Sounds
1. shave
2. bangs
3. hair
4. which
5. Feeling
6. Fighting
7. bugs
8. stand
9. scares
10. takes

3 Which Word Does Not Fit?
1. month
2. English
3. catbird
4. scribe
5. start
6. Anne
7. queen
8. wrist
9. cure
10. pound

4 Vowel Sounds

Long Sound for *ea*	Short Sound for *ea*
1. bean	1. bread
2. beat	2. breakfast
3. easy	3. dead
4. please	4. instead
5. squeak	5. sweat

5 Compound Words
1. bath + room
2. big + wig
3. break + fast
4. cat + bird
5. check + book
6. every + thing
7. ginger + bread
8. girl + friend
9. short + stop
10. sun + burn

Lesson 7

1 About the Reading
1. The liquid comes from two pouches under the skunk's tail.
2. A skunk can spray his liquid from a range of ten to twelve feet.
3. He has to wait one week before he can spray again.
4. A skunk sprays his liquid to ward off danger.
5. He faces whatever he thinks is chasing him.
   He stamps his forefeet.
   He raises all but the tip of his tail.
   He raises the tip of his tail and sprays his liquid.
6. You can bathe in tomato juice.

2 Words That Mean the Same
1. munch
2. hidden
3. creep
4. dim
5. sprint
6. touch
7. bluff
8. friendly
9. trouble
10. form

3 Word Opposites
1. a nobody
2. late
3. hard
4. nothing
5. sink
6. stand
7. find
8. forget
9. saved
10. lovely

4 Compound Words
1. bed + room
2. blood + stream
3. cow + boy
4. home + work
5. May + flower
6. note + book
7. side + ways
8. some + one
9. sun + light
10. what + ever

5 Silly Verses
1. state, straight, sky, cry, dates
2. France, pants, tried, cried, dance
3. sour, hour, life *or* wife, life *or* wife, shower

Lesson 8

1 About the Reading
1. Otherwise the older baby chicks might kill the younger ones.
2. They are timing their hatching.
3. Air must get into the eggshell.
4. Someone in the first book of the Bible thinks the chicken came first.
5. The man who wrote this story thinks the egg came first.
6. In this story, *clutch* means a brood of baby chicks or a group of eggs.
7. *Clutch* can also mean a pedal on a standard shift vehicle, a strong grasp, or to hold tightly.

2 Word Sounds

1.	laying paying saying	laying	6.	fail mail pail	fail
2.	shell smell spell	shell	7.	bust dust just	just
3.	pounds rounds sounds	pounds	8.	bends lends spends	spends
4.	bite kite white	white	9.	cared glared scared	scared
5.	claw raw thaw	raw	10.	hatch patch scratch	hatch

3 Which Word Fits Best?

1. glass
2. sky
3. pack
4. upset
5. England
6. Wednesday
7. armchair
8. foot
9. school
10. lung

4 Compound Words

1. babysit
2. copycat
3. handwriting
4. hideout
5. lifetime
6. necktie
7. nickname
8. rainbow
9. touchdown
10. wristwatch

1. touchdown
2. necktie
3. wristwatch
4. hideout
5. copycat
6. handwriting
7. babysit
8. nickname
9. rainbow
10. lifetime

5 Word Sounds

Book	School
1. foot	1. groom
2. hood	2. pool
3. took	3. shoot
4. wood	4. spoon
5. wool	5. tooth

Lesson 9

1 About the Reading

1. California
2. John Sutter
3. 1849
4. forty-niners
5. one ounce

2 Word Sounds

1.	bread dead spread	spread	5.	leans cleans means	means
2.	bought fought thought	thought	6.	boil soil spoil	soil
3.	blind find mind	find	7.	beached preached reached	preached
4.	fool's cool's pool's	fool's	8.	leaks sneaks speaks	speaks

3 Vowels + the letter /

1. belt
2. tall
3. roll
4. milk
5. gold
6. bulb
7. wall
8. bell
9. cold
10. bald
11. Jill, hill

4 Marking the Vowels

1. līc¢
2. egghĕad
3. wăx
4. wĭthĭn
5. flōat
6. rēason
7. rāis¢
8. grāv¢
9. knēē-dēēp
10. nĕst
11. Frănc¢
12. brāk¢
13. betwēēn
14. jŭst
15. hătch
16. tĭp
17. sĭnc¢
18. wēak

5 Matching

1. coffee
2. peach
3. chocolate
4. bigwig
5. yolk
6. March
7. kneel
8. lice
9. news
10. hangover

Lesson 10

1 About the Reading

1. Boston
2. 1760
3. No
4. to carry soup
5. to taste the soup before the queen tried it
6. They ran off to get married.
7. The rhymes had been around for hundreds of years before they were called Mother Goose rhymes.
8. Answers will vary. Children like their rhymes, rhythms, and content.

2 Word Sounds

1. born	horn	6. block	clock	
corn		clock		
horn		shock		
2. die	pie	7. door	door	
pie		poor		
tie		floor		
3. close	nose	8. free	three	
nose		three		
rose		tree		
4. bed	bed	9. cane	lane	
fed		crane		
red		lane		
5. feet	street	10. drum	plum	
sheet		plum		
street		slum		

3 Which Word Does Not Fit?

1. California	6. leaves	11. cowboys
2. snow	7. ice	12. smoker
3. spring	8. straw	13. beach
4. pound	9. air	14. punt
5. eggs	10. wool	

4 Silent Letters

1. knit	5. wrong	9. meant
2. breath	6. thumb	10. heart
3. clutch	7. wrist	11. lamb
4. crane	8. climb	12. watch

5 Words That Sound the Same

1. red, read	5. bear, bare
2. see, sea	6. way, weigh
3. weak, week	7. break, brake
4. through, threw	8. sense, cents

Review: Lessons 1-10

1 Choosing the Answer

1. soundly	6. sin
2. though	7. main
3. shame	8. spoil
4. peeped	9. guess
5. burp	10. hunch

2 Words That Mean the Same

1. shut	5. spoil	9. melt
2. glitter	6. break	10. slim
3. tease	7. dirt	11. rhyme
4. guide	8. brake	12. during

3 Word Opposites

1. death	5. thaw	9. forgot
2. cloudy	6. evening	10. crooked
3. rare	7. messy	11. weak
4. against	8. shut	12. lies

Lesson 11

1 About the Reading

1. We are trying to draw in more air.
2. a. Body heat goes down.
   b. Brain waves become more even.
3. a. The heart rate slows down.
   b. The body relaxes.
   c. Breathing becomes very even.
4. Most dreaming happens during the deepest stage of sleep called REM.
5. You would take quite a few seconds to move.
6. You would probably become quite sick.
7. Answers will vary. Everyone dreams. Dreams are often related to recent events or needs the dreamer has.
8. Answers will vary.

2 Word Sounds

1. paws, claws
2. thaws, straw
3. jaw, law
4. dawn, lawn
5. pawns, yawn
6. lawful, awful

3 Long and Short Vowels

1. breathe		4. scrap	
breath		scrape	
2. bathe		5. gripe	
bath		grip	
3. tap		6. twin	
tape		twine	

4 Putting Words in Order

1. Mr. Clark couldn't go to sleep.
2. First he tried counting sheep.
3. Then he fixed himself a cup of tea.
4. He still couldn't fall asleep.
5. The next day he was fired for sleeping on the job.

Lesson 12

1 About the Reading

1. 10,000
2. a. queen lays eggs
   b. workers build hives, get food, and care for the young
   c. drones mate with the queen
3. queen and workers
4. drone
5. worker
6. in the fall
7. Drones mate with the queen so she can produce worker eggs.
8. They starve to death.
9. It would not survive because the queen couldn't lay worker eggs.

2 Word Sounds

1. brands   glands
   glands
   lands
2. buck   suck
   suck
   tuck
3. dive   hive
   five
   hive
4. gives   gives
   lives

5. fly   fly
   shy
   try
6. ground   pound
   pound
   round
7. honey   honey
   money
8. Drunks   Skunks
   Punks
   Skunks

3 Words That End in -y

1. sleepy
2. watery
3. sticky
4. corny
5. creepy
6. worthy

1. spicy
2. shiny
3. noisy
4. bouncy
5. flaky
6. wavy

1. sunny
2. snappy
3. piggy
4. kitty
5. buddy
6. foggy

4 Words That End in -ly

1. brotherly
2. calmly
3. nearly
4. sharply
5. bravely
6. weekly
7. barely
8. lonely
9. cheaply
10. commonly

5 Common Sayings

1. bat
2. bee
3. gold
4. lark
5. the nose on your face
6. beet
7. snail
8. fox
9. sheet
10. kite

Lesson 13

1 About the Reading

1. a. He looks at the slant.
   b. He studies the direction of the writing line.
   c. He studies the size and width of the letters.
2. a. false   d. false
   b. true   e. false
   c. true   f. true
3. a. Answers will vary.
   b. Answers will vary.
   c. Answers will vary.
   d. Answers will vary.
4. Answers will vary.
5. Answers will vary.

2 Words That Mean the Same

1. employer
2. large
3. barely
4. allow
5. bright
6. certain
7. present
8. double
9. marry
10. scream

3 Word Opposites

1. asleep
2. sunny
3. birth
4. uphill
5. bright
6. begin
7. won
8. young
9. yesterday
10. summer

4 Vowel Sounds

Star	Air	Ear
1. are	1. bear	1. beer
2. carve	2. fair	2. dear
3. hard	3. stare	3. deer
4. heart	4. their	4. here
5. march	5. wear	5. peer

Lesson 14

1 About the Reading

1. 1863
2. a. They had nowhere to go.
   b. They had nothing to live on.
   c. They had no background in looking out for themselves.
   d. They had nothing to work with.
3. The crowd wasn't prepared to handle all the rain and the ex-slaves didn't know what to do with their freedom.
4. Answers will vary.

2 Choosing the Right Heading

Farms   Baseball   Soups   War
Games   School   Lights   Christmas
Snacks   Water

3 Words That End in -er

1. sticker
2. hanger
3. heater
4. cracker
5. mower
1. miner
2. diver
3. maker
4. dancer
5. freezer
1. trapper
2. batter
3. dipper
4. zipper
5. swimmer

4 More Words That End in -er

1. coaster
2. dresser
3. folder
4. rubber
5. campers
6. slippers
7. corner
8. lighter
9. poker
10. checkers

5 Putting Sentences in Order

1. When I was fifteen years old, I was put up on the block for sale.
2. A white man was there who was very rich and mean and owned many slaves.
3. He was so mean that many white and black people hated him.
4. When he bid for me, I talked right out on the block.
5. "If you bid for me, I will take a knife and cut myself from ear to ear before I would be owned by you."

Lesson 15

1 About the Reading

1. Hold Fast, Saw Tooth, Wrap Around, Brink Twist, Necktie (any three)
2. He gold-plated them and sold them to a big store.
3. Their main goal is to own at least one strand of every kind of barbed wire ever made.
4. a. The doctor gets into his helicopter.
   b. He flies over miles of fence looking for barbed wire.
   c. He sees something that looks good.
   d. He sets his helicopter down in a field.
   e. He takes out his wire cutters and snips off a strand.
5. the way they looked.
6. farmers
7. They used it to keep cattle away from their crops.

2 Words That Rhyme

1. cold, gold, folded, sold
2. brink, drink, sink, stink
3. tent, bent, went, rent
4. Mack, rack, lacked, sack
5. cared, share, bare, spare
6. Sutter, utter, cutters, butter
7. tucked, stuck, sucked, luck
8. king, bring, sting, sing
9. wiped, griped, swiped, ripe
10. crook, look, hook, book

3 How Do You Say It?

1. flock
2. loaf
3. deck
4. pack
5. pot
6. herd
7. school
8. batch
9. bunch
10. quart
11. pair
12. can
13. bar
14. book
15. load

Review: Lessons 1-15

1 Choosing the Answer

1. sticky
2. flaky
3. foggy
4. repaid
5. filed
6. crosses
7. nowhere
8. grouches
9. batter
10. bid
11. grape
12. drones
13. Fourth of July
14. North and South

2 Silent Letters

1. wrote
2. dumb
3. badge
4. Dutch
5. young
6. build
7. knee
8. dodge
9. batch
10. writer
11. witch
12. certain

3 Matching

1. rainbow
2. oven
3. mower
4. towel
5. fence
6. stamp
7. alphabet
8. piggy
9. wax
10. pepper

4 Word Sounds

1. whose
2. certain
3. allow
4. bath
5. soup
6. heading
7. flood
8. ginger

5 Compound Words

1. lipstick
2. babysitter
3. sunglasses
4. ashtray
5. firecrackers
6. overdone
7. stagecoach
8. cheesecake
9. underline
10. busybody

Lesson 16

1 About the Reading

1.

	Fish	Whales
a. Breathing	in the water	out of the water
b. Blood	cold-blooded	warm-blooded
c. Birth	lay eggs	young are born alive

2. Cold-blooded means the temperature of the blood changes as the temperature of the environment changes.
3. Warm-blooded means the temperature of the blood stays the same even when the temperature of the environment changes.
4. a. true   g. true
   b. true   h. true
   c. false   i. false
   d. true   j. true
   e. false   k. true
   f. false
5. Answers will vary. Frequently such animals are declared endangered species and killing them is forbidden.

2 Changing the y to i

1. busier   busiest
2. noisier   noisiest
3. happier   happiest
4. luckier   luckiest
5. sleepier sleepiest

3 Changing the y to i

1. happily
2. busily
3. noisily
4. sleepily
5. Luckily

4 Silly Little Stories

1. swear, sweater, sweat, swell
2. lot, lost, locked, loss
3. Dan, dam, dashed, damp
4. band, bank, bang, banker
5. crust, crushed (or crunched), crumbs, crunched (or crushed)
6. witch, without, wished, wings, winked

5 Which Word Fits Best?

1. people
2. mammal
3. find
4. horses
5. flower
6. football
7. cow
8. wood
9. tomorrow
10. hardly ever

Lesson 17

1 About the Reading

1. Charles
2. eight years
3. more than thirty
4. teaching
5. about two thousand dollars
6. He intended only to scare the driver.
7. a. He made careful plans.
   b. He always worked alone.
   c. He never held up stagecoaches near home.
   d. He never told anyone about his plans.
8. A teacher earned about one thousand dollars.
9. Answers may vary.

2 Words That Mean the Same

1. limbs
2. bold
3. earn
4. clue
5. robbery
6. alive
7. all right
8. cause
9. high-class
10. ton

3 Word Opposites

1. under
2. dozed
3. scared
4. full
5. awful
6. harmful
7. leave
8. fresh
9. froze
10. cool

4 The Ending -ful

1. successful
2. truthful
3. mouthful
4. thoughtful
5. sinful
6. cupful
7. forgetful
8. hopeful
9. wasteful
10. spiteful

5 A Verse from Black Bart

This is the way I get my money and <u>bread</u>.
   When I have a <u>chance</u>, why should I refuse it?
I'll not need either when I'm <u>dead</u>,
   And I only tax those who are <u>able</u> to lose it.

So <u>blame</u> me not for what I've done,
   I don't deserve your <u>curses</u>.
And if for some cause I must be <u>hung</u>,
   Let it be for my <u>verses</u>.

Lesson 18

1 About the Reading

1. The earth is more than two billion years old.
2. They can tell the age of the rocks that make up the earth's crust.
3. The heavy matter in the center of the earth is liquid iron.
4. Life began in the ocean.
5. a. The earth was a ball of hot whirling gases.
   b. The gases began to turn into liquid form.
   c. The outer shell of the earth changed from liquid to solid.
   d. The rains fell.
   e. Oceans and seas filled with water.
   f. One-celled forms came into being.
   g. Worms and starfish came into being.

2 Word Sounds

1. sprinted, spray, sprawled, sprained
2. stranger, strong, streets, strike
3. swung, swiftly, swimming, switch
4. scraped, screen, screamed, scrubbing
5. squirrel, squeezed, square, squirt

3 The Ending -less

1. sleeveless
2. breathless
3. sleepless
4. worthless
5. thoughtless
6. meatless
7. cloudless
8. useless
9. hairless
10. Needless

4 Same or Opposite?

1. same
2. same
3. same
4. opposite
5. opposite
6. same
7. same
8. opposite
9. opposite
10. same
11. opposite
12. same
13. opposite
14. opposite

5 Spelling Check

1. March
2. crown
3. universe
4. stork
5. January
6. nerve
7. iron
8. drone
9. rainbow
10. cheese

Lesson 19

1 About the Reading

1. a. They used galleys to guard the coast.
   b. They used galleys to remove ships wounded in battle.
2. Note: The details below may be listed in any order. Other details may be included as well.
   a. The galley was mainly an open boat for four hundred men.
   b. Convicts manned the oars that made the galley move swiftly.
   c. Each oar was manned by five convicts.
   d. Sometimes the convicts rowed for twenty-four hours without any rest.

e. Nobody ever washed.
3. a. They would work at their respective trades.
   b. They would get some food from the nearest town.
   c. They would get much needed sleep.
4. They used steam when it became available because it was faster.

2 Words That Sound the Same
1. be, bee
2. know, no
3. Ann, an
4. thrown, throne
5. cent, sent
6. cell, sell
7. hear, here
8. where, wear

3 Which Word Does Not Fit?
1. question
2. dry
3. person
4. hidden
5. soap
6. work
7. one-half
8. port
9. dirt
10. gripe
11. bumped into
12. water

4 Words That Begin with *un-*
1. unmated
2. untie
3. unmade
4. unarmed
5. unfriendly
6. unsafe
7. undress
8. unable
9. unfolded
10. unfair

5 Common Sayings
1. good
2. old
3. will
4. hatched
5. away
6. ton
7. play
8. heard
9. worth
10. thousand
11. heart
12. Home

Lesson 20

1 About the Reading
1. February 11
2. February 22
3. bodyguard
4. swearing
5. New York City
6. 2 terms
7. 1789
8. He was the first president of the United States. He commanded the Continental Army in its effort to gain independence from England. He also served as president of the convention that wrote the Constitution.
9. four years
10. the one dollar bill

2 Vowel Sounds
1. born, barn, burned
2. crook, crack, creaking
3. time, tame, team
4. slum, slim, slammed
5. truck, trick, track
6. slung, sling, slang
7. peeled, pail, pile
8. store, stared, stars
9. While, wheel, whale
10. drank, drinks, drunk

3 The Ending *-ly*
1. nearly
2. Surely
3. hardly
4. swiftly
5. lovely
6. really
7. badly
8. friendly

4 Compound Words
1. body + guard
2. country + men
3. check + book
4. every + where
5. cat + fish
6. busy + body
7. police + man
8. some + one
9. in + land
10. hide + out
11. under + line
12. star + fish

5 More Common Sayings
1. flies
2. boils
3. put, basket
4. wool
5. back
6. say
7. friend
8. hole
9. pod
10. candy, baby
11. speak
12. easy

Review: Lessons 1-20

1 Twenty Questions
1. George Washington
2. February
3. Fourth of July
4. Mayflower
5. galley
6. scribes
7. El Dorado
8. California
9. forty-niners
10. warm-blooded
11. cold-blooded
12. quarts
13. pints
14. ounces
15. alphabet
16. B.C.
17. Pinocchio
18. bigwig
19. drone
20. New Year's Day

2 Words That Mean the Same
1. nearly
2. bold
3. munch
4. deserve
5. rim
6. buddy
7. present
8. guide
9. cause
10. utter
11. slim
12. worthless

3 Word Opposites
1. simple
2. remember
3. thaw
4. shrank
5. deadly
6. spiteful
7. ugly
8. spicy
9. certain
10. overdone
11. bold
12. crooked

4 Which Word Fits Best?
1. peep
2. hour
3. chew
4. writing
5. cross
6. oars
7. gills
8. firecracker
9. March is to February
10. water is to ice

5 Words That Sound the Same
1. through
2. be
3. sent
4. weak
5. thrown
6. bored
7. cents
8. weigh
9. brake
10. know

Answer Key for Book 3

Lesson 1

1 About the Story

1. Steven drives a van for a living.
2. He has had this job for five years.
3. His sister's name is Ruth.
4. Steven sees Ruth once a week, on Thursday night.
5. a. The exercise class would help Steven feel more relaxed.
   b. The class would also give him an opportunity to meet new people.
6. At first, Steven gets angry.
7. At the end of the story, Steven decides to give the class a try.
8. A pact is an agreement or bargain.
9. Answers may vary. Ruth may be encouraging Steven to "get out more, do things and meet some new people" because she enjoys these activities. On the other hand, Steven does visit her every Thursday and she may be trying to prevent him from getting into a rut like she has.
10. Ruth tells Steven that he is still young, and he has been driving a van for five years. Therefore he is probably in his mid-twenties.

2 The Ending -ing

1. blessing	1. bathing	1. bedding
2. building	2. lining	2. clipping
3. clearing	3. paving	3. fitting
4. dressing	4. wiring	4. cutting
5. stuffing	5. coming	5. padding
6. washing	6. icing	6. wedding

3 How Do These People Earn a Living?

1. teacher	6. waiter
2. baker	7. boxer
3. farmer	8. manager
4. fiddler	9. teller
5. miner	10. lawyer

4 Compound Words

1. road + work	6. dish + pan
2. side + walk	7. pig + pen
3. tool + box	8. man + kind
4. rose + bud	9. home + made
5. back + fire	10. news + paper

Lesson 2

1 About the Story

1. Steven's best friend is Jerome.
2. Steven is taking a yoga class at the Y.M.C.A.
3. He wandered into the yoga class by mistake.
4. Jerome thinks yoga has stranger exercises.
5. Jerome didn't laugh at Steven for taking the yoga class.
6. Jerome seems to have let himself into Steven's apartment, and he helps himself to the stew Steven has made for dinner.

2 Adding -est to Words

1. finest	1. proudest	1. saddest
2. rudest	2. shortest	2. biggest
3. nicest	3. cheapest	3. thinnest
4. latest	4. greatest	4. dimmest
5. ripest	5. meanest	5. maddest
6. sorest	6. highest	6. hottest

3 How Do These People Earn a Living?

1. reporter	5. tailor	9. shortstop
2. carpenter	6. babysitter	10. fisherman
3. bodyguard	7. trainer	11. scribe
4. actor	8. clown	12. doctor

4 Compound Words

1. pay + check	7. class + room
2. tooth + paste	8. under + shirt
3. under + stand	9. flash + light
4. corn + starch	10. cook + book
5. chalk + board	11. work + shop
6. short + cake	12. hand + shake

Lesson 3

1 About the Story

1. Jerome hadn't been in a library for twelve years.
2. All Jerome ever did in the library was flirt with the girls.
3. She said she thought he belonged in a reform school.
4. He wanted to find out more about yoga because he wanted to talk Steven out of taking a yoga class.

5. At first Jerome thought yoga was yogurt.
6. The ladies are pleasant, smiling at him when he almost knocks over the flag.
7. He feels awful while in the library even though no one is giving him a hard time.
8. A vow is a promise.
9. Going to the library brings back bad memories of being kicked out of the high school library, but Jerome signs out the book on yoga without incident.

2 **Adding -y to Words**

1. tasty	1. grouchy	1. runny
2. shaky	2. stuffy	2. doggy
3. shady	3. bossy	3. patty
4. stony	4. rainy	4. knotty
5. edgy	5. squeaky	5. woolly

3 **Who Uses What?**

1. flashlight
2. punch
3. towel
4. ashtray
5. folder
6. oars
7. notebook
8. sponge
9. Bible
10. charm
11. jet
12. buggies

4 **Compound Words**

1. black + board
2. ear + ring
3. house + wife
4. fruit + cake
5. over + grown
6. grown + up
7. sun + light
8. suit + case
9. eye + strain
10. ring + side
11. bob + sled
12. free + way

Lesson 4

1 **About the Story**

1. Jerome was studying up on yoga.
2. It is a way to relax and free oneself from the phony nonsense in this world. He also tells her that some people claim it improves their sex life.
3. Jerome says he always goes to her place.
4. a. She is waiting for a call from her new manager.
   b. Jerome's place looks like a pigpen.
5. Ginger hangs up on Jerome.
6. Jerome won't stop clowning around.
7. Answers will vary.

2 **Changing the y to i**

1. grouchier   grouchiest
2. rainier   rainiest
3. icier   iciest
4. stuffier   stuffiest
5. bossier   bossiest
6. rosier   rosiest

3 **The Ending -y**

trashy	1. hairy	salty	6. brainy
bloody	2. jumpy	brainy	7. salty
hairy	3. puffy	tricky	8. bloody
jumpy	4. risky	puffy	9. tricky
risky	5. trashy	woody	10. Woody

4 **Who Uses What?**

1. iron
2. leash
3. grill
4. plow
5. spices
6. putty
7. globe
8. gloves
9. platter
10. sails

5 **Compound Words**

1. rail + road
2. basket + ball
3. under + ground
4. grand + mother
5. dream + land
6. grand + father
7. cheap + skate
8. wood + pecker

Lesson 5

1 **About the Story**

1. It got you thinking about what kinds of information the story might contain.
2. She sang with a band, wrote songs and gave voice lessons.
3. She had met Jerome six months ago in a hardware store.
4. Jerome worked as a clerk in the hardware store.
5. Ginger was in love with Jerome.
6. No one knows for sure how Jerome felt about Ginger.
7. Ginger's mother thought her daughter's apartment didn't look at all homey.
8. Ginger had not told her mother how wealthy she was.
9. Answers will vary.

2 **The Ending -ly**

lately	1. properly	wildly	6. costly
madly	2. shyly	oddly	7. lately
truthfully	3. truthfully	costly	8. lively
peacefully	4. madly	shyly	9. peacefully
properly	5. wildly	lively	10. Oddly

3 **Words That Mean the Same**

1. plead
2. brink
3. edgy
4. shove
5. frighten
6. notice
7. bright
8. gaze
9. beginning
10. dense
11. pledge
12. healthy

4 **Compound Words**

1. tooth + brush
2. Thanks + giving
3. over + board
4. gum + drop
5. flower + pot
6. bill + fold
7. snow + ball
8. snap + shot
9. high + way
10. cross + walk

Lesson 6

1 About the Story

1. This story takes place in the hardware store.
2. It is evening.
3. a. Ginger might stop being angry with him.
   b. It might encourage her to paint her apartment.
4. The lid came off, and paint spilled all over Jerome, the counter, and the floor.
5. Tony laughed very hard.
6. It took seven hours to clean up the mess.
7. Answers may vary. The first paragraph of the story suggests that Jerome wants to take the paint now and perhaps pay for it when he gets his next paycheck.
8. Answers may vary.

2 The Ending -ly

freshly
hourly
neatly
tightly
thickly

1. neatly
2. rarely
3. hourly
4. certainly
5. freshly

rarely
squarely
successfully
mildly
certainly

6. squarely
7. mildly
8. tightly
9. thickly
10. successfully

3 Word Opposites

1. hairy
2. costly
3. grownup
4. frozen
5. rarely
6. skinny
7. ugly
8. phony
9. tense
10. risky
11. loose
12. dumb

4 Compound Words

1. dish + rag
2. finger + nail
3. tail + spin
4. any + more
5. over + head
6. drug + store
7. finger + print
8. in + side

Lesson 7

1 About the Story

1. Steven had a slight cold and apparently wasn't feeling too well.
2. He was catching on to the yoga exercises quite quickly.
3. Holly asked Steven if he wanted to go out for a cup of coffee.
4. The sugar in it could make people grouchy, restless, fat, and unhealthy.
5. He apparently has decided not to order the chocolate cake when he says, "Well, so much for the chocolate cake."
6. Steven learned that yoga is a whole way of life. He also learned that in becoming involved with yoga he had a lot more to think about than he imagined he would.
7. a. Steven's apartment
   b. The Y.M.C.A.
   c. a coffee shop

2 The Endings -ful and -less

A. restless
stressful
sugarless
spotless
armful
peaceful
harmful
tasteless

B. 1. stressful
2. tasteless
3. harmful
4. armful
5. peaceful
6. restless
7. spotless
8. sugarless

3 Same or Opposite?

1. opposite
2. opposite
3. same
4. same
5. same
6. same
7. opposite
8. same
9. opposite
10. same
11. opposite
12. same

4 Compound Words

1. knock + out
2. ship + wreck
3. life + guard
4. match + book
5. light + house
6. door + knob
7. rest + room
8. come + back
9. eye + sight
10. knee + cap

Lesson 8

1 About the Story

1. This story takes place in Ginger's apartment.
2. It probably takes place in the morning since Ginger was fixing breakfast.
3. Gail wanted to stay at Ginger's for a day or two.
4. Gail goes to see her parents only when she wants money.
5. She had banged her head against the front door.
6. Ginger suggested that Gail ought to think about how she is treating her parents.
7. We know that Gail doesn't live with her parents because the story said she visited them only when she wanted money.
8. Probably most students will feel that Gail is not treating her parents very well and that she should be more considerate.

2 The Endings -ful and -less

A. countless
faithful
homeless
joyful
painful
painless
spoonful
sunless
watchful
worthless

B. 1. homeless
2. spoonful
3. sunless
4. faithful
5. painful
6. watchful
7. joyful
8. countless
9. painless
10. worthless

3 Same or Opposite?

1. opposite	5. opposite	9. same
2. same	6. opposite	10. opposite
3. same	7. same	11. opposite
4. same	8. opposite	12. same

4 Compound Words

1. coffeecake	5. scoreboard	9. crybaby
2. newsstand	6. waistline	10. kinfolks
3. washcloth	7. leapfrog	11. cheapskate
4. meatballs	8. pitchfork	12. spendthrift

Lesson 9

1 About the Story

1. Jerome was feeling lousy because he hadn't heard from Ginger in four weeks.
2. At first, Jerome thought Ginger was calling him.
3. Jerome wasn't pleased.
4. Steven spoke sharply, indicating he was angry.
5. Steven had called Jerome to invite him to Holly's party.
6. Going to Holly's party was better than sitting in a bar by himself.
7. Jerome is disappointed at first. At the end of the phone call, he is glad to be going to Holly's party rather than sitting in a bar by himself.
8. Probably the most obvious answer is that Jerome won't call a woman after they've had an argument. Instead, he waits for her to call him.
9. Answers will vary.

2 The Ending -en

1. frozen	7. weaken
2. forgiven	8. written
3. sunken	9. threaten
4. forgotten	10. loosen
5. broken	11. moisten
6. chosen	12. mistaken

3 Which Word Does Not Fit?

1. buddy	6. speak
2. ice cubes	7. worm
3. blouse	8. trip
4. chocolate cake	9. breathing
5. beef	10. play

Lesson 10

1 About the Story

1. a. Finding a parking place was difficult.
   b. The machines might not work properly.
   c. You have to be careful not to lose anything.
2. Holly was writing "Out of Order" signs for the machines that didn't work.
3. Holly had tried two washing machines.

4. a. The four quarters and two dimes ($1.20) she lost suggests she tried two machines — sixty cents in each machine.
   b. She was writing two "Out of Order" signs.
5. Since she had hung up on him, he felt she should phone him to apologize.
6. Jerome wants to see her, so he should call her.
7. Jerome wasn't taking any steps to get what he wanted.
8. Answers may vary.

2 The Ending -en

1. driven	5. bitten	9. given
2. fallen	6. eaten	10. ridden
3. shaken	7. spoken	11. Risen
4. straightened	8. beaten	12. rotten

3 Which Word Does Not Fit?

1. newspaper	5. pest	9. ivy
2. month	6. drum	10. season
3. deck	7. saucepan	11. whale
4. building	8. highway	12. Rome

4 Spelling Check

1. breakfast	6. coffee
2. alphabet	7. wedding
3. mammal	8. mirror
4. Christmas	9. Swiss
5. doctor	10. thirteen

Lesson 11

1 About the Story

1. a. Ginger had had her phone taken out.
   b. She had gone camping.
2. She was daydreaming about never having to work again.
3. a. She is going to buy a phone for every room.
   b. She is going to paint her walls.
   c. She is going to read all the newspapers she can find.
4. Life in the city looks safer than camping in the woods.
5. Ginger had gone camping to perk herself up after her trouble with Jerome. When she thought she heard a growling sound, she became scared and ran away as fast as she could.
6. Answers will vary.
7. Answers will vary.

2 Words That Begin with re-

1. react	6. recall
2. refuse	7. recover
3. remarks	8. repeat
4. respect	9. rejected, rejection
5. reveal	10. require

3 Words That Mean the Same

1. lousy
2. respond
3. boast
4. rejoice
5. nervous
6. faithful
7. juicy
8. require
9. recall
10. mistaken

4 What Is Where?

A Laundromat
1. bleach
2. coin machines
3. dryers

A Library
1. bookshelves
2. newspapers
3. records

A Diner
1. grill
2. oven
3. tips

5 What Is Where?

A Circus
1. clowns
2. dancing bears
3. side shows

A Concert
1. drums
2. flutes
3. stage

A Baseball Game
1. center field
2. pitchers
3. scoreboards

Lesson 12

1 About the Story

1. Steven's boss had given him the free passes.
2. The Colts and the Cowboys were playing.
3. a. She asked if they could sit behind the batter's box.
   b. She didn't recognize the coach.
   (Note: The story contains additional evidence that Holly doesn't know anything about football.)
4. When the man next to Steven bumped him, the popcorn spilled, landing on his coat and trousers.
5. "The Star-Spangled Banner" is played.
6. Holly probably knows a little about baseball. She knows the term *batter's box,* but doesn't seem to realize it is associated only with baseball.
7. Answers will vary.

2 Words That Begin with re-

1. revive
2. remove
3. report
4. repair
5. refreshed
6. reduce
7. retired
8. related
9. recovery
10. return
11. retreat
12. reply

3 Word Opposites

1. forgive
2. wilt
3. nervous
4. moldy
5. reveal
6. fallen
7. scratchy
8. listen
9. sunless
10. wasteful

4 Compound Words

1. footprint
2. quarterback
3. eggshell
4. deadline
5. homesick
6. daybreak
7. standstill
8. wastebasket
9. blacktop
10. courtroom
11. lukewarm
12. playground

Lesson 13

1 About the Story

1. Jerome thought it would be a way to see Ginger.
2. Tony was supposed to invite Ginger to the party.
3. a. He got rid of the cockroaches in the kitchen.
   b. He swept the cobwebs from his bookshelves and ceiling.
   c. He cleaned the carpet.
4. Jerome's party really started at ten o'clock.
5. It ended at four in the morning.
6. Ginger never arrived. Everyone else had a great time and didn't notice that Jerome was miserable.
7. Answers will vary.

2 Words That Begin with in-

1. inhale
2. invent
3. invade
4. invite
5. increase
6. instruct
7. inquire
8. infect
9. intend
10. inspire

3 Which Word Fits Best?

1. chirp
2. neck
3. Boston
4. coffeecake
5. look down upon
6. lung
7. land
8. steam
9. stale
10. present
11. roar
12. year

4 Consonants

1. gŭt • ter
2. măt • ter
3. sŭm • mer
4. hăp • pen
5. mŭg • ger
6. cŭt • ting
7. măm • mal
8. căt • ty
9. pĕp • per
10. slĭp • per

Lesson 14

1 About the Story

1. He didn't get along with her very well. He stayed in a motel during the week and came home on weekends only to see his children.
2. Mrs. Darkpill began to cut down Tony's chestnut tree. He tried without success to talk some sense into her.
3. She complained that he had whipped her daughter.
4. Her name seems most fitting. Her personality is far from cheerful.
5. Answers will vary.

2 The gh and ght Words

1. might, right
2. right
3. neighbor, sighed
4. ought, daughters
5. dough, rough, cough, tough
6. sleigh, height, eight, bright
7. enough

3 Same or Opposite

1. opposite
2. same
3. same
4. opposite
5. opposite
6. opposite
7. same
8. same
9. opposite
10. same
11. same
12. opposite

4 Double Consonants

1. stŭt • ter
2. clŭt • ter
3. bĭt • ten
4. wrăp • per
5. thĭn • ner
6. hĭt • ter
7. lŏb • by
8. shăt • ter
9. trăp • per
10. cŏm • mon

Lesson 15

1 About the Story

1. Ginger is parked in front of her driveway.
2. She accuses him of having girls in until all hours of the night.
3. coffee
4. booze
5. Ginger puts her arm around Mrs. Darkpill to lead her to the couch.
6. The neighbors, hearing the uproar, called the police.
7. Students will probably agree.
8. Answers will vary.

2 The *ea* and *ear* Words

1. beard, heart, feared, head
2. repeated, nearby, pleaded, freak
3. leather, dread, feather, mincemeat
4. mean, cheap, headed, beach
5. heard, beard, dreadful, preach
6. beat, sea, leap

3 Syllables

1. card • board
2. bright • ly
3. cheer • ful
4. sub • way
5. proud • ly
6. in • hale
7. un • clear
8. stair • way
9. cob • web
10. fair • ness
11. sad • ness
12. in • vade

4 More Work with Units

1. months
2. hours
3. seconds
4. quarts
5. ounces
6. feet
7. letters
8. rooms
9. states

Lesson 16

1 About the Story

1. a. peanut butter balls
   b. prune whip
   c. date-nut bread
2. Holly was writing a cookbook.

3. peanut butter balls
4. prune whip
5. He complains rather than taking action to make life better.
6. He is living by a set of outdated rules.
7. The bread was burned.
8. Answers may vary.
9. Answers may vary.

2 The Sounds for *ow*

1. flowerpot
2. bowling
3. bowl
4. crowbar
5. scarecrows
6. pillow
7. elbow
8. shower
9. grownups
10. towel rack
11. rowboat
12. cow

3 Syllables

1. yesterday
2. woodpecker
3. Cinderella
4. helicopter
5. laundromat
6. recipe
7. hangover
8. thrifty

4 Brain Benders

1. false
2. true
3. false
4. true
5. true
6. true
7. true
8. false
9. false
10. false

Lesson 17

1 About the Story

1. a. Tony's apartment
   b. a diner
   c. a men's clothing store
2. Mr. Dennis is Tony's boss.
3. Since Mr. Dennis answered the phone in an "extremely unfriendly voice," we can assume he was in a bad mood.
4. Tony tells Mr. Dennis that he is coming down with the flu.
5. He decides to check out the sale at a men's clothing store.
6. Mr. Dennis sees Tony at the store when he is supposed to be home sick.
7. Answers will vary.
8. Answers will vary.

2 Sounds for *ow*

1. dishtowel
2. landowner
3. blowout
4. snowplow
5. washbowl
6. townspeople
7. downpour
8. wildflowers
9. showoff
10. lowdown

3 Which Word Does Not Fit?

1. peas	7. shelter
2. unfriendly	8. relax
3. knees	9. nervous
4. purse	10. destroy
5. weak	11. conceal
6. rain	12. mute

4 Syllables

1. con • fess	9. win • ner
2. booth	10. pay • day
3. ex • treme	11. home • sick
4. ex • treme • ly	12. rest • room
5. shop • per	13. o • ver • board
6. flu	14. un • friend • ly
7. six • teen	15. bas • ket • ball
8. yes • ter • day	

Lesson 18

1 About the Story

1. Steven thinks Jerome can't admit when he's made a mistake and take the initiative to straighten out things with Ginger.
2. Steven is trying to get Jerome to understand that he will have to take some action in order to get what he wants out of life.
3. Jerome thinks Ginger might have started the fight with Tony's neighbor just to get out of going to his party.
4. Jerome only complains and won't do anything to get back together with Ginger.
5. Jerome seems to decide Steven is right. Evidence of this is Jerome's deciding to call Ginger.

2 Short Stories

1. discussed, expands, disagreed, extra, convince
2. exceeding, exchanged, unfriendly, unfit, extra
3. exhausted, uncertain, unhealthy, expenses, income

3 Who Uses What?

Baker	Barber
1. cake pans	1. chair
2. dough	2. clippers
3. oven	3. comb
4. pie plates	4. mirror
5. rolling pin	5. shaving cream

Carpenter	Fisherman
1. boards	1. bait
2. drill	2. boat
3. hammer	3. hooks
4. nails	4. net
5. saws	5. rod

4 Spelling Check

1. thumb	5. potato
2. August	6. Cinderella
3. wallet	7. waltz
4. paycheck	8. cheapskate

Lesson 19

1 About the Story

1. Jerome decides to go see her rather than calling her.
2. Most of the story takes place at the nightclub where Ginger is singing.
3. Ginger is sitting next to the piano player when Jerome first sees her.
4. At first, Jerome tells Ginger he came to see her because he wanted to hear her sing "September Song."
5. Ginger threatens to have the bouncer throw Jerome out of the club.
6. Ginger touches Jerome gently on the cheek and goes to sing "September Song."

2 Months of the Year

1. January	8. June (or May)
2. December	9. March
3. December	10. June
4. November	11. September
5. February	12. December
6. Answer will vary	13. Answer will vary
7. September (or August)	14. Answer will vary

3 The Four Seasons

Spring	Summer
1. April	1. August
2. Easter	2. beach
3. flowers blooming	3. Fourth of July
4. spring training	4. the All-Star game

Autumn	Winter
1. falling leaves	1. Christmas
2. October	2. December
3. schools open	3. ice skating
4. Thanksgiving	4. snow storms

4 Twelve Questions

1. upstairs	7. content
2. indoors	8. included
3. infield	9. overlook
4. income	10. replying
5. disposing	11. request
6. overdone	12. deflate

Lesson 20

1 About the Story

1. Holly is giving a party to celebrate signing a contract for her cookbook.
2. Jerome asked Holly if he could bring anything to the party.
3. Holly is sick of all the health food she had to eat while testing recipes for her cookbook.
4. about midnight
5. She had to sing at the nightclub.
6. prune whip
7. chocolate cheesecake
8. Ginger likes the people from the yoga class.
9. Jerome is happy for a change.
10. Jerome seems to have learned that life has its ups and downs, and a person never knows what will happen next.

2 Compound Words

1. passport
2. Passover
3. homebody
4. backpack
5. backbone
6. firetrap
7. dishpan
8. drumstick
9. teaspoons
10. overalls

3 Words That Mean the Same

1. find
2. tired
3. overweight
4. hardly
5. hurled
6. rough
7. lance
8. wander
9. singe
10. pout

4 Word Opposites

1. female
2. sour
3. morning
4. heat
5. freeze
6. crawl
7. common
8. bored
9. certain
10. contract

5 Feelings

1. cheered. The fans were happy to see a member of the opposing team thrown out of the game for unsportsmanlike behavior.
2. excited. At last, Joan could apply for a job that really appealed to her.
3. angry. He had gotten nothing for his quarter.
4. overcome with feeling. Charles's emotions reflected his happiness at winning the money.
5. rejected. John felt his neighbor didn't want him at the party.
6. happy. His boss's leaving would remove that source of irritation.
7. thankful. She was very aware of how fortunate she was to have her son found unharmed.
8. Answers will vary.

Review: Lessons 1-20

1 Word Study

1. c	6. b	11. d
2. b	7. a	12. a
3. d	8. c	13. a
4. a	9. a	14. c
5. b	10. c	15. d

2 Words That Mean the Same

1. loyal
2. fussy
3. nervous
4. fib
5. poor
6. beg
7. content
8. hoist
9. grab
10. pledge

3 Word Opposites

1. straight
2. spotless
3. shrink
4. quiet
5. underneath
6. fancy
7. complex
8. loosen
9. phony
10. costly

4 Syllables

1. cloud • less
2. suc • cess • ful
3. rob • ber
4. side • ways
5. thir • teen
6. thought • ful
7. re • tire
8. hand • shake
9. sit • ter
10. peace • ful • ly

5 Word Sounds

1. walk
2. city
3. gentle
4. great
5. good
6. plow
7. could
8. certain

6 Spelling Check

1. courtroom
2. highway
3. England
4. eggshell
5. school
6. ear
7. cookbook
8. ashtray
9. kitchen
10. El Dorado

Answer: cheesecake

Answer Key for
Book 4

Lesson 1

1 About the Reading

1. a. true   f. false
   b. false   g. true
   c. true   h. true
   d. false   i. false
   e. true   j. false

2. The person is putting a strain on his heart by making it beat harder and faster.
3. 1,660,000 people in the U.S. die from heart disease.
4. Answers may vary.

2 The Human Body

1. artery   6. bloodstream
2. vein   7. nerve
3. nose   8. ribs
4. brain   9. lungs
5. elbow   10. spleen

3 Adding -er

1. dealer   1. trader   1. runner
2. reader   2. shaker   2. drummer
3. blender   3. hiker   3. bidder
4. printer   4. liner   4. flipper
5. performer   5. believer   5. patter

4 Syllables

1. book • cāse   6. hōpe • less
2. wĭn • ner   7. nor • mal
3. strong • ly   8. for • gĭve
4. clŭt • ter   9. cŏp • per
5. lō • cāte   10. per • form

5 Brain Benders

1. kind
2. want something badly
3. a snob
4. full of pride
5. strongly moved
6. agree with your friend
7. insist on having your own way
8. teasing you
9. hurts your feelings
10. angry

Lesson 2

1 About the Reading

1. Baltimore
2. a reform school
3. the Boston Red Sox
4. Yankee Stadium
5. fifteen years
6. His legs gave out.
7. cancer
8. 53
9. Answers may vary. The reading suggests he lacked self-discipline and maturity — particularly as evidenced by the way he managed money.

2 Games and Sports

1. quarterback   6. height
2. outfield   7. racket
3. yards   8. paddle
4. bases   9. checkers
5. squares   10. dice

3 Words That Mean the Same

1. perform   6. conceal
2. car   7. wrong
3. brag   8. message
4. normal   9. trousers
5. gloomy   10. female

4 Word Opposites

1. conclude   6. increase
2. edge   7. restless
3. built   8. smooth
4. dull   9. plump
5. normal   10. brand-new

5 The Ending -er

1. buzzer   1. wiper   1. digger
2. jumper   2. insider   2. gunner
3. killer   3. outsider   3. logger
4. learner   4. invader   4. jogger
5. broiler   5. tuner   5. skipper
6. strainer   6. breather   6. snapper

6 Syllables

1. grāve • yard   6. tĕn • nĭs
2. dĭs • turb   7. brĕak • fast
3. wrăp • per   8. fĭd • dle
4. ĭn • quīre   9. păd • dle
5. ŭn • dĭd   10. trāin • ing

Lesson 3

1 About the Reading

1. *Concept* means a thought or idea about something.
2. They are afraid something serious has happened.
3. "A long time" can be anything from a few days to ten or twenty years.
4. They think "a long time" means thousands of years.
5. They think the person is rude or unfit for his job.
6. The Pueblo Indians begin something when they feel the time is right.
7. He had to wait until 2 A.M. for the dance to start.
8. Different groups of people have different concepts about time.
9. Answers will vary.

2 Time

1. spring, summer, autumn, winter
2. Tuesday, Wednesday, Thursday, Friday
3. dawn, noon, dusk, midnight (or *midnight* may come first)
4. New Year's Day, Easter, Fourth of July, Christmas Eve
5. second, minute, half-hour, hour
6. July, August, September, October
7. day, week, month, year
8. wristwatch, alarm clock, grandfather's clock, sun
9. free time, a normal working day, time and a half, double time

3 More about Time

1. steal
2. earned
3. save
4. waste
5. use
6. spent
7. lost
8. blown
9. lend
10. borrowed

4 The Ending -y

1. soapy
2. dusty
3. sandy
4. curly
5. bushy

1. breezy
2. wheezy
3. scary
4. nervy
5. greasy

1. peppy
2. potty
3. fatty
4. choppy
5. clammy

5 Syllables

1. wrĭst • watch
2. South • wĕst
3. clăm • my
4. short • cŭt
5. ŏb • jĕct
6. brĕath • less
7. rē • quīre
8. săd • nĕss
9. hōpe • full
10. mĭs • trŭst

Lesson 4

1 About the Reading

1. 800,000
2. where it is cold or in salt water
3. Insects have six legs.

4. three
5. feelers
6. They help plants to grow by carrying pollen from one flower to another.
7. a. They serve as food for a number of animals.
   b. They return matter to the soil.
   c. They give us honey, silk, and wax.
8. a. Some bite.
   b. Some sting.
   c. Some carry diseases.
   d. They can mess up kitchens, etc.
   e. Some destroy crops.
   f. Some harm forests.
9. There are fewer insects in colder places.
10. There are so many of them that if they were larger they might overrun an area.

2 Name That Insect or Bug

1. bee
2. termite
3. ladybug
4. spider
5. tick
6. housefly
7. butterfly
8. grasshopper
9. ant
10. cockroach

3 Which Word Fits Best?

1. tick
2. huge
3. ocean
4. orange
5. fish
6. comfort
7. water
8. sand

4 Word Endings

1. speedy
2. rusty
3. silky
4. creamy
5. leafy
6. flowery

1. choosy
2. scaly
3. spongy
4. pasty
5. mousy
6. bony

1. baggy
2. Tommy
3. gummy
4. smoggy
5. floppy
6. sloppy

5 Syllables

1. cŏck • rōach
2. pĭc • nĭc
3. ter • mīte
4. mouth • part
5. ĭn • sĕct
6. pŏl • len
7. flŏp • py
8. cŏn • cĕpt
9. out • look
10. ŭn • lĕss

Lesson 5

1 About the Story

1. dots
2. ten
3. one-third
4. can be unaware of what is happening
5. brain
6. We can be affected by things that we're not even aware of.
7. Subliminal advertising such as this can make us do things we might not do normally.
8. Ads may influence people to buy items they normally would not purchase.

2 Putting Sentences in Order

1. She checks the *TV Guide* to see what time the program is on.
2. She also reads what channel the program is on.
3. She turns on the set. (May also be #1.)
4. She turns the knob to the right channel.
5. The picture is not clear at all.
6. She plays with the knobs to get a better picture.
7. The program turns out to be very dull.
8. She falls asleep on the couch.

3 Syllables

1. out • stand • ing
2. un • der • ground
3. yes • ter • day
4. but • ter • fly
5. Wash • ing • ton
6. com • mand • ment
7. grass • hop • per
8. per • form • er
9. re • mem • ber
10. a • part • ment

4 Working with Headings

Spending Time with Friends

Reading   Hiking   Playing Ball
Cooking   Talking on the Phone   Going to Night School
Making Things   Going to a Concert   Going out for Dinner

5 Words That End with -*y*

1. cooky
2. bunny
3. panty
4. battery
5. belly
6. muggy
7. brandy
8. moody
9. bully
10. gravy

Review: Lessons 1-5

1 Answer These Questions

1. vein
2. artery
3. Indian
4. Yankee
5. swamp
6. desert
7. termite
8. grasshopper
9. oxygen
10. carbon dioxide

2 Word Study

1. going on and off
2. a quarter
3. hero
4. George Washington
5. Baltimore
6. United States
7. tennis courts
8. meadow
9. museum
10. the American Southwest
11. gummy
12. flowery
13. insider
14. a jogger
15. Mother's Day

3 Words That Mean the Same

1. perform
2. underneath
3. meadow
4. locate
5. upper
6. concept
7. message
8. jogger
9. total
10. chat

4 Word Opposites

1. hero
2. townspeople
3. straight
4. cause
5. disease
6. exhale
7. prompt
8. scaly
9. baggy
10. aware

Lesson 6

1 About the Reading

1. false
2. true
3. true
4. true
5. true
6. false
7. false
8. true
9. false

2 Working with Headings

Solids	Liquids	Gases
1. chestnut trees	1. blood	1. air
2. ice	2. orange juice	2. carbon dioxide
3. rocks	3. water	3. oxygen
4. steel	4. wine	4. steam

3 Compound Words

1. starfish
2. moonlighting
3. moonshine
4. skyscraper
5. skylight
6. cloudburst
7. skyline
8. sunstroke
9. sunflower
10. suntan

4 The Ending -*ing*

1. spelling
2. crossing
3. drawing
4. coloring
5. coating
6. belonging

1. pleasing
2. mining
3. merging
4. boring
5. daring
6. carving

1. beginning
2. jogging
3. rigging
4. bidding
5. topping
6. matting

5 Confusing -*ing* Words

1. staring, starring
2. baring, barring
3. gripping, griping
4. hoping, hopping
5. filling, filing

Lesson 7

1 About the Reading

1. Ohio
2. February 11, 1847
3. Michigan
4. three months
5. Al
6. He wanted to see if his friend would fly when he passed a lot of gas.
7. She was angry that his teacher thought he was crazy.
8. He had caused a fire in the baggage car.

9. He could concentrate without being interrupted by a lot of noise.
10. a. light bulb
    b. phonograph
    c. moving pictures
11. 84
12. He spent so much time working that he didn't have much time for a family.

2 Compound Words
1. hourglass
2. padlock
3. dishwasher
4. handcuffs
5. boxcar
6. screwdriver
7. jackhammer
8. sandpaper
9. pacemaker
10. gearshift
11. airplane
12. mousetrap

3 Which Word Fits Best?
1. disease
2. part
3. knapsack
4. liquid
5. ears
6. dinner
7. state
8. stare
9. result
10. stage

4 Syllables
1. re • ceive
2. sky • line
3. dish • wash • er
4. wor • ship
5. rail • way
6. be • gin • ning
7. deaf • ness
8. com • pound
9. jack • ham • mer

Lesson 8

1 About the Story
1. the spoon
2. Italy
3. People carried a knife with them that was used for everything, including cutting meat.
4. A knife goes to the right of the dinner plate.
5. a. soup
   b. to cut meat
   c. meat
   d. two
   e. one
   f. cutting the salad
6. how we came to use knives, forks, and spoons.
7. Answers may vary.

2 The Last Word on Knives
The Johnson boys' table manners are so crude that they probably would not be invited to a fancy dinner party.

3 Food for Thought
1. potatoes
2. boiling
3. stew
4. deep frying pan
5. pound
6. berries (possibly oranges)
7. Italy
8. teaspoon
9. breakfast or picnic
10. Thanksgiving

4 Singular and Plural Words
1. singular
2. plural
3. plural
4. singular
5. singular
6. singular
7. plural
8. plural
9. singular
10. plural
11. singular
12. singular

5 One Knife/Two Knives
knives
lives
shelves
leaves
loaves
halves

1. life
2. loaf
3. lives
4. loaves
5. knives
6. shelf
7. half
8. leaf
9. leaves
10. knife
11. shelves
12. halves

Lesson 9

1 About the Reading
1. Children would rather act the way they want to rather than the way adults want them to act.
2. Answers will vary.
3. Answers will vary.

2 Which Word Does Not Fit?
1. ice cream
2. manners
3. release
4. dinner
5. beet
6. pockets
7. food
8. billionth
9. automobile
10. pacemaker
11. Huron
12. feet

3 Recipes

Fried Chicken
1. Put flour, salt, pepper and chicken in paper bag.
2. Shake until chicken is well coated.
3. Melt butter or fat in deep frying pan.
4. Brown chicken slowly until skin is crisp and golden.
5. Drain on paper towels.

Green Salad
1. Wash greens and throw away any stems.
2. Tear into bite-size pieces.
3. Chill greens in bowl until serving time.
4. Just before serving, pour ¼ cup dressing over greens.
5. Toss lightly until dressing coats leaves.

4 Singular and Plural Words
1. bubble
2. channel
3. concept
4. desert
5. effect
6. league
7. meadow
8. menu
9. message
10. pocket

1. batteries
2. children
3. heroes
4. museums
5. spiders
6. strawberries
7. tongues
8. waitresses
9. women
10. Yankees

5 More about Manners

1. d
2. a
3. b
4. c
5. d
6. b
7. b
8. d
9. c
10. Answers will vary.

Lesson 10

1 About the Reading

1. France and the state of Washington
2. 1947
3. The man in Washington saw nine discs, whereas the Frenchman had seen only one.
4. a. weather balloons.
   b. small meteors
   c. large hailstones
5. A group connected with an Air Force base in Ohio studies flying saucers.
6. It is hard for some people to imagine things they have not experienced for themselves.
7. Answers will vary.
8. Answers will vary

2 More about Meteors

piece, space, hot, shine

because, stars

200,000,000 entering, explode, heard

collected, outside

3 Choosing the Right Word

1. disc
2. morning
3. stony
4. sun
5. related
6. Earth
7. cloudburst
8. concept
9. record
10. sunglasses

4 Word Study

1. racket
2. use
3. wind
4. wound
5. tears
6. racket
7. use
8. wound
9. lying
10. wind
11. lying
12. Tears

Review: Lessons 1-10

1 Answer These Questions

1. star
2. gases
3. disc
4. reach the Earth
5. the light bulb
6. deaf
7. Italy
8. Thanksgiving

2 Word Study

1. worship
2. drawing
3. crudely
4. inventor
5. medicine
6. fork
7. Italy
8. tongue
9. whirling
10. record

3 Words That Mean the Same

1. enter
2. dining
3. continue
4. connected
5. release
6. pretend
7. sloppy
8. sudden
9. beam
10. tale
11. swirl
12. entire

4 Word Opposites

1. worried
2. daring
3. release
4. skyscraper
5. believe in
6. sloppy
7. swallow
8. immense
9. bottom
10. lying
11. downward
12. narrow

5 Syllables

1. pocket
2. waitress
3. Michigan
4. medicine
5. America
6. cavemen
7. cranberry
8. strawberry
9. atmosphere
10. Huron

6 Menus

Breakfast	Thanksgiving Dinner	Picnic
1. corn flakes	1. apple pie	1. hamburgers
2. oatmeal	2. cranberry sauce	2. ketchup
3. orange juice	3. dressing	3. pickles
4. poached eggs	4. sweet potatoes	4. potato salad
5. toast	5. turkey	5. ants

7 The Sound for le

little, middle, able, gentle, apples, bubble, gobble, Bible

struggle

single, double

table

Lesson 11

1 About the Reading

1. a. false
   b. false
   c. true
   d. false
   e. true
   f. false
   g. false
   h. false
   i. false
   j. false
2. Answers will vary.
3. Answers will vary.

2 Changing the y to i

1. happier   happiest   happiness
2. lazier   laziest   laziness
3. lonelier   loneliest   loneliness
4. easier   easiest   easiness
5. moodier   moodiest   moodiness
6. busier   busiest   business

3 **Word Endings**

1. friendship	1. disagreement	1. deafness
2. worship	2. basement	2. loneliness
3. battleship	3. agreement	3. laziness
	4. statement	4. blindness
	5. apartment	5. happiness
		6. business

4 **Silent Letters**

1. g̶nat   6. thumb̶
2. k̶neel   7. w̶rist
3. w̶rench   8. lamb̶
4. dumb̶   9. w̶ren
5. w̶rap   10. numb̶

5 **Happiness!**

1. barbers   6. February
2. Easter   7. happy
3. eighteen   8. moon
4. mammal   9. sign
5. knives   10. innings

Quote: Every human being is in some form seeking happiness.

Lesson 12

1 **About the Author**

1. Holland
2. twenty-five
3. Hitler
4. kill all Jews
5. Six million Jews were dead by the end of the war.
6. World War II
7. They needed to take many clothes with them, but they didn't dare carry a suitcase.
8. It was a small attic in Mr. Frank's office building.
9. a. They were loaded into cattle trucks.
   b. There was only one place to wash for 100 people.
   c. There were not enough bathrooms.
   d. Men, women, and children all slept together.
10. the English radio
11. Answers may vary. By giving her diary a name, it became sort of a friend she could talk to.
12. Answers will vary.

2 **Word Beginnings**

1. bookworm   7. Everywhere
2. committed   8. backfired
3. homeless   9. downfall
4. cattle   10. remind
5. misjudged   11. concept
6. unlikely   12. doormat

3 **Words That Mean the Same**

1. basement   6. perhaps
2. inmate   7. truly
3. M.D.   8. excite
4. inflate   9. dozen
5. slaughter   10. depressed

4 **Word Opposites**

1. disagreement   6. depressed
2. attic   7. accept
3. fever   8. blindness
4. outskirts   9. North Pole
5. cheap   10. glance

5 **Words That End in Hard or Soft *g***

Soft *g*		Hard *g*	
badge	gorge	beg	jog
binge	misjudge	brag	shrug
garbage	verge	egg	underdog

Lesson 13

1 **About the Reading**

1. Anne seems to have the most trouble with her mother. Her mother apparently criticizes her with words and looks.
2. a. Peter wanted to see a movie.
   b. Peter's father and Anne's sister wanted a hot, leisurely bath.
   c. Peter's mother wanted to eat cream cakes.
   d. Anne's mother wanted a cup of coffee.
   e. Anne's father wanted to see a friend of his. (Also the dentist wanted to see his wife; Anne wanted a home of her own and the chance to return to school.)
3. She was not in Germany when the war broke out.
4. She believes that people are really good at heart.
5. Answers may vary.
6. Answers will vary.
7. Answers will vary.
8. Answers will vary.

2 **World War II**

money, changes, history

fifty, wounded, armed

invaded, countries, bombed, declared

3 **Cities, States, and Countries**

Cities	States	Countries
1. Amsterdam	1. California	1. Egypt
2. Baltimore	2. Hawaii	2. Germany
3. Boston	3. Michigan	3. Holland
4. Detroit	4. Ohio	4. Japan
5. Rome	5. Washington	5. Spain

4 Word Endings
1. picture, nature
2. attic, picnic
3. foolish, selfish
4. cattle, terrible
5. swallow, meadow
6. total, chemical
7. manager, message, baggage
8. wilderness, kindness, sadness

Lesson 14
1 About the Reading
1. the camel
2. Asia and Africa
3. fat
4. seventeen
5. a. Its lids and lashes protect its eyes.
   b. Its nostrils can close, protecting its nose from sand.
   c. Its strong teeth can chew nearly anything.
6. twenty-five miles
7. one thousand pounds
8. a. Camels can carry cargo across the desert.
   b. Its hair is used to make cloth, blankets, and tents.
   c. Its skin can be made into leather.
9. It has a bad temper.
10. Answers will vary.

2 Compound Words
1. duckpin
2. pigtail
3. beeline
4. foxhole
5. mousetrap
6. snakebite
7. piggyback
8. dogwood
9. fishbowl
10. birdhouse
11. sheepskin
12. monkeyshines

3 Word Endings
1. bracelet, blanket
2. produce, reduce
3. America, Africa
4. channel, camels
5. curdled, paddle
6. narrow, borrow
7. affected, rejected, collected
8. heaven's, dozen, chickens, kitchen

4 Syllables
1. car • gō
2. cur • dle
3. shăg • gy
4. kīnd • ness
5. cŏn • fūse
6. thŭn • der
7. frēe • ly
8. at • tăck
9. Ger • man
10. of • fice
11. in • māte
12. per • hăps
13. ŭn • păck
14. Hŏl • land
15. Ăm • ster • dăm
16. ō • ver • hang • ing

Lesson 15
1 About the Reading
1. a. southpaw   e. twenty million
   b. Italy   f. right-handed
   c. 1903   g. left
   d. hooker   h. oxygen

2. a. false   f. false
   b. true   g. false
   c. true   h. true
   d. true   i. false
   e. true   j. true

2 "Handy" Sayings
1. c   5. d
2. a   6. b
3. b   7. c
4. a   8. d

3 "Handy" Words
1. handlebar   6. handcuff
2. handball   7. handsome
3. handshake   8. handle
4. handbag   9. handy
5. handful   10. handpick

4 Singular and Plural Words
Singular	Plural
1. leaf	leaves
2. half	halves
3. employer	employers
4. ox	oxen
5. lash	lashes
6. deer	deer
7. diary	diaries
8. bicycle	bicycles
9. unit	units
10. cow	cattle

Review: Lessons 1-15
1 Answer These Questions
1. Adolf Hitler
2. 1945
3. Japan or Italy
4. Anne Frank
5. Holland
6. camel
7. Asia and Africa
8. fat
9. southpaws
10. twenty million

2 Word Study
1. throw it high
2. piggies
3. the United States
4. past
5. Yellow
6. breathing
7. start a fire
8. wet
9. solid
10. culture

3 Matching

1. Mr.   5. etc.
2. IOU   6. A.M.
3. Ms.   7. Dr.
4. Mrs.   8. B.C.

4 Matching

1. English   3. German   5. Dutch
2. French   4. Greek   6. American

5 Meet Ms. Brown

1. kindhearted   5. handicapped
2. lazy   6. moody, accepting
3. selfish   7. clumsy
4. foolish   8. confused, loneliness

6 Spelling Check

1. Holland   5. radio
2. Texas   6. dentist
3. truly   7. student
4. wages   8. Germany

7 Syllables

1. hand • cuff   9. fish • bowl
2. pro • tect   10. duck • pin
3. pig • tail   11. lone • li • ness
4. state • ment   12. un • com • mon
5. there • fore   13. wil • der • ness
6. de • press   14. mis • fit
7. bee • line   15. a • gree • ment
8. it • self   16. dis • a • gree • ment

Lesson 16

1 About the Reading

1. a   3. b   5. c   7. b   9. d
2. a   4. c   6. c   8. b   10. b

2 About the Reading

1. A living thing is badly hurt.
2. Hormones are released.
3. There is no pain
4. The living thing becomes calm.
5. Death happens without a struggle.

3 The Ending -ly

differently   awfully
narrowly   nervously
suddenly   entirely
foolishly   strictly
mostly   promptly

1. narrowly   6. strictly
2. promptly   7. suddenly
3. entirely   8. mostly
4. nervously   9. awfully
5. foolishly   10. differently

4 The Ending -ly

1. easily   5. unluckily
2. bodily   6. speedily
3. busily   7. happily
4. greedily   8. clumsily

5 Compound Words

1. deadline   6. sunset
2. newsstand   7. neighborhood
3. overheard   8. lowdown
4. campground   9. jackhammers
5. freeway   10. outhouses

Lesson 17

1 About the Reading

1. 1856 to 1917
2. as a salesman
3. He collected diamond jewelry.
4. He planned to eat all the desserts on the platter.
5. His stomach rubbed against the table.
6. The doctors advised him to eat properly.
7. He thought that eating reasonable amounts of food would take all the fun out of eating.
8. He died in an Atlantic City hotel of overeating.
9. Answers will vary.

2 Food for Thought

1. Apple   6. dough (bread)
2. lemon   7. beef
3. chicken   8. honey
4. toast   9. crab
5. bread (dough)   10. Cheese

3 The Ending -ful

bagful   shameful
colorful   spiteful
delightful   successful
faithful   tearful
graceful   wishful
respectful   wonderful

1. colorful   7. tearful
2. Faithful   8. respectful
3. successful   9. shameful
4. wishful   10. delightful
5. spiteful   11. graceful
6. bagful   12. wonderful

4 Working with Syllables

1. vegetables   6. vanilla, chocolate, strawberry
2. oyster   7. restaurant
3. yogurt   8. spaghetti
4. doughnuts   9. menu
5. salad   10. breakfast

Lesson 18

1 About the Reading

1.	false	6.	false
2.	true	7.	true
3.	true	8.	true
4.	false	9.	false
5.	false	10.	false

2 More about Potatoes

writer

mountains, wheat, pieces, instead, bread

explored, Spain

brought, 1621, Ireland, settled

3 Where Would You Find It?

1.	vines	8.	purse
2.	fork	9.	piano
3.	Italy	10.	Holland
4.	restaurant	11.	ocean
5.	bottle	12.	stadium
6.	jail	13.	street
7.	hotel	14.	New England

4 The Ending -less

hitless   priceless
faultless   speechless
sugarless   strapless
pointless   treeless

1.	sugarless	5.	hitless
2.	priceless	6.	speechless
3.	Strapless	7.	faultless
4.	treeless	8.	pointless

Lesson 19

1 About the Reading

1.	pints	6.	large intestine.
2.	small intestine.	7.	What the person likes to eat
3.	relaxed.	8.	solid to liquid
4.	waste.	9.	glands.
5.	makes food soft.	10.	how food is digested.

2 More about Digestion

1. Teeth — break up food into small bits
2. Stomach — turns the food into a semi-liquid mass
3. Small intestine — digests the food
4. Large intestine — stores waste from food

3 Cause and Effect

1. The stomach has to work harder at churning the food.
2. It passes into the large intestine.
3. The person feels tired and upset.
4. The body can become diseased.

4 The Human Body

1.	stomach	6.	large intestine
2.	glands	7.	heart
3.	lungs	8.	muscles
4.	liver	9.	pancreas
5.	small intestine	10.	spleen

5 Word Endings

1. mentioned, digestion
2. Moments, agreement
3. continued, blue, tissues
4. settled, bottle, apple
5. pocket, blanket, racket
6. America, soda, saliva
7. handle, paddle, muscles
8. managed, message, cabbage
9. certain, curtains, mountain
10. ideal, hospital, chemicals

Lesson 20

1 About the Story

1. She was angry at him.
2. She was happy with him.
3. The young man has won her over with his charm and his soup.
4. He gives her the nail and tells her not to use it until she has nothing else to eat.
5. Answers may vary.
6. Nail soup, in this story, is a vegetable soup. The nail served only as a catalyst to obtain the other ingredients.
7. The young man is not a beggar. Granny willingly offered him the ingredients he needed for the soup.

2 May I Take Your Order?

1. a. $2.50
   b. $5.05
   c. $1.80
2. Iced tea is not available. (It's out of season.)
3. Probably you would try to talk a young child into ordering "Kid Stuff."
4. Answers will vary.
5. Answers will vary.

3 Same or Opposite?

1.	same	9.	opposite
2.	same	10.	same
3.	same	11.	opposite
4.	opposite	12.	opposite
5.	same	13.	opposite
6.	same	14.	same
7.	opposite	15.	same
8.	opposite		

4 **Word Endings**

1. onion, million
2. tongue, leagues
3. magic, Atlantic, picnic
4. extra, vanilla
5. dangerous, delicious
6. culture, nature
7. forgotten, broken, frightened, happen
8. statement, disagreement, payment
9. requested, digest, inquest, forest
10. faucet, bucket, wallet, pocket

4 **Four-letter Words**

1. disc		7. Asia	
2. hero		8. soda	
3. item		9. busy	
4. toes		10. mitt	
5. acre		11. view	
6. Ohio		12. menu	

5 **Syllables**

1. child • hood
2. won • der • ful
3. tis • sue
4. nar • row • ly
5. de • light • ful
6. hard • ship
7. re • spect • ful
8. ner • vous • ly
9. cham • pagne
10. mid • morn • ing

Review: Lessons 1-20

1 **Matching**

Group 1

1. swamp	5. hormone
2. artery	6. champagne
3. vein	7. carbon dioxide
4. saliva	8. oxygen

Group 2

1. Yankees	5. Huron
2. Thomas Edison	6. Fourth of July
3. Pearl Harbor	7. Pueblo
4. New England	8. North Pole

Group 3

1. Ms.	5. A.M.
2. Mrs.	6. Dr.
3. etc.	7. B.C.
4. P.M.	8. TV

2 **Word Study**

1. oars	8. scaly
2. turtle	9. Diamond Jim Brady
3. Japan	10. Africa
4. polo	11. Santa Claus
5. diagrams	12. moodiness
6. released	13. planet
7. object	14. culture

3 **Which Word Does Not Fit?**

1. sidewalk	9. mention
2. rare	10. newspaper
3. dunce	11. turtle
4. Midwest	12. silky
5. nostrils	13. sun
6. El Dorado	14. skyscraper
7. split	15. roast beef
8. pocketknife	